CATHOLICS CAN COME HOME AGAIN!

A Guide for the Journey of Reconciliation
with Inactive Catholics

CATHOLICS CAN COME HOME AGAIN!

A Guide for the Journey of Reconciliation with Inactive Catholics

Carrie Kemp

Paulist Press
New York/Mahwah, N.J.

Book design by Lynn Else

Cover design by Nick Markell

Library of Congress Cataloging-in-Publication Data

Kemp, Carrie, 1938-
    Catholics can came home again : a guide for the journey of reconciliation with inactive Catholics / Carrie Kemp.
        p. cm.
    Includes bibliographical references and index.
    ISBN 0-8091-3955-3 (alk. paper)
    1. Church work with ex-church members—Catholic Church. 2. Catholic Church—United States—Membership. I. Title.

BX2347.4. K45 2000
282—dc21

                                                                                                00-062377

Published by Paulist Press
997 Macarthur Boulevard
Mahwah, New Jersey 07430

www.paulistpress.com

Printed and bound in the
United States of America

Contents

Foreword

I stayed away from the church for nearly 30 years. I am a 51-year-old, pre-Vatican II cradle Catholic, the youngest of five children. My parents came from strong Catholic families; my father was Irish and English and my mother was French Canadian. We all attended parochial schools where, for eight years, we were required to attend Mass every day. My brother and sisters went to Catholic high schools. Mass and confession were always required of us in our family.

I have good memories of growing up Catholic. A wonderful priest in our parish, Father Simon, encouraged me to learn "Mass Latin" when I was in the fifth grade so I could become an altar boy. In those days, no girls were allowed to serve Mass, and women were not even allowed in the sanctuary. I loved being an altar boy. It was often scary, depending on which priest was saying Mass. But I always felt very special when I was serving.

Our family moved the summer before I started ninth grade. Because my parents couldn't afford to send me to a Catholic high school, I started junior high in the public schools. What a change for a Catholic boy who had never known anyone who wasn't Catholic! I remember the other students laughing at me the first time I stood up to answer a teacher. It was unthinkable to *not stand* when we answered the nuns, and we had to rise whenever a priest came into the classroom. And I couldn't believe all the fooling around in class. In parochial school, the punishment for that kind of behavior would have been swift and painful.

I battled with my father all during my high school years and, during that time, watched my sister, a year older than I, die from some mysterious disease. When I finished high school, I couldn't leave home fast enough. The Vietnam war looked like a way out. At the age of 18, I enlisted in the Coast Guard and left home for boot camp.

I never attended Mass again, except for my sister's funeral. I have no idea why. I just stopped going, probably because there was no one to make me go. I remember feeling guilty but I kept pushing the guilt further and further back in my mind. As soon as I was on my own, I became a nonpracticing Catholic. But I always felt that I was a Catholic. When I made my First Communion, my mother gave me a religious medal on a stainless steel chain. One side of the medal said, "I am a Catholic. Please call a priest." I am still wearing that medal 42 years later. Even in the Coast Guard, with dogtags clanging around my neck, I always wore my Catholic identity medal.

I met Jeanne after three years in the Coast Guard. We fell in love very quickly and not long after we met decided to get married. The only problem was that Jeanne's father was an American Baptist minister. You can imagine his feelings when his oldest daughter brought home a Catholic sailor and announced that we were going to be married. Jeanne had told me a story about a Catholic boy inviting her to go to a dance when she was a high school junior. Her father asked her not to go, warning, "If you date a Catholic, you could end up marrying one of them."

We had to postpone our wedding because I was shipped to Alaska for a year. During that time, without telling me, Jeanne went through an RCIA program and became a Catholic. We had never even talked about religion, which may be an indication of how far my Catholic guilt had been pushed into my subconscious.

When I came back from Alaska, Jeanne and I were married in a Catholic church in the small town where her father was the pastor of First Baptist Church. He did not participate in the ceremony. Jeanne just wanted him to be her father that day. Our marriage caused a lot of gossip in the community— the Baptist minister's daughter marrying a Catholic! Fortunately, Jeanne's father is one of the most wonderful, caring, loving people I've ever known. Our relationship often seems more like brothers than father-in-law, son-in-law. Once while doing the dishes together about a year after the wedding, he told me about how hard it was for him to accept our marriage, referring to that time of his life as his Gethsemane. Then I really understood how trying it was for him.

Our wedding ceremony was only the second Mass I had attended since leaving home, but it wasn't the start of my return to the church. I didn't attend Mass again for many years, although I always knew that if I ever went back to church, it would be to the Catholic church. I knew that no matter what, I would always be a Catholic.

For the next 25 years, I made little progress in my spiritual life. Occasionally I would try to go to Mass but it never felt right. I was away from the church when all of the reforms of Vatican II were taking place, and I felt like a stranger there. I never found a parish that welcomed or offered to help "fallen away" Catholics. Then, in the fall of 1994, my older brother invited me to meet the rector of the Basilica of Saint Mary, Father Michael O'Connell. My brother was not an ideal Catholic and I couldn't believe he was asking me to join him and a priest for lunch!

I still don't know why I said yes to the invitation, but I did. By that time, with the help of a psychologist, I had come to understand and accept many events in my life. We often talked about spirituality and religion, and although I told her about my Catholic background, I was convinced I would never go back to the church. Yet I had this fear that I would die before I returned to the church and straightened things out with God. The guilt I carried from not going to church and participating in the sacraments for so many years was overwhelming.

We had lunch with Father Michael on a lovely October day, just the three of us in a beautiful dining room in the rectory. Conversation was focused primarily on fund-raising but it was a very soft sell, concluding with a tour of the basilica. Just as I was leaving, Father Michael asked me where I went to church. It was obvious that my vague answer about going to several churches didn't fool him. He suggested that I might be interested in a program starting in a few weeks called Catholics Coming Home. He gave me Carrie Kemp's name and phone number.

That's how I met Carrie. I called her that same day and asked her about Catholics Coming Home. I was really frightened about taking this step, but after talking to Carrie I found the will to keep going. In just that first phone conversation with her, I knew that she understood how I felt. She knew about fear and guilt and a yearning to return to the church.

The first meeting of Catholics Coming Home was really scary. There were about 20 of us sitting in a circle in a room with no windows. We each introduced ourselves and talked about our history with the church, good and bad. Everyone in the room had experienced something in their Catholic life that had driven them away from the church. I set the group record for being away the longest, 28 years! Once the painful introductions were out of the way, Carrie took over and we were on our way. It was hard to meet only once a week. Now that I had taken the first step to come back, I wanted things to move faster. I knew that something very special was happening.

The one thing that stands out in my mind is when Carrie said it was all right for me to come back. She actually apologized for the church driving Catholics away, whether by guilt or some action that alienated or excluded someone. She talked about how the church was the people, all of us, not some hierarchical bureaucracy. And she spoke about her own struggles with the church. It was evident that she loved the church and that she really wanted to help all of us to resume our spiritual journeys. Only if we wanted to.

Father Dale Korogi participated in a number of our meetings. During the second-to-last session of Catholics Coming Home, Father Dale took us into the basilica sanctuary where we prayed together. Then he anointed each of us with oil. There were just 15 of us in the basilica that evening. It was a powerful moment for me. I knew I was really coming home.

Our group was invited to attend the basilica's Communal Reconciliation Celebration on the night of our final meeting. The week before we had talked about the three forms of reconciliation. Having been away since before Vatican II, I didn't know anything but "black box" confessionals. I found it hard to believe that this sacrament could be a positive experience. But Father Dale said something I will never forget: "By the time you think about asking God for forgiveness, God has already forgiven you." What a concept! A loving, caring, forgiving God had taken over.

The reconciliation service was another milestone for me, an inspiring experience. Our Catholics Coming Home group met afterward to talk about how we felt. Based on my pre-Vatican II training, I knew I had to go to "confession" before I could come back to the church. I had always dreaded that hurdle but the experience of reconciliation was peaceful, healing. I asked Father Dale, "Did that really work?" In a very kind, understanding way, Father Dale said, "Yes, Phil, it really worked." I knew then that I was officially back in the church.

I started attending Mass regularly from that evening on. I loved being in the basilica so much that I looked forward to Mass, very much as I had when I first became an altar boy. Since that time, I have never felt that I have to go to Mass. I look forward to it and to anything going on in the basilica. There is so much peace there. Jeanne and I joined the Basilica Community in 1994, and within a short time we were both invited to participate in ministries there. I was invited to become an acolyte (new word for altar boy). I couldn't believe it. I started right away and hope to continue until someone tells me I'm too old.

In August 1996, I was diagnosed with non-Hodgkin's lymphoma, a very aggressive form of cancer of the lymphatic system. Treatment began immediately. I received chemotherapy for three months and radiation treatment for one month. The cancer appeared to be gone. Exactly two years later, it was back, only worse. I did my research about recurring lymphoma and I knew this was serious. The treatment was almost six months of aggressive chemotherapy. I had my share of bad days during both treatment periods. I remember lying in bed one day just after receiving chemotherapy. I felt terrible and my 11-year-old dog, a black Labrador, was lying on the bed with me. I told her that I never thought she would outlive me, but she probably would.

I have kept a very positive outlook during most of the past three years and I was able to work much of the time I was receiving treatment. And I didn't miss many of the Masses I was scheduled to assist at. Since I didn't have any hair, I figured people would think I was a monk. I have just about recovered from the last round of chemotherapy, and I can honestly say that I was never afraid of dying. That's not to say that I wanted to die, but I wasn't afraid of it. My faith has grown strong during the past five years.

I know now that God is love. During my illness, the support of Jeanne and of all the staff and parishioners at the Basilica of Saint Mary carried me through a very difficult time. My faith grows stronger every day. Without Carrie Kemp and Catholics Coming Home, I would still be lonely in many ways. I no longer live in fear of death and the unknown. Catholics Coming Home gave me hope and love and peace.

Philip Perkins

Introduction

I decided to write this book on a late July evening in Rome, the first stop of an Italian vacation our kids gave us. I had been there before but it was Gary's first time. We catered to jet lag the afternoon of our arrival, and savored pasta and vino at a sidewalk ristorante. We then headed back to our pensione for a good night's rest. Since our bus stop was close to the Vatican, we decided to stop there for a while to prepare ourselves for the next day's tour of the Vatican Museum and St. Peter's Basilica. I was eager to observe Gary's reaction when he saw it. A converted Methodist, his love for all things catholic—with a small "c"—energizes my sometimes heady Catholic experience.

Only one or two steps into a darkened opening in an ancient wall, we were greeted by a Swiss guard who asked us to stay back a few paces; he was more than willing to talk with us from the appropriate distance. "A church greeter," we mused to ourselves as we continued toward St. Peter's Square. Church has become so ingrained in our lives and our marriage that we sometimes find ourselves not only living but observing church in unison.

And then we saw the square, mellow lights casting comforting shadows in the ancient archways that surround it. The basilica bells were tolling a tired, ancient sound of beckoning so unlike the vigorous, melodic bells recently hung at the Basilica of Saint Mary in Minneapolis, our home parish. How many people, we wondered, had heard those bells over the years? St. Peter's was wrapped in scaffolding and safety netting, in anticipation of a face-lift for the Jubilee Year. The magnitude of the structures and the historic symbolism were overpowering and deeply personal. We were two of only a dozen people in that entire square. I had expected throngs to be there, based on my recollections from previous daytime visits. Congestion and crowd distractions had been my lasting memories of the Vatican. This time, it was as if we were part of something intimate and sacred. We forgot about catching the 10:00 P.M. bus.

Instead, we sat on the cobblestones by the fountain and I realized my soul was at that moment uniquely centered on my church. Not the building, but what it represented, the people, all those who have come before and all those who form the church in the world today, and all those who will love one another into church during the millennium to come. I felt connected to all these good people in a way I never had before. I thought about my Italian grandmother whose unconditional love had shown me the face of God over and over again, a simple, uneducated woman whose heart was never separated from her friend Jesus and from the church she knew he loved. I thought of the thousands of people who have blessed me with their trust during these past 15 years of ministry, who have shared their faith journeys with me, those who have mentored me and have been living examples of Christian discipleship.

It was a humbling experience to realize that I, too, am a part of all that meets in the symbolism of that square. My call to ministry, birthed in great struggle and love for the church, has had new meaning for me since that night, a deeper sense of participation in the Body of Christ. This is where I belong. My soul is at home here. I was overcome with the realization that others are longing for that same reassurance of belonging and participation.

Over the centuries we have followed paths away from the gospel vision. There, beside the fountain, tears burst forth as the stories of seekers flooded my thoughts, destroying the sense of well-being that had pervaded my soul. I wanted to hold on to the velvety euphoria of the darkness, to know only what was good. But the stories kept coming, woven between recollections of a history filled with church failure, human failure. I was losing the vision and its promise...until I realized that that is the way the church works. As long as human beings have the vision to guide them, they will succeed in bringing it into being. There will be failures, and missteps, and errors, and wrong judgments. But the Spirit of God will continue to draw us back on course, forgiving and loving us into people with eyes to see and ears to hear the message and the hope the world longs for. Human sacredness will prevail over human failure.

I began to feel at peace again, reassured that just as I was sitting at the center of the symbolic crossroads of our church, the church itself is at the crossroads of its past and future. The people of God will journey into the new century with confidence, assured that the church, a sacred mystery, will continue to fill history with the presence of God through their human hearts.

In a powerful way, it became clear to me that the seekers need to be a part of that journey and that I am called to be a voice for them in this church I love. It is a sacred call and I am grateful for it.

It is my prayer that in the pages that follow you will hear their voices, see their goodness, and be touched by their faith. If you are a seeker, may you find hope and nourishment for your journey in the courage and honesty of all the seekers who have come before you.

For all who share a
belief in the Vision,
especially the Community of the Basilica of Saint Mary
where my soul finds rest and nourishment.
And for the seekers, whose trust
and love
consecrate my ministry.

I myself will pasture my sheep; I myself will give them rest, says the Lord God.
The lost I will seek out, the strayed I will bring back,
the injured I will bind up, the sick I will heal.
Ezekiel, 34:15-16

Chapter 1
Sharing the Gift

Jesus sent these men on a mission as the Twelve, after giving them the following instruction: "Do not visit pagan territory and do not enter a Samaritan town. Go instead after the lost sheep of the house of Israel.... **The gift you have received, give as a gift.**[1]

Matthew 10:5–8

In the decade since *Catholics Coming Home* was published, the lost sheep of our church have taught me more about the sacredness of our faith than all the theology lectures and books that prepared me for my vocation as a lay minister in the church. For it is in the yearning, the anger and the sadness, the hope and the despair of baptized Catholics who no longer sit in the pews with us during weekend liturgies that I have come to know who we are as a eucharistic people.

We call them alienated, former, lapsed, fallen away, but only rarely do we call them to talk with us, to tell us their stories, to know their goodness and their pain. Unrecognized, the millions who are alienated from our Catholic family become a gaping wound in the Body of Christ—a hemorrhage of anger, frustration, pain, and rejection. Without opportunity for reconciliation and healing, ongoing struggles with the church eventually erode into spiritual deadness, isolation, and hopelessness.

Historically, we have placed little emphasis on ministering to those who don't feel welcome at our doors, or at the eucharistic table. Judgments are rendered about their lack of faith, their lack of zeal, their

1

having made wrong choices, always something wrong with "them." They are often resented at Christmas and Easter liturgies when they are publicly chastised for "crowding" the pews, making it uncomfortable for the "more deserving," those who show up every Sunday. Some of them are beginning to refer to themselves as "Christmas and Easter Catholics." They appear apprehensive when we gather, not sure they will be welcomed.

I have come to think of these people we have rejected, as well as those who may have rejected us, as *seekers,* because most of them are truly seeking an honest relationship with God and are exploring the church's role in that relationship. They are men and women, blue collar and professional workers, some in their 20s and others in their 80s, some who have been away more than 40 years. We find them everywhere: on airplanes, at family gatherings, at our workplaces; they are the people who come into our homes to fix our appliances and who take care of us when we are ill. Some of them are our own children or parents. Perhaps you are a seeker, wondering whether the church really means it when it says, "You are one of us."

I meet seekers daily in my parish ministry, adults who grew up in strict Catholic homes, couples coming for marriage preparation sessions or bringing their children for baptism; the separated, divorced, and remarried; gays and lesbians; those who struggle with grief and loss and addiction in their lives. There is no common denominator with which to describe these seekers except for the one event that is central to their search: the gift called Eucharist.

"Prophets" is what Father Bill McKee, C.Ss.R., has called the seekers. "They are calling attention to the abuses or evils in the church which should be remedied." And at the very core of this abuse is the denial of the gift—Eucharist—to spiritually starving members of our baptized family. The seekers are good, faith-filled people, often confused by what they perceive to be the church's efforts to control their decisions and their lives. Given an opportunity to reclaim their belovedness in the heart of God, to sort out issues of confusion, guilt, and shame, many choose to live out the rest of their lives in harmony with God and church.

In a format we call Catholics Coming Home, we are privileged to facilitate an ongoing discovery of the relationship between the seekers and the church during this critical, unwritten period of church history.

This ministry doesn't require elaborate seminars, many dollars, or glossy handouts—only our own humble acceptance of the gift of Eucharist in our lives.

The church needs to be a place where we can not only bring our burdens, but where we can sort them out, finding acceptance during our reflection and the encouragement to continue on the journey. The people who are the church must provide hope for inner peace in lives torn asunder by heartache, loss, indifference, and despair. Parish communities must offer a sense of intimacy and belonging to all, acknowledging that many of the seekers need an opportunity to understand the church and forgive it. I am always amazed at how willingly they forgive, once they feel accepted, and I am deeply grieved by how much some of them have to forgive.

For the seekers, a breakthrough occurs when they begin to realize that the church is *us, the people of God*. They begin to comprehend church as people on a journey of faith instead of a closed institution; this allows them to embrace their own story as part of the journey too.

All of us who are called to active ministry in the church need to notice the seekers we meet in our daily encounters. They are at the bedsides of the sick we visit, in the families of the bereaved we comfort, sitting in the pews while their children celebrate sacraments, even standing at the altar during the weddings we celebrate. They watch passively while we receive the gift, Sunday after Sunday, reinforcing their isolation and exclusion from community. A quiet word, an invitation to converse, a reassurance that we miss them may prompt their journey of reconciliation. Parish liturgies must acknowledge their presence in a loving way, and offer opportunities for reconciliation and healing. It can be as simple as a bulletin insertion stating, *"We're glad you're here. If you are troubled because you feel you cannot receive the Eucharist, please call..."*

Seekers rarely find spiritual peace far from the gift that defines us as church, the Eucharist. There are too many empty places at our table, so we need to break bread with these good people, to shelter them in our spiritual family. They have much to teach us about faith, about truth, and about forgiveness.

With each passing year we receive an increasing number of inquiries about our ministry to inactive Catholics. I am heartened and excited as I listen to Catholics proclaiming the message of healing and reconciliation more vigorously in dioceses all over the United States.

The millennium has become a mile-marker for us as people called to promote forgiveness and healing for all inhabitants of the world, and it is appropriate that we should begin with our own.

Since our first effort 15 years ago to invite inactive Catholics to discuss their dissatisfaction with the church, the ministry itself has continuously changed and evolved, always in response to the seekers and their issues, or problems. Our original three-week series has doubled in duration and could easily last longer. Parishes are discovering a need to provide ongoing adult education for these people. Once they return to the fold, their thirst for spiritual nourishment, continued education, and opportunities to serve send energy throughout the parish communities who welcomed them. At the Basilica of Saint Mary in Minneapolis, where our ministry has been based for the past six years, Father Dale Korogi, associate pastor, observed one day, "The seekers are everywhere." They are Eucharistic Ministers, lectors, RCIA sponsors, Hospitality Ministers, faith formation teachers, members of parish councils, boards, and commissions. They are living their faith, bringing about the reign of God in their daily lives and in their church communities.

To welcome people back to the church requires full acknowledgment and disclosure of the "messiness" evident in a faith community comprised of human beings. No longer a staid, predictable institution, the church is a "work in progress," to use a popular phrase. Vatican II opened wide the doors to a deeper understanding of what it means to be fully human, yet infused with God's power and love. The scriptures have been and continue to be researched, examined in their early context and original languages with far-reaching implications for our lives as individuals and as church. The realization that we all belong to one another through this God-ness within us is rooting itself in Catholic Christians and making a difference in the world. As the millennium begins, we hear continuous talk of healing, restoring, and mending within the Body of Christ. Catholics are no longer content to sit passively in the spectator section of the church arena. We have work to do, a kingdom to build.

It is a confusing time to be a Catholic, active or inactive. The word itself becomes a catalyst for argument, questioning, doubt, and insecurity. I am fascinated by the reaction I elicit when I respond to those who ask me what my work is, whether it is the person next to me on a plane, a new acquaintance at a social function, or even my husband's work associates. Catholics and non-Catholics alike react similarly: first, horror stories they've heard about the church, then questions concerning my role as woman in the church. Often these people turn out to be inactive Catholics, testing the waters to see whether they dare reveal to me their inactive status in a church to which I commit my life on a daily basis. Sometimes the conversations are respectful; often they are not. I am somewhat stunned by the freedom with which people comment on the Catholic church in social settings. In or out of it, the church touches their lives. This phenomenon does not exist in other denominations to the degree that we are experiencing it as Catholics. I have never heard Presbyterians or Lutherans bombarded by criticisms of their denomination in public settings. Nor does it seem that other denominations engage in the amount of scrutiny to which we Catholics subject ourselves. Encounters between informed Catholics produce instant, thought-provoking discussion. There is so much that is alive in the church today that everyone seems to have something to say, an opinion to offer, a concern to express. This is something I have grown to love about the church; all this energetic conversation is very healthy.

I used to be troubled by all of this Catholic upheaval, and suggested early in my ministry that the church seemed to be struggling through an adolescence marked by turmoil, rebellion, confusion, along with startling discoveries of its real identity and mission. In August 1998, Father Richard Rohr, O.F.M., conducted a two-day symposium at the University of Saint Thomas in Saint Paul, during which he suggested the church is a year old for every hundred years of its existence, moving it beyond adolescence to young adulthood. And in her book *Practicing Catholic,* Penelope Ryan claims, "...I am one of those people who believes that the church is still at the beginning stages of its growth and life. We are still *becoming* the People of God."[2]

No longer troubled by the intense momentum of disagreement and challenge within our ranks, I have come to accept these indications of new life and health. Just as a marriage without conflict and struggle is hardly functioning on the soul level of its partners, a church without members who speak from their sacred authenticity will have no soul. It is the soul of the Catholic Church that prevails throughout the ages.

For those who do not see signs of hope in this advent era of church, the result of this period of turmoil is alienation. In a very real sense, those most likely to separate from the church are the men and women whose Catholic heritage rests on a foundation of vague memories and fragmented truths. Although estranged from their perceived church, they still seek something deeper from life, something that will replace confusion and insecurity with purpose and serenity. Our American culture is marked by separateness and nonpersonal communication. People are looking for lasting relationships on the Internet; conversations with loved ones are replaced by television sitcoms and sporting events. Many are working too hard and don't even know what it means to celebrate life. Those who are blessed "with ears to hear and eyes to see" know what these seekers are looking for, and that they will find it only within community. Our biggest challenge as church today is not in the arena of doctrine and dogma. People's hearts are not changed by words, but by relationships. Our growing edge as church is to *live* the gospel.

I identify easily with the seekers because my life, from its very beginning, did not fit easily into the Catholic community. Although a cradle Catholic, my mother's Protestant background created a continuous tension in my religious upbringing. I attended public schools during a time when to do so raised questions about our salvation! I can remember well-intentioned sisters expressing deep concern about this during the two-week summer classes we attended each year while we were in elementary school. From that early age on, I learned to dichotomize my religious expression, saying what I knew people wanted to hear while inwardly qualifying what my heart truly believed. I loved learning answers to the questions in the Baltimore Catechism, even though I hardly understood what I memorized. I recall being elated when, during sixth-grade confirmation preparation, I earned the coveted prize, a statue of Our Lady enshrined in a papier-mâché-covered oatmeal box. It was an indication that I had arrived. I was Catholic after all. My sense of belonging didn't last long, however. When our confirmation pictures were taken, those of us who attended public schools were told to stand behind the parochial school students, and sternly reminded that when the bishop asked questions, we were to remain silent and let the Catholic school kids respond.

I also knew that I was not as Catholic as my cousins who were told in parochial school not to join in meal prayers at our house. "Come, Lord Jesus, be our guest" was not a Catholic prayer. I thought it quite strange that they quickly crossed themselves and then muttered a prayer that sounded stiff and formal. I loved their word, *bounty,* but at those tender ages, none of us had the slightest idea what it meant. We only knew it was Catholic.

By age 19, I was married to a Protestant whose denomination taught that Roman Catholics were not saved. Only after 22 years of marriage did I learn that he believed that his marriage to a Catholic jeopardized his own chances for salvation. He was a decent person and when that marriage ended after two decades, we were both broken and devastated. That was 20 years ago. Catholic women didn't get divorced in those days.

Once again, I began to question my right to belong to this church. Throughout my years as wife and mother, I had been very active in the parish near our home. Our children went to public schools (it had become acceptable by then), and I committed hundreds of hours to what we used to call CCD (Confraternity of Christian Doctrine). But as a divorced woman, my status changed. Lifelong friends avoided my glance when we went to Mass. There were no phone calls of consolation or confrontation. Just silence. It was a shunning that left searing wounds on my already broken heart. The kids started to question why we were using a different church door and I felt ashamed to tell them it was because I didn't want to see the people we usually saw when we entered the church every Sunday. (That was when the church you attended had to be the one nearest your house.) It became so painful I decided to leave not only the parish but the Catholic Church as well.

When I expressed this decision to the therapist I was seeing, she cautioned me not to leave too quickly. She suggested that my Catholic roots might be deeper than I realized, a revolutionary assessment that brings smiles to me in retrospect. At her recommendation, I journeyed to a parish in Minneapolis on Mother's Day, knowing I could not, on that particular Sunday, face all those blank glances from people who had been my church family all my life. My kids joined me under protest. They knew I never drove to Minneapolis from our St. Paul home and this trip seemed absurd since our church was at the end of our block. But our little red Volkswagen found its way to the small, inner-city parish, where we were welcomed warmly. How different from our big suburban parish where people simply filed in and out without noticing anyone.

The best was yet to come. As Father began his homily, I felt the dread seeping through my body, knowing the kids would have to sift through his comments about mothers in order to find a context for what was going on in our lives. Divorcing parents have their own pain. But the inability to neutralize the pain of their children is the most profound agony of all. To my surprise, Father quickly honored all the mothers gathered there and then said he wanted to focus on particular mothers that day, single mothers! The pew vibrated as my kids nudged one another and then began to tune in. For the first time in months, they heard their mother's life not only dignified but held up as an example of a way some are called to live out their discipleship. He spoke of the sacrifices required to parent children alone, face economic hardship, the scorn and judgment of others. Father not only understood, but was helping the entire congregation understand the plight of single parents.

I was hooked. I had come home again to the church I was only beginning to know, one that has honed and formed all the days of my life since that conversion moment. My story is commonplace in the American Catholic experience. What sets me apart from many thousands of others is that people helped me find my way back not only to the church, but to a totally new awareness of what it means to be Catholic. Their outreach planted the seeds of the ministry that eventually unfolded. At that very church, we were to begin a small effort to reach out to others whose lives were suspended in spiritual limbo because of unresolved church issues.

In the beginning we were unaware of the sheer numbers of inactive Catholics. Various polls and studies indicate that the number in 10 years has grown from 15 million to 17 million today. Bishop Norbert Gaughan states, "The second largest denomination (in the United States) is comprised of fallen away Catholics."[3] When I read this 10 years ago, it was startling. Today, it grieves me. The staggering reality of these numbers has a profound effect on every member of Christ's body, the church.

Whether we call ourselves the "one, holy, catholic and apostolic Church," the "people of God," or "the Body of Christ," *church* means all who have been baptized into the Catholic faith community. In its purely historical and universal sense, it means even more. The church is all of us. The rootedness of our faith in the lived experience of Jesus

Christ demands that love, forgiveness, reconciliation, and celebration be offered to all; to exclude anyone is to impair the full promise of what the church can be for the rest of us. I see too many families torn apart, too many generations lost to the church forever. I see too many children being herded through sacramental programs while their parents sit uncatechized and disconnected in the pews, the result of a breach that may have occurred more than a generation before.

Almost as significant as the phenomenon of inactive Catholics itself is the increased interest among active Catholics to provide encouragement and hope for the seekers and for all of us who minister to them. Tandem to my work with the seekers is an ongoing interaction with active Catholics who want to know them, understand them, and invite them back. This seems to be a laity-driven concern and response, perhaps because it is our families that are most affected. While older, more abstract concepts of church are being challenged, defended, and redefined by clergy and hierarchy in this millennium era, lay women and men are crying out for healing of the church's wounds, and they want that healing to begin now. We can be proud of our Holy Father's challenge to invoke forgiveness and healing on a worldwide basis, extending to the economic indebtedness of the Third World. These global challenges take on more credence, however, if the church fosters forgiveness, healing, and reconciliation with our own baptized members.

If you are an inactive Catholic, it is our prayer that these pages will offer you promise and resurrected hope in your faith journey, along with a new understanding of what it means to be Catholic. This book is also intended for all Catholics who want to make the road back easier for their inactive family members, neighbors, or friends. The deep interest and caring for inactive Catholics among active parish members is a continuing source of encouragement to many.

Perhaps you are a member of a pastoral staff, either in a parish or diocesan office. Or you may be a religious sister or brother, or a lay person, educated and experienced in church and ministry. We trust that the ideas presented here will help you to begin active outreach within your community.

Our plea also reaches out to priests and pastors, whose role in this evolving church is a vital and difficult one. To the seekers, you represent the official church. Therefore, it is often to you, personally, that they look for the final word of reassurance and reconciliation. In my most recent parish position, I watched a recently ordained associate pastor move from a stance of apprehension to a compassionate, relational ministry as he celebrated the sacrament of reconciliation with seekers I referred to him. He commented shortly before he left to take on his own pastorate, "These people who have experienced some process in returning to the church are completely different to work with than those who just show up in the confessional, listing sins reminiscent of childhood teaching, with little or no understanding of how the sacrament, the church, or even they have changed in the meantime." Priests and pastors who have participated in the Catholics Coming Home process speak willingly of the mutual blessing derived from this ministry, when they get to know the seekers, listen to their stories, and experience their touching expressions of gratitude to all who helped them along the journey back.

Finally, we address the bishops of the United States. We encourage you to find the time and the means to connect your lives with the seekers and their stories. We believe they will inform your ministry, touch your hearts, and expose you to the fresh, new faith energy that these people bring with them on the homeward journey. Pope John Paul II has set a unique example for all of us in his open admission of the church's sins throughout the ages, urging forgiveness and promising reconciliation. Will you carry his message to the men and women in your own dioceses, providing referrals and resources for seekers who want to pursue reconciliation and healing? Most inactive Catholics are wary of making phone calls on their own behalf and may spend many years away from the church because they don't know how or where to begin the process of reconciliation. We need ministries that offer this outreach; we need to see that our local chanceries have information that will connect the seekers to the help they need. It is time for all of us who consider ourselves church to acknowledge the seekers' absence, their pain, and their goodness...and to ask for their forgiveness. Their absence should be noted and mourned in every parish. They deserve to be invited back.

There are others far more qualified than I to document data on those who leave, why they leave, and why they return. I prefer to speak directly from my ministry experience over the past 15 years. There have been obvious changes over those years, in the church, in the seekers, and in me. This ministry has informed every other aspect of my ministry because of the particular lens through which I have come to view my own church experience.

Since our ministry is not one of preaching absolutes, but rather helping the seeker take responsibility for his or her own faith journey through scripture, prayer, church teaching, and ongoing reflection, a starting point can be somewhat skewed by all the conflicting definitions of *church* that influence Catholics today. It was simpler when *church* meant the same thing to everyone. By the end of our process, however, the seekers come to respect the challenge faced by a church that commits itself to celebrating diversity. After only two or three sessions, they realize that they have embraced that same diversity among themselves.

The seekers have changed in a number of significant ways. We have fewer coming now who are irate about Vatican Council II. We see people who have been away since the early 1960s who don't know what Vatican II was. And some are outraged because of strong feelings about what the church should be, only to discover through our process that they have pretty much described what the church is! "That's not the way I was taught" is a familiar refrain during our sessions. Seekers come today with higher levels of education both in and out of church. They question more and they have a broader world picture. They are looking for information, not answers. While they enjoy free-flowing discussion, they want input that challenges them, guides them toward more depth and understanding.

The average age of the seekers is a bit younger, with most in their 40s or early 50s, although we still get some people in their 70s. We are getting more and more people in their thirties who are asking, "Is the church relevant in my life?" This group is exciting to work with. Having received their religious education in the immediate post-Vatican II era, most of them learned very little that was absolute. They feel no identity and no loyalty to the pre-Vatican II church and know little about its history. They are dry sponges, thirsting for spiritual stimuli and, surprisingly enough, community. In a culture defined by individualism, belonging takes on new significance. This age group is our future as church and they are generous with their gifts and talents once they see the connection between discipleship as a way of life and church as a means of spiritual sustenance. They do present a particular challenge, however, because there is little common historical or theological framework from which to draw. Their Catholic identity is not as self-defining as it was for their parents.

It was uncommon for the seekers we saw 15 years ago to have had any religious experience outside the Catholic Church. Now many of them have had experience with other denominations or religions. For many, experience with Protestants provided a first encounter with faith based on personal relationship with Jesus. They speak openly about the life-changing ramifications of that and wonder whether that same kind of relationship with Jesus is celebrated in the Catholic Church.

Our ministry is not concerned with those who have found inner peace and a sense of belonging within other Christian denominations. We speak for those who have no church home, who have been away from church for generations. Yet they pause when they are asked to complete a simple form that asks for their religious affiliation. They know that they once called themselves Catholic but they are uncertain about their right or their desire to claim that identity. Many tell us they leave that space blank, creating a twinge of discomfort because of the void it reveals.

Reconciling a broken relationship with the church is not terribly different from mending any other significant relationship. It takes time, commitment, honesty, and great risk if trust is to be renewed. Without that trust, the mending is only superficial, or temporary at best. However, if securely rooted, renewed trust opens the seeker to the possibility of faith exploration filled with conversion and life-changing discovery. Rather than seeking reconciliation with the church as a goal, we suggest that the entire process be viewed as the beginning of a lifetime journey. Whether they return to the church or not, it is always our hope that they are stronger and more at peace with their God. They go with our friendship and our blessing.

Chapter 2
Tell Me the Story

"Tell me the story of Jesus..." I can hear my Lutheran mother singing this refrain throughout my childhood. As I reflect on the sacredness of the stories shared by seekers—those who search for meaning, for purpose, and for God in their lives—those words keep popping into my thoughts: "Tell me the story of Jesus." The story of Jesus is the story of the seeker and, in the most hopeful sense, there is a seeker in all of us. What is the powerful connection between each seeker's story and the story of Jesus?

For inactive Catholics, the story becomes a bridge from isolation to connection with community and recollections from childhood, to long ago reminders of who we are and where we came from. Alienation often causes us to throw out the good with the bad, resulting in unnamed losses, unspent grief. Reflection on our story helps us reconnect with what was good, invites healing into those areas long ago sealed off by pain. The value of the story is twofold: (1) the listener is learning more about the teller, about God, and about his or her own life; (2) the teller receives personal validation and awareness that life does have significance and value.

Blessed daily by seekers' stories, I am struck by how seldom a story's sacredness is noticed by the teller until it is processed through a listening, Christ-filled heart. Sanctification reveals itself in the relationship of hearts and minds bound by trust and validation of one another's goodness. When your story connects with mine, a powerfully sacred bond begins to form, one rooted in the promise of Matthew 18:20:

"Where two or three are gathered in my name, there I am in the midst of them." The power of Jesus' story becomes fused with our own!

This is the mystery of the stories we call scripture. Their sacredness is not derived from any power the church has given them. Rather, the words themselves—from the ancient stories of all who struggled to know God and live in relationship with one another—have bestowed sacred power upon the church. For the church is neither the institution nor the laws that have evolved over centuries, but real people of faith with real stories, and their sacred stories will bless and benefit the church for as long as human beings continue to search for meaning in their lives. Their ongoing stories give life to local parish communities; they are what keep our faith communities fresh, vital, and filled with purpose.

We are spiraling with great speed toward a society in which one's identity can be reduced to statistical information, denying the true meaning of daily struggles. The result is often an inward focus on our human weakness and failure, causing us to withdraw even further, hiding our real selves from one another. Human weakness, however, is divine strength! Our faith assures us that we are created with a craving to be in relationship with one another—and with God. Our story becomes the vital link toward the intimacy we desire. Our story is the story of Jesus. We are born, we suffer, and we die. This pattern repeats itself over and over again as we discover new truths, overcome more obstacles, and embrace more questions on our journey toward holiness.

But our stories, like the story of Jesus, include the undying hope of a happy ending, the resurrection. With Jesus, we will live again not only in the world to come, but in new and deeper awareness of our own sacred calling right here in this life.[1]

I invite you to listen *with Christ-filled hearts* to the stories that follow. I was deeply touched by the seekers' responses when asked to tell their stories for this book. They were eager to share their faith stories with the Catholic community, but I was not prepared for the emotion that would pervade each taped interview. Tears, laughter, anger, and insightful reflection revealed the depth of these faith journeys. We walk on holy ground when another trusts us with their story. It is the trademark of evangelizing ministry, that ongoing cycle between minister and recipient that nourishes the very soul of the minister.

To protect confidentiality, identifying information has been changed. Some stories are woven from composites of several seekers' stories, and there has been no fabrication of events and experiences. After all, who could contrive anything as beautiful as the lived experience of the seekers themselves?

Irma

Irma came to the first session alone. She was cordial, but very quiet, saying little when she introduced herself. But when we got into her reasons for coming, she had much to say! Born in Poland, her Catholic roots were strong. She holds the distinct honor of having been confirmed by the bishop who would one day become Pope John Paul II. Her heritage, her connection with the Holy Father, and her sense of betrayal by her church had become one tightly knit ball of spiritual confusion.

She married very young in Poland and came to the United States with her husband, a world away from everything and everyone she knew. They both worked, they both struggled with the language, and both found their own ways to cope with the daily difficulties of finding a place in their new world. She turned to reading, learning, whatever she could do to become a mainstream American. He turned to alcohol. Her growth threatened him, and he hurled all of his feelings of inadequacy, anger, and frustration at her. Shortly after their second child was born, she faced the hard truth she had known a long time: her physical and emotional survival—and that of her children—demanded that this marriage end. She went to the parish priest, but he disagreed with her. God had put this marriage together and it was her responsibility to keep it together. But the drinking and the abuse intensified. In the finality of divorce a few years later, she became the sole emotional, physical, and financial support of her children. Their father evaporated from the children's lives. But in the embers of her fear, Irma began to sense sprouts of hope and opportunity. She went to school and worked and raised her children, but she also went to church less and less. Compared to the new friendships and the support network she was developing, her parish community seemed cold and indifferent. Her foreign accent seemed to fend off the very people she wanted to accept her. There was no way she would trust them with the story of her divorce! When she went to Mass the old loneliness reappeared, along with the sense of deep loss—of her country, her family, her marriage. She drifted away from church without ever deciding to leave.

Until she got an emergency call from her mother several years later. Her brother, in his late 20s, had died in an accident. Her minimal savings could wrap themselves around only one plane ticket, so close friends offered to take care of her children. Not until she sat with her family in the house where she had grown up did she learn the details surrounding her brother's death. Just as she had hidden the troubles and problems of her new life in America from her family for years, they had hidden the truth about Tony from her. He was an alcoholic and had spent most of his last years in a drunken stupor, unable to work, totally out of touch with everyone. But there was more, and it was worse. Their lifelong pastor told them that Tony could not be buried in the church because he was an unrepentant alcoholic, a drunk.

Irma was stunned by this brutality. She knew what faithful Catholics her parents were and she knew their hearts were breaking over Tony's life and death. Accustomed to rejection from the church, however, it didn't occur to her to confront the priest, to try to persuade him to reconsider. Everyone now knew Tony was in hell. Filled with shame and deeply-burrowed seeds of anger, she helped her parents arrange a secular funeral and then returned to her children as soon as she could. The experience severed her ties with the church and in some unexpected way, her ties with her native country. Her future lay in this land.

When she finished school, she took a job in the Midwest. There was no money to go back home, and barely enough to keep her little family together. But things would get better. She did well at work and they were integrated into the neighborhood community. Her children were happy and at times she realized she truly was too. Emotionally, she distanced herself more and more from her parents and her roots. Too much darkness there, too much pain.

She fell in love with a man who was Protestant, and his entire family embraced her and her children. She grew to love them as well. There was no question about where the marriage would take place. Her Catholic roots were ruptured, and besides, she was a divorced woman. The church had no place for her. It really didn't matter anymore. The church was entwined with too much that was wrong in her life. She had learned to trust new beginnings, knowing that God blessed her with strength and courage every time she ventured a risk and grew. Irma's faith had never wavered; it had intensified in spite of the chasm between herself and the church.

Their marriage was a happy one and they found a home in their Protestant faith community. Her husband's work flourished and he was a good father to her children. She thanked God often every day for bringing this angel named Steven into her life.

Nearly two decades went by before she noticed our invitation in the newspaper. She ignored it at first, then found herself tearing it out without understanding why. She had no interest in the church; in fact, the mere reminder of her association with it brought rage to the surface. Besides that, she and Steven had a wonderful life. She enjoyed being a part of their church community, the weekly worship services, and the volunteer work she was doing there. Her children had no idea she had ever been a Catholic. She had always felt a sense of relief that they were free of the kind of darkness she associated with her church experience.

But she came to our meeting. Only a small part of her story tumbled out that first night. She was given a place of good-humored honor by the group because of her unusual connection with the pope. She seemed surprised to find compassion and understanding flowing freely in a Catholic gathering. And there were others who were "living in sin," hurting because the church had judged them unworthy to receive what they had been taught was essential spiritual nourishment. It was a kind of spiritual death sentence, they all concurred, death by spiritual starvation. She would later reflect that the analogy had startled something within her, a hunger she had not wanted to address because there was no way that hunger could be satisfied. Her bridges were burned behind her.

She came back the second week where our focus on images of God and Jesus brought out more of her story and more of her strong faith. It was fun to watch her defense mechanisms melt into amiable humor with others in the group, and it touched us when she allowed herself to admit there was something very Catholic still alive in her and she didn't know what to do about it. I invited her to meet with me during the week, and she pulled out her calendar with enthusiasm. We set a time to meet at my home.

There, in a comfortable old rocking chair, she filled in the rest of the story, the pieces she hadn't shared with the group about her brother, about her happy marriage, and about the fact that Steven was very suspicious of her coming to the basilica for these meetings. He sensed an ominous threat to the happy life they knew. She had never said anything about wanting to return to the church. Now, he was concerned. She was uncomfortable about her desire to continue the series and confused by the conflict this was causing in their relationship. "I fully intended to just come and blow off steam about the church for one night," she reflected. "I had no idea all this would happen inside of me."

When I suggested she invite Steven to come to the next session, she seemed surprised. "I don't think he will come," she said, "but I'll ask." Steven came and fended off any attempt at conversation with team members or seekers. He sat with his arms folded across his chest, watching Irma connecting with her new friends. Steven chose not to participate in the small groups that evening and said nothing during the large group presentation and discussion. I feared Irma would not be coming back the following week and it saddened me. Her energy and enthusiasm had begun to invigorate the entire group and I knew they would miss her. Affectionately claiming her as their personal papal emissary, they were beginning to see her as a leader. When we finished the session, Steven hurried toward the door. The doorway was congested with seekers in discussion and I nonchalantly positioned myself in the only exit area. I thanked him for coming and asked if he had any questions. It was the first time he had allowed me to speak directly to him all evening. His face was firm and he looked me straight in the eye, "I came here for one reason, to see what kind of lightning rod Irma is being attracted to." End of conversation. My heart was heavy.

The following week, Irma and Steven were the first to arrive. Irma was jubilant. They had been talking all week long about God, about church, and about each other. Steven seemed more relaxed, less threatened, but still cautious. Except for welcoming him back, we gave him a lot of space. He seemed to enjoy the honesty coming from all corners of the group, the exposed vulnerabilities, the questioning. He began to share some of his own experience and doubts from his Protestant background, and before long he was as involved as the rest of them in the evening's agenda. He left with good humor and said he was coming back. Irma winked at me.

The next day, Irma was called back to Poland. Her mother was in a nursing home because of Alzheimer's disease, and her death was imminent. Her father was frantic because the priest wouldn't give her Viaticum. "After all," Father explained, "she doesn't know what it means." Irma was to learn that the priest had refused to bring communion to her mother during the final months of her illness for the same reason. She was livid.

But Irma was no longer submissive and compliant. In just three weeks, she had reclaimed her eucharistic roots. She was a woman on a mission, "a Catholic woman," she realized during her flight. Her new-found confidence was too much for the aging priest and he relented. Her mother died in the arms of her husband and daughter and her church. Irma realized that was how she needed to die too, but feared during the homeward journey that it could never happen. We hadn't discussed annulments yet; all she knew was that forms had to be completed and information had to be substantiated. Her entire sacramental history had been lost in a political bombing of the church where she had belonged.

Irma had many questions at that next session. She looked tired and drained, but Steven was with her and they had talked through the night. Could the two of them schedule an appointment with me to talk about how Irma could come back to the church? She desperately craved the Eucharist. They were confused; she had bonded deeply with her Protestant community and could not fathom wrenching herself from those relationships. What about her children, now grown? What would this do to their marriage? Was it too late? Was it possible?

Again in the old rocking chair, Irma listened intently as I explained what annulment means. This woman couldn't wait until we covered it in our meetings. She needed to know now! Armed with a new understanding of conscience from the previous evening's session, she was beginning to believe she had a chance. I explained the various kinds of annulments: external forum, internal forum, and lack of form or defect of form. (These are explained in Chapter 5.) It seemed like a lot for her to take in considering her emotional exhaustion, but she listened intently. I gave her some reading material and asked her not to rush into any decisions about anything. If there was anything I was certain of, it was that God would not call her to anything that would be divisive in her relationship with Steven.

Steven brought me something the following week, a cross made out of nails and copper wire. He made it, he said, "for the lightning rod that had been attracting Irma."

They worked hard to track down her records in Poland, but it was impossible. The church didn't respond to her calls, faxes, or letters.

What Irma wanted most at this point was for the church to recognize in some way that this marriage to Steven was centered on God, that she was not living in sin, and that she could reclaim her Catholic heritage. I gave her the name of a wonderful, elderly priest, a healer and shepherd. After several visits, Irma asked him to facilitate an internal forum solution. He agreed. Several weeks later, that same priest attended a small gathering at Irma and Steven's home where we all acknowledged the presence of God in their union and the blessing of these people to each other, to their family, and to all of us. What a celebration!

A year later, Irma was stunned when Steven said he wanted to be part of the RCIA process and the two of them journeyed toward the Easter Vigil together. I don't know whose face was brighter that night, Irma's or Steven's. They are active members of the Catholic faith community now. Steven is a Lector and Irma is a Eucharistic Minister. My throat swelled last Holy Thursday when I saw the two of them washing the feet of fellow parishioners. What a gift they are to us, what an example of faith.

They have made it a point to stay connected with their Protestant faith community, and have been surprised at the interest and support they received from their friends and family there. Their children are cautious, but curious about all the changes in their parents' lives.

"All that anger and rage I brought there, Carrie," Irma mused during our last visit, "it's gone now. I still have lots of church issues, but they are not important. What is important is that the church has room in it for people like me, people whose lives don't fit in the rule books." Steven winked at me, adding, "and we found out that your lightning rod was Jesus."

Tom

He was in a relaxed, happy mood when he arrived for our appointment one Saturday after having breakfast with his adult children and grandchildren. He obviously values his relationships with all of them; they are a vital part of his life. That same relaxed demeanor had intrigued me the evening we met, the first night of our series. Many seekers exhibit extreme discomfort in the beginning, but Tom appeared to be a man who not only knew himself, but was comfortable with who he is. I hadn't thought of him as a grandfather then, but he does exude the gentle strength and confidence so characteristic of grandfathers.

Throughout the series I was struck with the vast spectrum of knowledge he had about church and societal issues. He didn't speak often, but when he did, the group clearly recognized *wisdom*. This was a man who thinks and reads, who reflects and discerns. It was evident that he was firmly rooted in Christ-centered spirituality. I wondered how he could have been attracted to our series since he seemed so capable of reasoning things out on his own and it was evident he knew much more about the Catholic Church than most seekers.

He was born into an upper-middle class family in a suburb, and looks back on his childhood as a happy, complacent time. His mother was Irish Protestant; his father, Irish Catholic. Not until he was grown did his mother tell him how painful it had been for her to sign the document promising to raise her children Catholic. Although she continued to worship in her own church throughout his childhood, she was a strong support in their Catholic nurturing. Tom and his siblings attended Catholic elementary schools and high schools. He graduated from a Catholic college. He never doubted his faith. In fact, he was convinced during his early years that there was something better about being Catholic. On rare occasions when the family attended functions at "Mom's church," he reflects, "I had this feeling, even when I was very young, that this was different. What could I have possibly known about theology at age six? Yet, I felt just a little uneasy about being in a church without statues. It was confusing to me because the people were so nice to us and I enjoyed myself, but my earliest recollection was that uneasiness about whether or not it was as good as my Catholic Church."

When I asked whether church was a good thing for him back then, his response was an enthusiastic "Yes!" A few seconds of silence followed and he added quietly,

> There was a certain amount of fear of hell. But even in grade school I would write the answers on the test I knew they wanted me to put down, knowing that I didn't really believe what they wanted me to at times. I guess from very early on I learned to pick my fights and I knew those were fights I couldn't win so I just went along with it, kind of an all right, whatever attitude. But in my heart there was always that question, "How do you know that,

what makes you so sure?" It was as if I had this sense that there was much more than all the rules even back then.

After he graduated from high school, Tom joined a religious order. When he left after a short time, the novice master insisted, "This is a mistake. If anyone in this class has a true vocation it is you." For years those words stayed with him, connected to a part of himself that considered them true. He contemplated returning from time to time, but his life just kept taking him further and further away. He finished law school, married, and the thoughts faded. But the church held out something mysteriously inviting to him.

Much later in life, Tom would find himself reading intensely about church and theology issues. He recalls reading a book on the history of the Catholic Church and concluding that much of what had been presented to him as absolutes were the results of political maneuvering, "one group contending against another and sometimes being bloodily put down by the orthodox." His eyes dance as he relates, "In grade school they taught us it was the Holy Spirit who was leading us to this knowledge. When I saw swords and burning books and people being banned, I didn't see the Holy Spirit!" Scepticism began to take hold, along with events in life inconsistent with the absolutes that had been drummed into him throughout his Catholic education.

His marriage crumbled after 12 years, a painful failure for him. He worked hard to recover and to maintain a close relationship with his children. He petitioned for an annulment that was granted. But he continued to avoid a reality that would bring an end to a second marriage and to life as he had known it.

> Most of my life I had to struggle with the denial of my sexual identity. I just couldn't be that! I couldn't even say the word. Church was very much a part of that dread from the earliest awareness, but it wasn't only the church. It was everything. It probably isn't a lot easier to deal with this issue today than it was then, but today there are resources, more education, even support. In the 50s, none of this was available. The word "gay" wasn't even used then, not even "queer"; it was [he uses an expletive] "____ queer" or "God-damned fag."

He cringes as he recalls how determined he was not to have any part of that life. Yet he knew something was different by the time he was in sixth grade. And that difference conjured up vague feelings of hell and damnation. Otherwise, he felt close to God, so he simply put that isolated issue "somewhere, shutting the door tight. That's what I did with it. I dated and tried to act like the other boys my age." In reflection, he surmises that the roots of his leaving the church were probably there then, even though he had no conscious issues that were serious enough to contemplate leaving at the time.

Devastated by the end of his second marriage, Tom sought counseling, a long and painful process that brought him to conscious acknowledgment of his true identity, and much later, acceptance of it as well. It was an agonizing experience that led him to a liberating inner peace with himself and God. But the church was something else.

Eventually, as he began to talk with other gay men and women, he discovered many of them had left the church. Tom began accepting their invitations to worship with them in other denominations. He liked the freedom he felt there, to be open and honest, to be accepted for who he was. Yet he felt pulled back to the Catholic Church, convinced he could make a difference, that his painful experience was somehow a call to work within the system toward a time when gay men and women wouldn't have to leave. He became active in Dignity, an organization of Catholic homosexuals, arguing with gay friends who insisted he wasn't welcome in the church. "But I don't feel that way," he countered; "I am a Catholic."

A fierce political battle with the local ordinary that resulted in Dignity being banned from its Catholic facility was a serious blow to the infrastructure of his Catholic identity. He seemed almost amused that he could ever have been so naive about what he calls "church politics." His strong church commitment and his legal background called him to serve as a spokesman for a cause destined to be crushed by a system far beyond his comprehension.

> Those men at the chancery were our spiritual leaders. We were dealing with a matter of our own identity, our core identity, and trying to find a way to reconcile that within the church because we loved the church. But they seemed to treat this whole thing as a two-cent political issue. Things would get so heated and I kept thinking, "Why doesn't he say, 'Let's pray together. Will you at least accept my blessing?'" But it never came. It was horrifying.

For the first time, Tom's serene face was contorted now, revealing a flood of emotions yet unresolved from that experience. Words began to tumble out so fast the listener could hardly keep up.

You cannot separate gay from who we are. I can never step out of my gay skin. I tried that for forty years and damned near killed myself doing it. Married two wonderful women who went through hell because of my denial. Thank God I have been able to make my peace with them and my children. I was about 43 when I came out. I can't step outside that skin but what I can do is say, "Okay, I'm gay. This is how God made me. Big deal. As the kids say nowadays, 'Deal with it!'" Then the real challenge is, "How do I integrate that into my life?' And that is a lifelong challenge. But there are a lot of positive things I can do. Human sexuality bridges a whole spectrum....I am never going to have the authenticity of a female or a straight male. That's just not who I am; I can never crawl into that skin.

I was blessed then and have been blessed by having the right people in my life at the right moments. During that time I was working with a psychotherapist because I just couldn't handle all this painful reality. I was like an adolescent discovering his sexuality. I was worried because I was in my 40s and acting like a 17 year old. He told me not to worry about it unless all that craziness was still going on a year from then. But it wasn't. I grew into who I was more easily than I could ever have dreamed, with good mentoring and a lot of prayer.

My church relationship was pretty ragged by that time, but I still thought I could hang in somehow. Then came the infamous document, defining all homosexuals as intrinsically disordered. When I read that, I said to myself, "Huh! When I was trying to be straight I was intrinsically disordered." I read that thing twice, asking myself, "Who is this guy anyway, this cardinal?" But then I saw those words that severed my relationship with the church completely, the notation that Pope John Paul II had read the document, approved it, and ordered it to be printed. It was the ultimate betrayal. I didn't even want that document in my house.

I stopped going to Mass immediately and became more involved in Unity, worshiping regularly at their services. Their churches are filled with former Catholics! But I was reading and looking at a lot of other options too. The gay issue led me to other issues that I hadn't looked at over the years. The Catholic system looked less and less Christian to me.

Eventually, I realized there was little grounding or substance to the theology at Unity. I started asking questions because everything seemed so ambiguous. I finally asked the minister whether they believed Jesus Christ is God or not. I thought that was a pretty straightforward question but he responded, "What do you think he is?" Hmm, I wasn't sure. I pressed a little and asked, "What does Unity believe?" Again back to me, he responded, "What do you need Jesus to be?" That was a challenging question to me and I spent a lot of time thinking about it, ultimately deciding I needed a religion that had a consensus on who Jesus is. Their core belief seemed to be whatever you need it to be.

Still searching, Tom began attending services at a Lutheran church led by a female pastor. "Female priests were never my issue, but after seeing her, I wondered, why not? I began to realize that part of my comfort there was because there were so many similarities to the Catholic Mass. But Lutherans don't do liturgy the way Catholics do. Yet it was more than just a matter of liturgy; something was missing and I couldn't put my finger on what it was."

Tom began to think his search was going nowhere; he had tried the Methodist, Unity, and Lutheran Churches. He even read Jewish books, but nothing fit. He describes that period of his life as a "spiritual holding pattern."

"Then one day I picked up the paper and it was like Bingo! There was the ad for Catholics Coming Home. I had learned at Unity that God works in mysterious ways sometimes, so I thought maybe I was supposed to go there and I went." He found the whole process was easier than he imagined it would be.

He smiles as he recalls his actual reentry:

I remember your saying one night, "Maybe after we're finished here you might want to peek into the church and see what it is like...go take a look...it's a beautiful building." At that point, I was thinking, "Oh, no. I don't know if I want to come back to this church or not....but what can it hurt to just look in there?" So I did.

That was Tuesday before Holy Week. I came back for Holy Thursday, Good Friday, and the Easter Vigil on Saturday night. And I have been there ever since. But it all started with that non-threatening invitation...I was not ready to make any kind of commitment.

His amusement grows and he teases me, "Just open the door and take a peek...you don't have to sign up....just take a peek."

Now, several years later, he considers his life as a Catholic:

For me, being Catholic is about liturgy. The liturgies at the basilica engage all my senses. I love the way we talk there about the smells and bells and laugh about it, but that incense is important if for no other reason than that it engages another sense. The decoration of the church engages us visually, the music engages us through sound and language, and all of that combined transports us into something very sensual. I didn't know that so much of our early understanding of church was based on the sensual human experience. I am careful who I use that word with because some people think I am talking about sex. I love liturgy that engages all of our senses.

I used to think of church being the hierarchy, and then there were the rest of us. That has changed for me. I look at the Catholic Church as an enormously big resource for me to draw on as I make my way. It is horribly rich in resources, more than any other organization I know of anyway: two thousand years of history, millions of people and their stories, plus the people who are there every Sunday. That's what I think of when I think of church now.

I suggest that it would be difficult to eradicate the history, breadth, and scope of the Catholic Church from the face of the earth and Tom quietly responds with a question: "How can you wipe it out of your own consciousness?" Touched by his answer, I ask whether returning to the church has changed him, whether it says anything new about who he is. Again he responds from the wisdom source deep within his soul, "I don't know if it says anything about who I am because I'm not sure I've changed a lot. What has changed is that I have become a lot more aware of who I am."

He is still finding his place in the church, discovering that when he thinks one issue is resolved another seems to pop up. He handles this with words his mother always taught him about life: "What do you benefit from sitting in the soup? It's okay to sit there for awhile but then you have to get up and move on." Reflecting on her words, Tom says quietly, "I guess I've sat in the soup a lot, especially with these church issues. Now I say, 'Okay, I'm done with that. I want to go on.'"

Tom has been meeting monthly with a Catholic monastic community, for prayer and spiritual discernment. He has determined that he is not called to monastic life, but knows there is something rippling deep within him. "Maybe there is something more in the church for me...and I have no idea what that could be. But that's what seems to be my next issue...."

Wayne

I was intimidated by Wayne's abrupt manner that first evening. It was a new church setting for us and we were unprepared for acoustical problems in the area assigned to us. Wayne was very annoyed because it was so difficult to hear. I wondered if he was typical of many older seekers we saw in the early days of this ministry, those who had been swept through Vatican II changes with no explanation or pastoral concern. They would come on like gangbusters, insisting the church was no longer Catholic, demanding we return to pre-Vatican II certitude about everything. Our basilica groups are getting younger and younger and although we do have a few seniors in every session, my heartbeat always increases when they arrive. Some of them are tremendously resistant to change, making our job very difficult. Change, however, turned out to be the least of Wayne's issues. He welcomes it!

His comments that night were fired in staccato-like phrases laced with anger, camouflaged hurt, and very little pleasantry. As the series continued, it was obvious that he was well read on many church issues. Although he boasted of having been away more than forty years, this man was obviously still connecting on some Catholic circuits at age 72. He seemed so awed by the new discoveries presented in Catholics Coming Home that he repeated the series a few months later. He doesn't let his defenses down easily, but when he does the deep faith and goodness of this wise man tumble out.

He was happy to accept my invitation to come for an interview, expressing surprise that I found him at all interesting. He began our interview with a statement of his own that would weave itself through our entire discussion: "Although I've been away officially for more than 40 years, it has really been much longer than that. We were brought up to believe the worst thing we could possibly do was go to communion without making a good confession first...that was the worst thing! Murder was nothing compared to that! Also, we were expected to know what was right and wrong and if we didn't know, we were just as guilty as if we knew we were doing something wrong."

He went on to describe an early church formation that was anything but nurturing. Raised in a rural community of fewer than 700 people, he was among the religious minority. There were five churches in town: Methodist, Baptist, two Lutheran, and Catholic. "The Protestants called us murderers, said we had guns stashed in our basement and we wanted to take over the entire country. They were sure of that. I grew up going to public schools that always had one token Catholic teacher."

Not to be outdone by their Protestant brothers and sisters, the Catholics left Wayne with an equally unbending attitude: "To be Protestant was to be wrong. You were not in the true church."

Wayne's family was poor. While his father barely eked out a living at a series of endeavors, his mother stayed home and raised the kids. The depression years were difficult, never enough money for necessities, much less a telephone or a car. His parents were very religious. As she lay dying a few years ago, his mother's only regret was that she could no longer say the rosary twice a day as had been her life-long custom.

World War II lured Wayne into the army shortly after high school graduation, an experience that left a deep impression on him. He was assigned to squadrons that provided gasoline for the "B-29s that flew over Japan." Some of that gasoline fueled the infamous flight of the Enola Gay, the bomber that dropped the atomic bomb on Hiroshima, Japan, in 1945. It is obvious as he speaks of it that he has wrestled with his part in that horror, and that he has found peace in believing it had to be done at the time. It is interesting that he included this thought during our conscience and sin discussions during Catholics Coming Home sessions.

After the war, Wayne enrolled in a teacher's college in the small community where he had grown up. He lasted two years but was terribly bored. A proud man, he reluctantly transferred to an expensive

Catholic university where his tuition, books, school supplies and a $75 per month stipend were provided by the G.I. Bill. It is evident that the government's investment in this man was well placed!

Reflecting on his church experience, Wayne recalls, "I remember as a kid thinking that I would probably end up in hell. Everything was a sin and we always had to go in that black box and tell the priest what *he* thought was wrong for us to do. And if we didn't tell him, we would be committing the worst sin that is possible to commit: making a bad confession and going to communion unworthily." This time, he concludes the refrain with a revelation so new it seems to surprise him: "I now go to communion for the first time in my life without being scared...for the first time in my life!"

A man who has been able to rationalize the horror of war is still trying to understand the horror of the confessional. He ponders this a bit, reflecting on those feelings, experiences he has carried with him for decades. "I never shared that fear with anyone, certainly not my brothers and sisters. We never talked about anything like that. And they left the church too. I have only one brother still living and when I told him about my experience with Catholics Coming Home he said he might like to come back too. I'll bet he is just as afraid as I was."

Wayne discovered other issues that troubled him as he grew up and saw how the church interfaced with the lives of the people around him. He considers many of the issues that upset him to be unjust, even punitive to the people affected, and he cites examples of people whose lives have been negatively impacted by the church.

He goes deeper, to an injustice that is difficult for him to talk about more than a half century later.

> My mother was the treasurer of the Altar and Rosary Society. The priest accused her of stealing money from the treasury [his voice breaks] from the pulpit during a sermon. A private accusation wasn't good enough for him...he did it in front of the whole parish community. We were all devastated. Of course, she took the books right to the bank president the next day and asked him to audit them. A Protestant, he had already heard what had happened and said he was scandalized by what the priest had done. He promised he would audit the books and do such a thorough job that it would stand up to any scrutiny when he was finished.

Years of considering the priest's motives have led him to conclude that he may have been an alcoholic. "A buddy of mine went to see him one time to ask permission to go to a dance and his parents found him still with the priest hours later, both drunk. Where's the justice in a priest doing that with a young high school kid?"

Wayne's litany of church transgressions is lengthy. I asked him if he just drifted away because of all the dis-ease with what he saw going on, or if he made a deliberate decision to leave. The familiar refrain returns:

> I made a decision and I can remember the day. I went to confession and the priest asked, "Is this confession similar to your last one?" I said it was and he said, "Why do you bother coming?" That was enough. My perspective on that was he was telling me I was wasting his time by not making a decent confession. And so I thought, "The hell with it. I'll just get out." This was when I was somewhere between 35 and 40. And, of course, I couldn't go to communion without confession...so!

His decision raised concern from his parents, which he rebuffed by declaring, "I'm not going to go back to confession. If I don't go to confession and at least make my Easter Duty, I'm going to hell. If I'm going to hell anyway, why should I waste my time going to church on Sunday morning?"

Even his father's offer to go to Mass with him failed. "Dad, the Catholic Church is so wrong that I don't want any part of it in any way, shape, or form." Wayne acknowledges the pain this must have caused his father, a man whose sister was a nun, and whose uncle and brother were priests. Tenderly, he recalls, "He was a man of deep Catholic faith."

Wayne declares the main reason he left the church is the result of "two things, hypocrisy and fear." Again, he reminds me, "Remember, this is the first time in my life that I have been able to go to communion without fear, without committing the worst sin there is." I asked him whether he realized all during that time that it was fear that kept him away, acknowledging that some people walk away from the church feeling freedom, not fear. He responds reflectively, "I lived with that fear the whole time."

Typical of his age group, Wayne didn't attend Protestant churches during all those years away. "But remember, there is a difference between leaving the Catholic Church and leaving God. I never left God. I continued to say prayers all the way through. Our Fathers, Hail Marys. I won't say I said them on a daily basis because I know I missed a lot of days, but I know there is a big difference between leaving God and leaving church." Wayne's honesty is unrelenting, sometimes contrasting his self-assurance and intelligence with a stroke of childlike naivete.

He married a Catholic girl and as the children came along, "Sundays were just another day of the week when Mary would take the kids to church and I would stay home. That's all. There was no discussion and no strong emotion about it." That statement is enveloped by a new thought, "I didn't receive Eucharist at my mother's funeral. Hey, I wasn't going to commit the worst sin. Do you see where I was at? During all that time, I didn't even want the Eucharist because I didn't see it as anything positive. It was something imposed on us as a judgment by people at the top of church who had no idea how it affected us. We were controlled by fear."

Through all those years away, he always read the church bulletins his wife brought home, and he read the diocesan Catholic newspaper from cover to cover every week. That's where he saw our ad. He cut it out but did nothing with it until late afternoon of the first meeting night. He called to get more information, still doubting it was anything he wanted to attend. "The receptionist who took my call made me feel like there was someone in the church who does give a damn about people. She talked to me for quite a while and encouraged me to attend the series. She made sure that I knew that she cared and that I was welcome. She did so much. It was the first time in nearly 40 years that anyone in the church cared about me!"

I asked whether he considered, as he was driving to the session that evening, that it would begin a journey back home to the church. "Oh, no! I thought it would be the journey that would be the final break. You said Welcome Back in your ad, so I thought you would try to drag me back to the church as it used to be. I had no knowledge of the kinds of changes that have taken place that specifically addressed my concerns. The church doesn't publicize that kind of information, not even for Catholics who go to Mass every week! Anyway, I had no intention of going back to all that fear and condemnation."

Now Wayne joins his wife at Mass every week and on holy days, but wants to make sure he doesn't misrepresent himself, "I don't want to create the impression that I'm going regularly during the week, although I do go now and then on a weekday. And every time I go, I receive communion! I feel very comfortable at Mass and I have absolutely no fear anymore. This is a huge step for me."

With good humor, he relates:

> After the first time, I waited to see if the fear would set in and it didn't. So I went the next Sunday. I still didn't feel fear. By the third Sunday, I still didn't feel fear, so I thought, "O.K., I'll keep doing this." At last, I am rid of the fear that what I am doing is absolutely going to send me to hell. I have a right to be there because I belong. I am a baptized Catholic. I don't have to be in a perfect state of grace to get the graces from communion! I'm starting to think of myself as a part of the Catholic community now. My wife is real happy but I am not doing this for her.

Wayne still feels some ambivalence about the church. On the one hand, he thinks the Catholic Church has driven people away by convincing them they don't deserve salvation. He thinks church gets in the way of God for too many people. Yet, he knows the church preaches things that are good. "Charity, we need a lot of that." He goes on to describe the volunteer work he does, including preparing tax returns for those who cannot afford to pay accountants. It is obvious that he cares about his clients. He explains, "Both my mother and mother-in-law were intimidated by taxes because they weren't able to go beyond grade school. As I helped them, I realized there were many others who deserved the same assistance. Now I realize that God gave me the ability to do this for others." His face softened and he seemed puzzled when I suggested that God's love was at work through him. It is obvious that this newly-reconciled Catholic has yet to discover that he, too, is a minister.

Lisa

I was hesitant about asking Lisa for an interview. She is a private person whose shyness might be interpreted as being distant. But she responded with a resounding yes when I finally approached her. A psychologist whose preparation for her profession provided a journey of self-understanding, Lisa determined long ago that the church was incompatible with what she believed to be a healthy, holistic approach to life. For her, church and psychology had to be compatible in order for her to embrace religion again.

> It was as if psychology replaced church for me; my concept of God became the loving interaction between people, what we do for each other. That concept didn't seem to fit with my Catholic experience, even though I know that church did have some good to offer me. When I started coming back to the church, I began reading a lot about spirituality and psychology because I wanted to see how the two mesh with what I understand about the world from my studies in psychology. I trusted psychology more than I trusted church. Part of my decision to become a psychologist was because I was a terribly shy little girl. Everyone commented on how I never talked.

As she speaks, I recall that just the Sunday before, she ministered as Lector for the entire basilica community. She had done a beautiful job, reading before a large congregation in that large building. I told her what I was thinking and she acknowledged that she has pushed herself to do this because it is hard for her. "Without that kind of push, I could see myself being a little shut-in somewhere. I realize now that this value I place on relationships, being with people in a healthy way, is also a part of my spirituality."

A math wizard in high school, she purposefully enrolled in a college psychology program because she knew she had to do the "hardest thing for myself. I think that comes from my Catholicism, a good thing from a bad experience." She giggles as she makes this assessment. "The therapists who have helped me are the ones who have pushed themselves, not the ones who just do their job. I think the people who help us in life are the ones who get it. They've been there...they've struggled and have some passion about what they are doing."

The oldest child in a large family, Lisa describes growing up in what was then considered a typical Catholic family in a middle-class neighborhood. She defines her father as a "stickler" to the rules of Catholicism, yet she doesn't recall either parent being very religious. They followed the rules and sent their children to parochial school. Her father worked hard at his profession and her mother gave up her nursing career to raise the children, seven in all. More laughter, even girlish giggles as Lisa suggests that her mother and father seem to love each other very much and are very attached to each other. There was a strong priority placed on family vacations and doing things together. Now they take vacations to visit their children and grandchildren. Their entire marriage has been child-focused.

> Every one of us left the church eventually. And at some point, my parents left. It was after I had gone away to college. When I came home for a visit, I found out they weren't going to Mass anymore. I suspect they just gave up after all of us had left the church in our teenage years.
>
> When I was very little, there were positive things about going to church. And I really bought into the nuns' teaching when I was in grade school. I became this scrupulous little girl, very sensitive, quiet, susceptible to the influence of everything they told me. I wanted to be good. Some of the things they said have stayed with me to this day, and not to my benefit. For instance, when I was about 12, Sister said something like, "The leaves falling in autumn are the number of souls going to hell." Then we would hear that "God is love." I was trying to sort that all out but I couldn't put it together. I have an accumulation of these little gems of wisdom that don't make sense except in a terrifying way.
>
> I also learned that an angry thought is as bad as an angry deed. Anger is bad and I had the most complicated, messy relationship with my little sister. I was always angry at her. So I became vigilant about every thought going through my mind, any feeling. I would tell myself I wasn't angry over and over again, when I was. Then I would go to confession and feel so good for one second. But the anger always came right back. This pattern had a terrible effect on me.

She pulled two snapshots out of her purse to prove her point, one taken when she was six years old. Her face was happy and she is smiling into the camera. In the next picture she is twelve years old and what she calls "a Catholic little girl." It is her brother's First Communion and she looks concerned, withdrawn, evidence of the conflict raging inside. "These two pictures symbolize what being Catholic meant to me, fear of anything that was real inside me."

She describes her family today as "close in a nonintimate way." They never discuss church. When one of her sisters married a Catholic and began going to Mass again, Lisa was convinced it was only to please her husband. "At the time of her marriage I was still separated from the church, yet always connected in an angry way. Now I'm no longer sure that my sister returned only for him." She hasn't told anyone in her family that she has reconciled with the church, a reality consistent with the fact she doesn't tell them much about any other aspect of her life either.

Lisa recalls a traumatic experience—now perceived to be a stepping stone toward leaving the church—that occurred in the fifth grade, while she was still trying to be the perfect little Catholic girl. She was in a class of sixty children and one exhausted teacher, a nun. There was a lot of chaos and disruption in the class and Sister would walk out of the classroom for five minutes as if to abandon them. "She had this crazy routine of rattling her rosary beads real loud so we would know she was coming back. It was supposed to signal us to be quiet." As if she needs to defend herself to me, she declares, "But I was always good, never disruptive."

> One day the class was supposed to focus on a metaphor. Now, I ask, what do 10 year olds know about metaphors? Sister told us some story that I didn't understand at all, asking us to explain what the metaphor meant. The only inkling that came to my mind seemed stupid, so I sank down in my chair and hoped she wouldn't pick me. Other kids were raising their hands, but she called on me and told me to stand up. I stood there thinking, "I can't say I don't know because that would be a lie, since I did have this stupid inkling." So I stood there silently while the other kids were yelling, "Sister, Sister, I know, I know." Sister growled back at them, "No, Lisa will answer the question!" I froze and couldn't say a thing. Finally, she screamed at me, "Get out of my classroom." [This quiet woman is yelling in my living room!] I knew that she didn't really want me to leave the classroom and that if I walked out the door she would be furious, but I couldn't stand there anymore so I walked to the back of the room.

I am touched by how painful it is for Lisa to recall this episode now, after all these years. I can only wonder how painful it must have been for that shy little girl who wanted only to be good.

"Pride is an awful thing," Sister screamed as Lisa dragged herself toward the back of the room. She stood there for hours, crying the

whole time. When it was finally time for lunch, she followed the class out of the room and Sister didn't stop her.

Later that afternoon the principal, also a nun, came into the room and asked to see Lisa. As the two of them walked out of the room, her teacher demanded to know, "Are you afraid of me?" Lisa lied, "No." In her office, the principal, a "nice nun who was a motherly person," asked Lisa if she was afraid of her teacher and Lisa admitted that she was.

> And then I realized she knew and I knew that I had lied. She was very nice to me but the whole thing was terribly confusing. Was I this conceited, proud, deceitful girl or not? I was so ashamed. The entire experience was shaming. Then the principal made some analogy between me and St. Therese, the Little Flower. I don't have a clue what she meant. She was comparing me to a saint and that made me feel good, but it didn't fit with what happened in the classroom. She told me to go and pray about it all and I went back to the classroom, scarred someplace deep inside me.
>
> It was more than 10 years before I ever told anyone that story; it just brought up so much shame in me. I really felt I was guilty of the sin of pride, I was too proud of myself. I was so confused and had no idea that I had a right to be angry at that nun. She had all the power and I had none. We were taught that these ladies were holy and knew what they were talking about, and I just didn't know what to make of it all. Sister had observed something very deficient in me and I had accepted her assessment. Believe it or not, I still haven't worked that all out.

The living room is silent. Lisa seems to be summoning her courage to reveal her thoughts. Finally, she speaks, "You know when you complimented me about reading at the basilica, Carrie? Others have said the same thing, but I still can't let myself feel good about it. Because if I do, then I'll be proud...you know. Oh, my God, that experience just killed me. After all these years and the work I've done to get healthy, it still brings up all this emotion." We turn off the tape recorder for a while and talk about how hard it is to believe we are the beloved of God when we have these scars on our souls.

Lisa's actual departure from church would come seven years later. "I left in a dramatic way, quitting the church when I was 17, during my junior year of high school." By that time she had become even more scrupulous, rarely feeling she measured up to anyone's expectations, certainly not God's. She joined her sisters and brothers as they left for mass one Sunday only to discover they had no intention of attending. One of them would run inside, pick up a bulletin, and they would all leave. She stood in the church vestibule, agonizing over wanting to be with them and doing the right thing, when a priest approached her angrily and ordered, "Go inside or get out of here." She got out of there for 27 years!

During all that time away, Lisa never went to another church and only rarely went to a Catholic Church. Although she went to her sister's wedding and her grandmother's funeral, she didn't participate in either liturgy. Her anger had turned by that time into a feeling of superiority over those who still bought into Catholicism. Her concept of God as a relational being was replaced with her newfound religion, psychology. "It never crossed my mind that I would come back to the church." She had become convinced that this church had "taken everything good about humans out and replaced it with a focus on our evil sinfulness."

Four years ago, the architecture of the basilica was the topic of conversation among new friends she had met at work. They decided to attend a Saturday evening liturgy together. Lisa dreaded the experience. "When I entered it felt foreign to me, but I loved the smell of candles. It connected me to something good in my childhood. The homily was all about love and forgiveness and my defenses were ignited: 'Don't suck me in with that kind of talk.'"

Shortly afterward she saw our ad in the *Minneapolis Tribune* and called me at home to ask whether it would be appropriate for her to come since was not interested in coming back to the church; she was just curious. Already three weeks into the series, I encouraged her to check it out for herself and invited her to schedule some time with me if she felt she wanted to be filled in on what had already transpired. I prepared the series team for the arrival of a newcomer and we must have overdone it because Lisa said the welcoming atmosphere was almost intrusive for her. She would have preferred our leaving her alone, but she sat quietly and listened. She came back for the rest of the series, each time a little more relaxed, less threatened. "I loved the humor there, that a woman was actually ministering out of a healthy connection with church, that you didn't try to deny or hide the ugly stuff."

I asked Lisa if her concept of church has changed during these years since she came back. "Oh, my God, yes! 180 degrees! The emphasis on love and forgiveness versus what we're guilty of. The challenge is still there, but it is a positive challenge. And people are encouraged to grow and learn about themselves, to be healthy in mind, body, and spirit."

And Lisa, has she changed?

> I'm more comfortable with myself. It has given me a lot, a grounding in a sense of values. It has helped me integrate who I am with what I do. This is an adult religion that makes sense to me. Sometimes when I am sitting in the basilica, I realize, "I have to be here. It feels good to be in this place, to reflect, to be at peace, to think about what I am going to do with my life. We all need to be reminded of who we are and where we are going from time to time. If the church can make this kind of difference for me, it would change the lives of other people too. I could not have returned to any other church. I have come home again, and am reconnecting with my roots."

Judith

It was the third week of our Advent series when I noticed someone new at the table. We had missed her when she arrived, an experience all too familiar in her 65 years of being a Catholic. No one ever noticed her. She had managed to find a name tag on her own but it was impossible for me to read it, the writing was so small. When I invited her to introduce herself to the group, she whispered that she had been away from the church all her life, but little else. Her body language, her sad eyes, and her quiet voice told me Judith wasn't at all comfortable about being in that church that night.

This was a particularly congealed group by that third week, with most of the seekers having been away a very long time. The first night had been a hard one. We had not seen that much anger, resistance, and preconceived conviction about all that is wrong with the church in a long time. While trust improved as the evening went on, their frustration level was high by the close of the evening. Nearly all of them came back the following week, expressing eager anticipation about this "new face of church" I had promised them we would begin to explore. As always, our second week focused on images of God, Jesus, and the church. Clustered in small groups, their stories were rich, filled with honesty and personal revelation. Most revealed a tremendously somber if not cruel God, a Jesus who seemed a distant historical figure rather than a living reality and a church of condemnation. During the wrap-up that evening, they all expressed surprise at how good it felt to talk so honestly about their religious experience. By the time they left that second session, this group was church! We were excited by their progress.

This is the group Judith encountered one week later. The pre-session conversation was energetic and free-flowing; the comfort level was high. But she was an outsider, the role she had learned to expect from any Catholic gathering. Except for her quiet introduction, she said nothing during the first part of the evening. I found myself observing her frequently as the material presented was discussed and processed. We looked at Catholic values, how they differ from cultural values, and we considered conversion as a lifelong process. The seekers were lapping it up, applying it to their experiences, and ministering to one another with their stories and affirmation. Judith looked more and more uncomfortable. I decided to call a break so I could talk with her.

Several seekers stayed around the table while others migrated toward the hallway or corners of the room where they continued their discussions. When I made eye contact with Judith, she said, "I don't think I belong here." That was obvious, but I asked why. She said she had been away from the church for more than 40 years and it was evident that "all these people are very active Catholics!"

"But you should have heard us the first night," the few who were in earshot responded, and they began to assure her that they were anything but active Catholics. Within that smaller group, Judith seemed more confident. She explained that it had taken her three weeks to get up the courage to come. She hadn't been able to make herself come the previous two weeks. She made it clear that it wasn't because of the long drive from her home, nor the dark, cold Minnesota November nights. She was convinced the effort would be futile; she simply would not be able to be reconciled with the church. It had been too long and she had distanced herself too far from God. The seekers assured her that was not the case; they were already filled with hope after long absences and serious issues.

She became more relaxed and began to tell us about herself. Born into an Irish Catholic family, her parents had baptized Judith and her only brother in the church. They were a small farm family who never attended church together. She does not recall her parents attending at all. Her mother did resume Mass attendance after her father died, but the subject was never discussed. Her father seemed very separated from the large family in which he grew up, and ghosts of that separation permeated all his relationships. Both parents died without discussing religion with anyone, perhaps not even each other, certainly not with Judith.

Yet they sent her on occasion to Mass with neighbors and for a time there were religious education classes in the summer. "A very nice priest came out to pick us up because it was the only way we would get there," Judith recalled. She remembers mostly learning that God had a low tolerance for people who didn't do what the church said. But it was hard for her to know what that was because her only church connections were those infrequent Masses and she didn't understand what was going on. "They were speaking Latin!" She remembers shame and a feeling of not belonging. And she remembers being sent, again with the neighbors, to make her First Confession. It was not a happy experience. The priest scolded her for not attending Mass every Sunday. In the darkness of that small box, her salvation chances slimmed to almost zero. A haphazard church connection continued throughout her early school years: infrequent Mass attendance with the neighbor family who offered her no sense of belonging other than transportation, and infrequent encounters with the dreaded black box. She began to long for the day when she would be an adult and "didn't have to be Catholic anymore." She was sure Protestant kids didn't have to feel guilty all the time.

Judith's wish came true after some attempts to reconnect with the church during college. For a time, she went to daily Mass at the Newman Center. Convinced from childhood recollections that the most damning sin of all had something to do with sex, she avoided relationships completely, focusing on her education and eventually her work. Church didn't fit into her life at all. For four decades Judith was convinced she was not worthy to be in the church. That also meant she had no entitlement to God. There was so much grief in her eyes at this revelation, I wanted to hold her and comfort her. But I wanted to respect her very private manner and we had to get on with the group. My heart was heavy.

Just before the larger group returned, I invited Judith to schedule a private visit with me and asked whether my home would be a reasonable drive for her. We were mutually surprised to discover she lived very close to the parish where I worked. I invited her to visit me in my parish office, promising that we would set up a private appointment before the series ended. It was hard to read her reaction; she seemed overwhelmed.

The following week, she remained apart from the group, sitting quietly with those same sad eyes and that apprehensive look. I made it a point to speak with her, reassuring her that I wanted to meet with her. By now, this was a need of mine. She exuded goodness. Her tenacity in trying to reconcile with the church was beyond understanding. How, in God's name, could we have rejected her so completely?

She participated more and more during the following two weeks we had together. The group was by that time quite close and congenial. The trust level was high. Judith joined in the laughter as they recalled the change in atmosphere from the beginning of the series. The pastor, a wonderful shepherd with an open heart and authentic humility, spent the last evening with the group. They loved him. One of the seekers agreed to role play "confession" with him, using a scenario we provided. Early into the role play, however, the comfort level moved her into a candid discussion about her own faith journey and Father moved right with her into her story. I watched Judith as we all listened. Hearts were being touched all around the table, the tissue box on a continuous circuit. Judith's eyes were on the priest.

We ended the series with a healing liturgy, a spirit-stirring ritual during which team members ask forgiveness from each seeker. Judith was clearly feeling at home in this Catholic environment. Before she left, I promised her that if she didn't call, I would call her to schedule our appointment.

She called the following week and came to see me. She began by expressing awe that so much had happened in three weeks after so many years of being "unable to connect the dots and be a good Catholic." In her totally nonaccusing way, more in awe than in judgment of the church, she cried, "Carrie, in more than 40 years, you are my first human contact with the church and the first Catholic to reach out to me in my lifetime!" That phrase will haunt me all the days of my life. How many Judiths are there out there, longing for human contact?

I expected her to tell me she had been divorced and remarried, thus the self-exile from the church. Not so. She has been married to the same wonderful man for 40 years, "the best thing that ever happened to me," and they have one grown son. She is a proud grandmother. Her husband was not Catholic and by the time she married, she felt so denounced by God and church that they were married by a judge. That act had sealed her fate. She could not be Catholic again.

I asked how she could account for her lack of bitterness toward a church that had rejected her all her life. Her quiet answer:

> It is the blessed mother. Ten years ago my son became very ill and I was terrified. It had been years since I prayed because I was sure I was not worthy to talk to God, but when he became ill, I simply had to pray even though I considered myself to be in mortal sin. It became clear to me: I could pray to Mary. (You know why, Carrie; you are a mother.) Mary had to watch her son suffer and even though I couldn't talk to God, she would understand how much I loved my son.

Her son recovered, a miracle she attributes to Mary's intercession.

That was five years ago. She tried to connect the dots then by scheduling an appointment with a sister at an area retreat center. "I wanted so badly to come back to the church by that time and thought they could help me." But they couldn't. In fact, Sister politely refused her stipend, telling Judith that their mission didn't include helping people reconcile with the church. Since they couldn't help her, they wouldn't feel right about accepting her check. Judith left, convinced she would never connect the Catholic dots...until she saw our ad.

There in my office, in the parish that was only minutes from her home throughout her exile, Judith and I began to connect the dots. First she wanted to celebrate the sacrament of reconciliation, to experience "something like what happened that night with our group." The role play gave her the courage to believe that a priest would be able to accept her within the sacramental setting. She scheduled an appointment with our associate pastor, a young man ordained only three years. My close association with Father Mark during that time assured me that he would know how to shepherd this lost, wounded sheep. And he did. Confessor and penitent were both moved by the experience.

The next step was the sacramental celebration of her marriage, more bureaucratically referred to as a validation. Father Mark met with Judith and her husband to complete the necessary canonical paperwork and plan the small ceremony. John was very cooperative, explaining that in all their years together he had no idea Judith wanted so badly to belong to the church. Like her parents before her, she simply did not discuss it with anyone. They asked John's brother and his wife, who had been their witnesses at their marriage, to witness their validation ceremony. Judith's sister-in-law was also a baptized Catholic who didn't attend church, and Judith added with a smile, "No, we never talked about it with each other."

Judith was radiant when they arrived for their wedding. She was, in fact, gleeful. Her sister and brother-in-law had just scheduled an appointment with Father Mark to begin arrangements to validate their marriage! They, too, had been married by a justice of the peace. Now they would celebrate their golden anniversary by being remarried in the church.

"But that's not all," Judith added between hugs, "John told me this morning that he wants to become a part of the church, to share this part of my life." A miracle she hadn't even prayed for.

Through my office window, I see Judith coming to daily Mass and am blessed when we share the sign of peace on those days when we are there together. She waited until "I could check 'married in the church'" before registering as a member, and then received Eucharist for the first time in 42 years. The dots are completely in order at last.

Judith and I met for lunch not long ago and she is still giddy about all that has happened since that cold November night. I asked her to help me, to help us as church, to learn what we need to learn so we don't have so many Judiths out there. She seemed surprised that the church would need any advice from her, but she did have something to say. "First," she clarified, "with me it wasn't about being angry, it was about me getting right with God." She tearfully recalled her "long, hard struggle with the church," adding, "The church only takes care of well people; that excludes so many of us." And she repeated, "...you were the only one in all those years!" We need to listen to this prophet's plea.

I asked Judith to give me a conclusion to her story and her face lit up, "It's overwhelming. God's love is simply overwhelming."

Michael

Although he arrived very early the first night of our series, he looked very unhappy about being there. Arms folded tightly across his chest, feet planted purposefully on the floor, he appeared to be forcing himself to face whatever was to follow. His face reflected a mixture of defiance and discomfort. Attempts at welcoming conversation were fruitless. Several times we thought he would leave before we got started. Although his dress and appearance indicated a confident man, probably in his early 40s, his demeanor suggested a frightened child. As others entered the room and were greeted by team members, he sat alone, eyes darting from one new arrival to the next.

When the group gathered to begin, he again chose a place removed from them. Yet, it appeared he was staying. It was our first night of the series so we were hearing the seekers' reasons for being away from the church, for questioning its role in their lives. He said nothing. His initial anxiety seemed overcome by an expressionless calm. While the others joined in conversation, topping one another's stories, and generally commiserating about their common Catholic heritage, he seemed untouched by anything they had to say. And when we invited those who felt comfortable doing so to join in a closing Lord's Prayer, he pulled even further away, making sure we knew he wanted no part of praying with us. He stood alone, arms still tightly folded across his chest, as we prayed. He left just before the Amen without a word to anyone.

It is the Michaels that keep us awake, the Michaels for whom we pray most fervently between sessions. I was sure he would not return. We had failed to connect on any level, even eye contact was abruptly rejected. Team members who tried to visit with him voiced concern during our wrap-up after the session. The message he sent out had been picked up by all of us.

You can imagine our surprise when he was the first to arrive the following week. We greeted him but honored the message he had sent out the week before; he did not want us hovering over him and he did not want to mingle. He picked up the handouts, made a name tag, and planted himself outside the circle we had prepared for the evening's discussion. Arms folded, same somber expression on his handsome, clean-shaven face.

We discussed images of God and Jesus that night, how they were formed, the people who influenced those images, the childhood images we had been dragging into adulthood that were not helpful. When the seekers broke into small group discussions, Michael chose not to participate, stating flatly, "I don't really believe in any of this stuff." But he didn't leave. He waited. And he listened to the frank, revealing feedback that erupted from those discussions. He left before the Lord's Prayer that night, having said only that one all-encompassing sentence the entire evening. Because he had chosen neither to sign in nor leave his address on our roster, I felt a sense of loss as I watched him exit. While the rest of the group had already begun to form community, Michael seemed only to feel more isolated by the process. More prayer and another restless night followed.

The ritual repeated itself the third week, with Michael's early arrival. Gary was able to do some "guy talk" with him that night and learned that he had been raised on the West Coast, worked for an international corporation in the Twin Cities, was married, and had children. We were making progress! But as the group spontaneously took their places, he repeated his retreat. This was the night we began talking about church, how it has been perceived in the seekers' individual lives. And the difference between faith and religion, the relationship between the two. Throughout our time with the seekers, we emphasize God's love and the belovedness of each one of us. Michael listened less passively, but he didn't participate. Sometimes he leaned forward almost as if he had something to say; sometimes he hugged his chest so tightly I felt sure he was protecting himself from receiving anything from any of us. Michael stood during our closing prayer that night. It wasn't the familiar Lord's Prayer, but an Advent prayer I had selected to help the seekers draw into the journey of anticipation. While he neither participated nor looked at the printed words, he did drop his defensive guard during that prayer, and he didn't leave before it was over.

Instead, he came directly toward me, shook my hand and said he was getting a lot out of the sessions and wanted to continue. I acknowledged his apparent discomfort and asked if there was anything I could do to help. "I want to talk to you alone...you and your husband...but not here," he answered, eyes down, shoulders hunched. Only in retrospect I realize what courage it took for him to ask for anything from anyone connected with church. That was truly a graced moment for us, one of countless reminders that there is a Spirit at work in this ministry beyond anything we can understand. We scheduled a time to meet with him two evenings later, at our home. He apologized for taking up our time, shook our hands again, and left without speaking to anyone else.

We were not prepared for what he shared with us that evening. Michael's life had been ravaged by sexual abuse by his pastor and subsequently brothers at a Catholic boarding school. The three of us wept openly as he pushed himself through his story, reliving the episodes and the church's compounded abuse in its refusal to provide advocacy, healing, or even validation of the ravage that had occurred. The weight of those experiences had colored his entire life, mostly in gray and black. "But," I protested, "you have survived; you have gotten an education; you are married and have a family. How have you accomplished all of that in spite of this horror?"

Eyes down, speaking slowly and deliberately, he began a litany of therapists, counselors, and individuals who had helped him along the way, none of them even remotely connected with the church. Even his parents were missing from the list. Confused and traumatized by their son's violation by the church they loved, their parental instincts to rebel and advocate for him had been paralyzed. He was quick to defend them. "It was a different time then; none of this was as public as it is now." This man's heart was capable of forgiveness. His love for his parents was even stronger than the damage that had been done to him. We marveled at that while we expressed our own anguish. We were walking on sacred ground with Michael. In spite of his mistrust of the church, he had invited us into his life. Victims of church-connected abuse usually project anger, even rage toward church, the offenders, even us. When I mentioned this, Michael responded, "Life has to go on. I carried that with me for a long time and all it did was compound the abuse, kept me from enjoying life, from letting anyone into my space."

I asked the obvious question, "Do you need to reconcile with the church?" We assured him that we didn't expect everyone to come home again; indeed, there are those whose mental health requires that they distance themselves from anything connected to church. After all he had revealed, Michael seemed to be one of those people. He had lived without the church for a long time and seemed to have a good life. Why did he need the church again?

> It's about my wife and kids. They mean everything to me. My wife is Catholic and I promised her we would raise the kids Catholic. That seemed easy when we were planning our life together years ago, but now it is hard for me. For years, I just let them go off to church together on Sunday mornings. A strange kind of loneliness swept over me every time. Finally, I decided to just go along with

them, but I couldn't even sit through an entire Mass. I would have to leave. My body would suddenly be up and out of there, without any willful thought on my part. When I saw your ad in the paper, I thought maybe you could just help me find a way to sit through Mass with my family.

By now, he was weeping again and so were we.

Church is always about belonging. And alienation is the antithesis of belonging. Michael's childhood scars were separating him from his family in the very place we Catholics celebrate our connectedness to one another. God was no help to Michael. From the onset of the abuse, he had known there was no God, only a church that had power over him.

He confided, "This God of love you talk about, Carrie, I've never heard that kind of talk before. And I hear you telling us in those classes that we are the beloved. Do you know I keep thinking about that and can't believe you are a Catholic! We don't even know the same God. I don't think I could ever believe again, but that loving God is the one I want my kids to know."

Our work with Michael had just begun. He attended all the rest of the sessions, participating, interacting, and obviously reading the information we sent home with everyone each week. The group accepted him and learned to enjoy his dry sense of humor. He never revealed his story to the others, but he did meet with us individually a number of times. In the safety of our home, he reflected that he was beginning to realize that the abundant love flowing between him, his wife, and his children must be from the loving God, so there must be a God after all. When, on the final evening, we invited the group to attend a Celebration of Reconciliation at the basilica, he apologized for not being able to attend. Later, he told me he could not go into the sanctuary; he was not ready for that.

That Advent series ended two weeks before Christmas. During the goodbyes after the session, Michael stood alone again, waiting until the others had left. "I don't want to promise you anything, but I think I am going to go to Christmas Mass with my family." He thanked us for what he perceived to be our patience with him, for giving him space, and for letting him into our lives. We promised him that he and his family would be in our prayers on Christmas, whether he went to Mass or not.

In January, I received a letter from Michael:

Dear Carrie,

On Christmas Day I went to the basilica with my family. I really did not feel inspired being there; in fact, I was getting angry at being there. Then, at the moment of the peace exchange, I started to shake people's hands around me and they mine, as we exchanged pleasantries. At that moment, I remembered what you kept saying throughout the seminars: We are the church. These good people and I are the church. I became more aware that they were all there to honor God, to be together in believing in a God of love. This was church to me and it was meaningful. From that point on I remained in touch with that community and its gratefulness. I have fought long and hard. At times, this warrior needs rest and food and at times I call the battle cry. This warrior has not quit fighting yet. Thank you for your rest and food. I feel much stronger.

It is not likely that Michael will ever be completely reconciled with the church. In his own words, though, he reveals the essence of what it means to be Catholic. Although unable to take his place at the table, he has begun to experience Eucharist through the community. Healing and reconciliation take many forms, and for seekers like Michael, sometimes years or even a lifetime. Through the love of his wife and children, he has opened himself up to God again, a loving God with whom he is just beginning to feel comfortable.

Roger

Roger's Catholics Coming Home experience was at times agonizing to observe, often presenting almost biblical images of a man who wrestles with God. Time and again, he would demand definitive answers, "Just tell me what the church's bottom line is on this!" And time after time we would encourage him to go deeper within himself to find the answers. Internal pressures that had built up during previous weeks exploded on the night we talked about adult conscience formation. His agitation was visible and his unusual silence told the group he was uneasy. This is not a man who hoards words! During a discussion on sin, the seekers revealed the dawning of a new awareness of sin, far removed from rules, regulations, dos and don'ts. They were seeing sin as something more internal, realizing this broader understanding precluded judging others. Only months later would he be able to admit that he had spent his life in a comfort zone, naming the sins of others, but rarely reflecting on his own authentic relationship with God.

But that night he finally blew up and cited the example of a murder case that was spread all over the newspapers and television broadcasts. It was a heinous crime, almost incomprehensible in its horror. "If there was ever someone who has to burn in hell, it is this person! These actions are not human." In anguish, he begged for consensus. It didn't come. Only stunned silence.

Gently, responding to Roger's pain, the seekers began to explain why they couldn't agree with him. The room was somber as one seeker after another spoke on a heart level, contextualizing within their newly discovered sense of conscience, responsibility, and God's unconditional love, their comments on the eternal plight of the murderer's soul. Roger backed his chair away from the group and cried out from somewhere deep inside, "Then why does anyone have to be good if God can forgive everyone?"

Again, only silence responded to his plea. I looked around the table and realized that all eyes were averted. Everyone sensed this was a moment not to be tarnished with simple answers or persuasive conversation, certainly not argument. The struggle was Roger's and all we could do was honor it. He looked at me, waiting for me to say something that would make sense with his "truth." I could only respond by acknowledging the awe I was experiencing as I watched his struggle, the respect I had for him as he allowed so much pain to surface, so much honesty to spill out, so much doubt and fear to poke its head through his comforting blanket of certitude. Deep inside, I knew that this evening's struggle would be a significant part of his faith journey. I suggested that we were all standing on holy ground in the sharing of that moment. One by one, the seekers gently concurred, speaking directly to Roger, assuring him of their prayers during the week, thanking him for trusting them so completely, for being so honest.

In retrospect, we had each considered during the week that Roger might not return. It would be easier to dull that kind of spiritual pain with an escape of some kind. But he came and he looked amazingly peaceful. He was greeted with a warmth that revealed deep respect and caring. Of course the evening began with Roger, who had lots to say. He had scheduled an appointment with one of the basilica staff members, confident that she would tell him that our group had gone awry, that he, indeed, was correct in his assessment of God's wrathful judgment on anyone who breaks a rule. Instead, he found another solid wall of disagreement, prompting him to reflect on what was going on inside him, on why he was so intent on a one-size-fits-all theology that imposed obedience and judgment on everyone. He related that the meeting had been excruciatingly painful, but after an hour and a half, "I got it!" He was jubilant though still having trouble putting into words what he "got." But he was at peace with the ambiguity. As we pursued concepts of healing and forgiveness that evening, he revealed a man changed by new discoveries within himself.

Months after the series ended, we met in our living room to talk about Roger's journey. As I read the transcript from that visit, I realize his words need little massaging from me. This is a man who speaks from his gut. A man who has made more than a million dollars, lost it, and made it again, he is at ease with power and control. Yet as he speaks he often reveals vestiges of that inner vulnerability and conflict so evident during that crucial session at the basilica. He prefaced his interview by admitting that the anticipation of it had given him an opportunity to think more about his faith journey, the church, and where he was headed.

Roger had already decided to return to the church by the time he came to Catholics Coming Home, but he wanted to know more about what the church taught, more about what he had missed during his 43-year absence.

> I hoped I would find what I needed to know about the rules and regulations. I didn't want to hear about personal responsibility and conscience issues! That was not what I came there for at all. I have this longing for rules...maybe because it is a lazy approach. It is easier if I know we have to believe this or that, to go back to the absolutes we were taught in catechism when we were kids. That's where I got my belief system, from the time I was seven until about ten years old when I learned the system and the rules. And they applied to everybody the same way! But what it boils down to, really, are the tough questions...it comes down to conscience, faith, living this stuff hands on.

His words shoot out like bullets at times, then silence, then a silky flow of quiet reflection that seems to come from another man, another time. Often he becomes animated, energetic, speaking with his whole body, even when the words have to push their way out through a swollen throat and unfamiliar tears. The flow seems endless, one thought nearing completion opens up another tributary of memories, feelings, thoughts, questions. Clearly, a dam has cracked in this man's soul and there will be no more holding back the rushing waters of God's spirit within.

"When you're gone for the extent of time I was..." He interrupts himself, "But it is important, Carrie, that you know that church never really did *go;* it was *always* there. Not a day went by in all those years that there wasn't some part of me that wasn't still rooted and grounded in the church. But all those years...if you glimpse at anything and put 43 years between, there are going to be major league changes." He gazes out our living room window and proves his point, "Even your yard has changed in 43 years!" It is as if he needs to convince me of truths he is in the process of discovering for himself.

> But I didn't want that! I wanted to come back to the church I left. I was adult enough to know that they hadn't put the tape on pause for me, and I was smart enough to know that this was going to be a very different church than what I had capsulized somewhere inside me all that time; I thought I had some semblance of what was going on since Vatican II. For me, the down side of the changes is the global picture. It seems like those bishops at Vatican II lowered our expectations of each other as human beings, down-graded our expectations of ourselves, tried to make things too easy for us.

Now comes a flow of insight from another direction:

> But on the other hand, what if they had just kept blindly plodding along? They would be as guilty as the Inquisition and all the sins connected with that if they kept blindly doing what they were doing just because they had some sense of authority that spanned 2000 years. There are two sides to that issue. A side that says those bishops were arrogant to impose all that change, for God's sake, and on the other hand, to stand back and say, they must be responsive. The church would *die* if they hadn't done what they did at Vatican II. I know that.

He is alternately shouting and whispering as he speaks. I'm thinking he has had this conversation with himself before, and often.

> One of the changes I really like is that we don't kneel so much anymore. I will never forget kneeling at the communion rail when I was a kid, about nine years old, waiting for the priest to get to my end. I walked home with a neighbor after Mass one Sunday and I said, "I got so sore from kneeling today," and she yanked me up by the collar and said, "That's nothing compared to the price that Jesus paid on the cross!" It was a message I never forgot. When my back gets a little sore, or I feel like I can't stand something for much longer, Mrs. Wilson's words come into my brain. Like I am nine years old again! But it straightens me up and takes away the fatigue when I think of it that way.

The river shifts directions again.

> Change isn't always good though. I'm not sure we understand sacrifice the way we used to. I'm left on my own and I'm not very good at doing it on my own. The church has to provide a structure, a place to get rules and regulations. I don't want church to be a social club and that's what a lot of parishes seem to be. Yet, I'm uncomfortable with too much of this soul-searching stuff about forgiveness and conscience. But in many ways the church is a better place than it was when I was young. It certainly is a friendlier place; a lot of people in the Catholics Coming Home group commented on that. The feeling of hospitality is much better today. And we can interact with everyone, even the priest. When I grew up our relationships with the priests and nuns were based on fear and respect, a mixed bag of things that aren't there today. But Father O'Connell is a parishioner like the rest of us. I think that is healthy. The playing field is leveled. But the church doesn't seem to hold us as accountable as it used to, and that makes it easier for me not to be accountable for myself.

Always, the struggle. And back to its source.

> I was the oldest child, kind of the family "pope" after my dad died. We were okay economically, and attended the parish school. Dad had a falling out with the church, some issue that was never discussed with us, although I knew it bothered my mother. But we

were still a Catholic family. Dad just wasn't in the loop. His attitude was, "I'm not participating in this but you are and your butt is going to get paddled if you don't." Dad was clearly the enforcer. He died in an accident when I was 17, without ever coming back to the church. He wasn't even buried from the church. By that time, my mother had drifted away as well. Once we all got out of grade school, she just gave up and let us do our own thing. But she is watching what is happening to me with serious interest. She's in her 80s now and I know she will come back. If all these seeds are in me, she must be the one who planted them! Her mother was a fanatical Catholic and lived with us for about two years when I was between five and seven years old. All my images of Grandma were of her praying and pacing by the hour, saying the rosary, this little old German lady wrapped in her shawl. When my mother would ask her why she prayed so much she would snap back, "Shut up; half these prayers are for you."

I don't know how or why church stopped for me. My memory is gone on the issue. I don't recall making a decision about it. I just drifted. And my sisters and brothers followed me. There were places I didn't want to go, though. Where I lived in the city, it was the in thing to be an ex-Catholic, but it was hard for me to visit Aunt Betty on the farm. She was a very important person to me. My mother's whole family held a special place in my heart. Mom would ship me there every summer, a farm in Iowa. They were German, rural Catholics. Two of my cousins became priests and two were nuns. When I went to church there, it took on a different meaning. We said prayers before we went to bed and we never did that at home. We said the rosary a couple of times a week. Religion was woven into their daily lives there. At home, religion was something we did on Sunday mornings and talked about at school.

His face changes when he talks about the farm. Even in memory, it provides an emotional haven.

I remember a wedding up there. It was one of my cousins and I desperately wanted to go. I'd been away from the church for about ten years, was married, and had the station wagon, the kids, and the mortgage. I can remember asking myself what I would tell Aunt Betty about church. So I didn't go. Then another cousin's wedding, and I couldn't stay away. But it was very hard. Not that there was ever any condemnation up there,...but I felt their disappointment and that was worse. You can argue when someone condemns you, but when you disappoint people...

"My wife wasn't religious either. She wasn't even baptized, but when the kids came..." His thoughts jump forward.

They bother me, my kids and my grandkids. I started working on our family history a few years ago and discovered that my kids are the first in 400 years to be raised outside the church. You can't imagine how that struck me. With the arrival of each grandchild I felt more compelled to come back. Holding these grandkids when they were born was awesome to me, the connection I felt with all these Catholic family members I'd been reading about, and I am the link that broke! When the last one was born, I just couldn't deny it anymore. I owe it to the kids. At least now they will know what they belonged to before I die.

I have no idea why, but we got married in a Protestant church. Not that we were giving any real commitment to that faith or anything either, but we just thought it would be better for the kids to be something. I didn't internalize anything for more than 25 years. I just ignored anything that had to do with faith. I wouldn't allow myself to think about that stuff because those questions were hard work. I had a good life, so what more did I need?

His voice drifts off and he speaks softly, to himself, "...not nearly as good a life as I could have had now that I look back." His face turns toward me and I see tears, "The waste of more than 40 years is just awesome to me."

When I go over and over the story in my mind, I keep asking myself, "How the hell did I end up Protestant in this process? Why didn't I just go back to the Catholic Church then?" But I know the reason: the Protestants didn't ask questions and there was no confession. I didn't have to confront anything. They made it just as easy as pie for me to continue this nonconfrontational, unexamined lifestyle. Confession was it! That's what kept me from coming back to the Catholic Church and that is exactly what I needed. The Protestant church had no confrontational rules, no corners I had to dig into and confront. So I tried to be a Protestant for the first half of my time away.

"I can tell you the day spirituality came back to my life because it is so memorable." He begins to cry openly, deep sobs that flow into words describing what he called an "extraordinary, painful experience," one that he insists he doesn't ever want to happen again. He seems to need the tears in order to continue the story. Head back, trickles of sorrow wetting his face, he relives the memory.

I had built a successful business, had lots of money, a wonderful family, everything going for me. I was on a business trip in San Antonio and found myself with two free afternoons. In all of my world travels, I made sure my schedule never included free time; I wanted to keep busy because my time was so important. So here I am with two afternoons I don't know what to do with. The first afternoon I went to the River Walk, wandering up and down, thinking it was fabulous to take all that in with no phones ringing. Thank God we didn't have cell phones then! I shopped for my wife and kids and realized I was actually looking forward to more free time the next day. That realization was confusing to me. I was looking forward to no appointments, no meetings, no family demands, no nothing! Just me, by myself, for a whole day of doing nothing that mattered. I couldn't wait, and when the next afternoon rolled around, I found myself heading toward the Alamo. I moseyed through it, enjoying the history, the folklore, and being alone. Then I walked down to the ancient mission church nearby. I rationalized that since I was sightseeing, I could go in this historic Catholic Church. I looked at the architecture, read the plaques, and crossed in front of the altar. Remember, this was 20-some years after I had left the church. But I genuflected as I crossed the aisle in front of the altar *and* made the sign of the cross! I sat in a pew and asked myself, "Where the hell did that come from?" I started bawling like a baby and couldn't stop. I think I sat there for a couple of hours. O God, it felt so good to be there. But I couldn't deal with how I would go back and tell that to my family. How could I explain how I felt about this strange church that none of them knew anything about because I had never mentioned it? I went back to the same old grind the minute the plane landed in Minneapolis. It was all over. I'm a workaholic and that's the way I avoided dealing with the pain. I was really confused. Why would God do this to me? I ignored all the signals but that was the beginning of coming back...20 years ago!"

We take a short break. Roger is wrung out from this encounter with his past. I ask if he would like to stop, but he finds refuge in his corporate demeanor, reciting facts that have occurred since the arrival of his grandchildren. His wife is open to his new self-discovery and has joined him on his journey, finding less conflict, less turmoil with the church, less baggage to unload and more freedom to embrace whole-heartedly the faith that Roger is still trying to define. Since this interview, they have had their marriage blessed and the two of them are considering various opportunities for ministry within their parish community.

With humor, he suggests, "I have to throttle back my enthusiasm. Nothing worse than recovering smokers and religious fanatics. I have to guard against pushing it. My kids all know what is going on and I haven't pushed any of them."

Calm now, he goes back to that dark old church in San Antonio and the fear rooted in that experience. "Will the newness wear off? I know I'm still in the euphoric, honeymoon stage. Will there come a time when it isn't new again?" I speculate that it will, that any love relationship has to be nourished, fed, considered on a daily basis in order for its roots to grow deeper. "You are right. I find myself hungry for more depth. Books I read keep getting deeper and heavier." He tells me about several of them and I am amazed at the theological depths which he is exploring after all those years he describes as shallow and meaningless. He asks why we don't do a Catholics Coming Home just for men, convinced that many men are as spiritually dead as he was, dulling their spiritual thirst with more and more busy work, making money, accumulating material evidence of wealth. He tells me about friends of his who have begun asking him about the church, men like himself who disconnected from church long ago.

He seems irritated with me when I minimize his suggestion with laughter. "I'm serious, Carrie. My life is not unusual at all among men in this country. My only regrets in life are the awesome emptiness of those 43 years. I could have had so much more than money, the big house, and a corporation." Quickly, he worries that he will get caught up again in addictive busyness. He has spent his life being busy and being successful. Now he knows the danger of not being still, not reflecting, not talking about what's going on inside.

> I didn't even pray during all those years, although there were times when I wanted to. Like when my kids were born, those times when you are so full you want to thank God for this gift. But the one thing you don't want to do when you leave the church is let God think that you need him only in these kinds of peak experiences. Catholics come home on their deathbeds. But now I realize that I am praying all the time, in a new and different way. I have become more aware of the signals that God sends me, many of which I don't pay attention to even when they are written on my forehead! Very good things are happening and I am able to see that there is more to life than the American Dream.

Chapter 3
What Are You Bringing Them Home To?

Those who've come undone, those going to pieces, those who are broken or breaking down find that they are lifted up and held safely and gently here. Fragile, tender, even raw, one is healed with hospitality here. At this table, there's a place for everyone. Those acquainted with judgment and rejection, those deemed "less distinguished" because of their race, economic status, their age, gender, or sexual orientation—the poor and the lame—they have a place of honor here. In this house, importance is not an issue; it's a given. In God's house, everyone is important and precious.

The leaders of this parish and its priests will come and go, as will their unique abilities and liabilities, their particular philosophies and idiosyncrasies, their personal passions and obsessions....What must endure through it all is the exercise of this community's preeminent charisma: its broad, deep, and humble hospitality. I beg you to continue to cultivate and nurture this inspired humility and hospitality: practice it, perfect it. Be quick to welcome those who cannot repay you. In that way, you will give the church and the city a glimpse of the kingdom and city of God—and you yourselves will be blessed.

Father Dale Korogi, Farewell Homily,
Basilica of Saint Mary in Minneapolis, August 30, 1998

I wish Father Dale's message could be read in every parish in the United States. He touched the very core of how the Basilica Community has come to define itself: a place where all are welcome. The impetus placed on that truth has changed who we are as a worshiping community and has changed our lives individually as well. For the more pragmatically concerned, it has proven that good church pays for itself economically too! In less than a decade an eight million dollar structural roof repair debt has been satisfied while once dwindling parish membership has increased to seam-bursting dimensions. An average of 50 new parishioners join the parish every month, most of them under 40 years of age. The basilica's membership roster spans 300 zip codes! Catholics are drawn by the basilica's fourfold mission: (1) to provide quality liturgy, religious education, pastoral care, and hospitality; (2) to preach justice and provide emergency relief to the poor; (3) to pursue interfaith relationships; and (4) to contribute to the cultural life of the community.

Ideally, every Catholic parish should be a center of welcoming, reconciliation, and healing, a place where any baptized Catholic will find welcome and support on his or her faith journey. Reality, however, is a long way from this ideal. Most parishes include in their membership many active Catholics who are angry at the church, seldom attend Mass, or who attend regularly out of obligation, experiencing very little spiritual inspiration from the parish community. While these parishes may not be ready to sustain an active outreach, they are fertile seedbeds for evangelization within their own membership.

The word *evangelization* makes most Catholics squirm! We have visions of television preachers, or door-to-door oracles concerned about our salvation. Yet, to understand any kind of outreach ministry effort, it is necessary to understand Catholic evangelization. Gary and I were most uncomfortable with this word when, shortly after our marriage in 1983, the Paulist Fathers invited us to be part of an evangelization effort in their Minneapolis parish. We feared they had some perception of us as the church's counterpart to Jim and Tammy, a husband/wife evangelical entity very much in the secular news at that time. We envisioned being asked to ring doorbells, preach our truth at people, and try to hook them back into the church. It was scary. Through their patient mentoring, the Paulists helped us to understand that evangelization is simply what Catholics are about. It is the way we build the kingdom of

God in this world. In their beautiful document *Go and Make Disciples,* the bishops of the United States declare evangelization to be the "reason for the parish's existence and the objective of every ministry in the parish."[1]

We have come to see Catholic evangelization as the ongoing response to the presence of God in our lives, not preaching our truth to others, but an effort to help others discover the good news of God's power *within themselves.* In essence, as evangelizers, we Catholics are called to be purveyors of hope, and that hope is Jesus Christ. This is the foundation of our ministry and every decision we have made for the past 15 years. People who identify themselves as a eucharistic people really haven't a choice when it comes to welcoming and hospitality. We are the Body of Christ. How can we do less than open our hearts to Jesus in others?

For most of us who were formed by the pre-Vatican II church, the assumption was that the reason for church was to insure the salvation of souls. We needed sacraments and priests and church in order to die in the state of grace. There wasn't much talk of community or of belonging to one another; our focus was on saving our own souls. But church was never intended to be one-dimensional. Being Catholic is about being the hands and feet and heart of Jesus, about building the kingdom in this life, about recognizing in our own sacredness the love that God calls us to share with one another. This may be a difficult concept for us to grasp in the United States because we are steeped in a culture that values individualism, the antithesis of community. Catholic evangelization calls us to build parish communities that provide a gospel *experience* to all who enter.

Outreach to inactive Catholics must be rooted firmly in the life and mission of the parish community. It serves little purpose to invite people back to a community that is incapable of supporting the seekers on their journeys of reconciliation. It is, in fact, harmful to extend invitations of hospitality to all, if in reality the church doors are barred to some. Many active Catholics live out their lives in parishes where only successes are noted, presenting a narrow vision of life. Christian community must encourage and support people committed to honest growth through human experience. Outreach activity that is laminated onto parish activities with little or no grounding in a welcoming community reveals itself to the seeker as superficial and does not engender an atmosphere of trust. Too often, such programs amount to busy work, with more burnout than results.

When we are invited to meet with parish representatives who want to evangelize inactive Catholics, we usually respond to their initial question "How do we begin?" with our own question, "What are you bringing them home to?" Sometimes the answer to our question reveals a parish fraught with strife, discord, or lethargy among the *active* members. Caught up in internal fighting and bickering, their liturgies often reflect tension and an absence of joy. The best place for these communities to begin is the confrontation and resolution of existing problems. Parishioners need guidance and permission to talk openly about parish problems. This kind of honesty will not only lead to more cohesive community, but will build trust as well. Too often parishes simulate dysfunctional families where the hurts and misunderstandings of the past are buried by activity and controlled effort to avoid honest discussion about serious issues.

We have seen dramatic changes take place in parishes that have decided to begin their reconciliation efforts with their own communities, to structure gatherings where participants can openly share the residual pain of bygone eras. Whether it was the abrupt imposition of sanctuary changes immediately following Vatican II, questions about the parish debt, a childhood school experience that permanently scarred self-esteem, alienation during a time of divorce, or the loss of a beloved pastor whose struggle with the priesthood and the church had been shared by the community, these issues need to be aired. A new pastoral appointment after years of leadership by a deeply loved priest can change the entire community's rhythm. Too often parishioners are counseled to forget the past, begin a new day, and go on. The issues troubling the hearts and minds of hundreds of parishioners are not spoken, and they hang like a dark cloud over every liturgy and parish gathering. There is no need to hide conflicts that arise within parish communities. They are a normal part of all healthy relationships and need to be resolved in a Christian manner. The alternative will result in permanent harm to the parish community and its ability to live the gospel.

In his book *A World Waiting to Be Born,* M. Scott Peck notes, "...an astonishing lack of interest on the part of the church in community building, yet a burgeoning interest on the part of business," adding, "most church-goers do not want to do the painful work that community requires. They want church to be pseudo community, and have no real desire to see the boat and their lives rocked."[2]

Building communities where honesty and genuine hospitality are extended to parishioners and nonparishioners alike may require some time and some uncomfortable changes, but the result is increased vigor, participation, and conversion among those who worship there. We have been delighted to observe these changes in parishes that have invited us back after committing themselves to inner renewal. On our return visit, usually a year or two later, we find a community filled with energy, a sense of identity and mission, and a renewed bonding of its members, the trademark of true gospel community.

Of course there is no perfect parish just as there is no perfect family. Preparing seekers for reentry to the church includes developing their awareness that the church consists of people and people are imperfect. So where do we begin active outreach to inactive Catholics? We suggest the following three steps for parish communities who are serious about this evangelization ministry: (1) evaluating and developing a welcoming parish atmosphere; (2) forming an evangelization or outreach team; (3) getting the word out.

1. Developing a Welcoming Parish Atmosphere

When we invite guests into our homes, we often make a mental inventory of our family's housekeeping and behavior patterns. We want our visitors to feel welcomed, comfortable, and free to be authentically themselves; in other words, relaxed. Parish communities need to engage in this same type of reflection before they invite people in. The seekers' initial visits must be comfortable, accepting experiences that provide confidence and reassurance. That caring, inviting atmosphere, however, needs to be present at every liturgy and parish event, not just conjured up for specific occasions.

Returning to Mass after years away can be traumatic. It takes courage to get that far in a journey of reconciliation. It takes faith for the seekers to believe there is heart room for them in the church after all, and it takes forgiveness to put aside the hurt that may have caused the breach in the first place.

Our experience indicates that people rarely reactivate where they were initially alienated. They need time to test the waters before risking attending the Eucharist among family and neighbors once again. If the root of alienation was a person or situation specific to their "parish of origin," they may never return to that parish. It is sometimes better for them to begin anew, away from the unpleasant associations of that parish community. It occurs to me that in the 20 years since I left the parish I had belonged to all my life, I have only been back for one wedding and two funerals. I am almost surprised at that realization since it is close to my home. But my spiritual journey has taken me far away from that community and I cannot imagine going back there to worship, even though I no longer feel the rejection and pain that caused me to leave.

The implication of this reality is that many of the seekers who come to Catholics Coming Home sessions may belong, in an ecclesial sense, to another parish. This is one of many positive aspects of the Catholic Church since Vatican II. Although parish boundaries may indicate otherwise, the seeker can feel a sense of belonging to the church through participation in liturgies and activities with a new, non-threatening faith community. They need to find positive worship experiences where they can move beyond old wounds. For many of them, their early parish experience is all that defines what it means to be Catholic. An invitation to worship at another parish may open the door to new understanding of the diversity that exists within each diocese.

Celebrating Mass again is usually the first public step in the reconciliation journey and takes on great significance for the seeker. Many tell us they have tried and tried again to attend mass, but have been confronted with so much anxiety, frustration, loneliness, or anger that they finally stop trying. Others have been locked into a pattern of avoiding Mass because of unpleasant confrontations with solicitous family members who are concerned about their salvation. Whether you are reaching out as a parish or an individual to someone who has been away from the church for any period of time, we recommend only gentle invitations, not confrontations. For those who have devoted time, prayer, and commitment to the reconciliation process, the eucharistic liturgy becomes something more than a weekly obligation. It is important that the liturgy they attend reflects their new understanding. While most are grateful for the invitation to attend with someone who understands their journey, others prefer to participate alone, remaining anonymous in their worship, being very cautious about all their options.

If the seekers feel no expectations regarding their participation or commitment, the burden of "What will others think?" is lifted. We encourage them to sit and observe, to participate only when it feels comfortable for them. We ask them to allow the presence of Jesus in the gathered community to minister to them, to feel all right about *receiving* what they need from the liturgy, the community, and from God, who understands all our needs. This is not the time to tell them about their responsibilities during the worship experience. This gentle approach removes pressure, fortifies the trust between the seeker and team members, and allows the Holy Spirit to permeate the situation, another affirmation that we are not in this ministry alone.

Perhaps it would help all of us to remember that there are seekers at every weekend Mass who are looking for a place to rest and be nourished. Here are some things to consider if your parish wants to convey an atmosphere of hospitality and acceptance to all who enter its doors.

Welcome Your Visitors

A greeting at the door by parishioners who understand the significance of their ministry is crucial. When we arrived at church to celebrate the First Communion of our grandson Nicholas, we were delighted to see entire families serving as greeters, welcoming us and asking us our names. Each greeter had a small clipboard with name tags on it. The 12-year-old girl who welcomed me asked me how to spell Carrie and then wrote it clearly on a name tag for me. Her family was doing the same for the rest of our group. The parish membership is very young, with an average parishioner age of less than eight years! But everyone seemed to own and manifest hospitality throughout our experience. There was joy and conversation both in the gathering area and in the sanctuary, right up until Mass began. Once again the presider welcomed us, acknowledging visitors present, and adding that some of us may not be accustomed to worshiping with so many children, and that some may have brought children with them for the first time. He stressed that children were welcome! (No one ever said that when I was bringing my four very young children to Mass!) He added with gentle humor, "If you have a screamer, you might want to take him or her out into the gathering area for a bit." Then he invited us all to greet the people around us, and because of the name tags that welcome seemed very personal. People used our names in their greeting and it felt good. The same adults who had welcomed us served as Eucharistic Ministers during that liturgy, calling us by name when we received the bread and again when we drank from the cup. The liturgy was joyful, easy to follow with the worship aids given to us, and inclusive. The children were escorted to their own Liturgy of the Word at the appropriate time, and when they returned the whole sanctuary joined in welcoming them back. They loved it and we felt great! After the Eucharist, the families who had greeted and served as Eucharistic Ministers mingled as hospitality servers, providing cookies, coffee, and juice

Being something of a church junkie, I lingered after the throngs had left and expressed amazement at the intimacy of our worship experience in spite of what some parishes would consider obstacles: a very large population of young families with young children and a tight budget that allows only three full-time staff, one of whom is the pastor! "But it's our church, so we do the ministry," I was assured by one of the Hospitality Ministers as his wife handed him a carpet sweeper and they began to clean up the inevitable cookie crumbs. The Hospitality Ministers were the clean-up crew too! That community considers all these tasks to be a part of welcoming. Families sign up for one liturgy during which they serve in all these ways. "It makes scheduling easier for everyone," they explained, very satisfied with the way it was working. Months later, we returned for the baptism of another grandson and things were very much the same. We felt at home after only two visits.

Smiling faces, the willingness to move into the pews when newcomers arrive, helpful sharing of hymnals and liturgy guides, and greeters who speak kindly and cheerfully all indicate that this is a community of believers, not just obligated members.

Since it is likely that inactive Catholics attend every Eucharist in your parish, an acknowledgment of that fact, along with an invitation to make your parish their home, may be all a seeker needs to come back for another visit. We especially encourage this kind of acknowledgment and invitation during the Easter and Christmas seasons. Can you imagine the fate of the prodigal son if his father had met him with veiled sarcasm instead of open arms?

Good Liturgies

I am not an expert on liturgy, but I know when a liturgy enhances my worship experience. I have also experienced those that do not. This is not about the expertise of the liturgy director but about the understanding and preparation of laity to assume their roles as ministers and participants. More and more seekers are citing liturgy and ritual as reasons for exploring their Catholic heritage once again. Inflexible rules and rituals can be exploitive and controlling. Liturgies that lift our hearts to God and give us a sense of belonging to one another prevent them from being boring and routine. Shortly after his appointment as Director of Worship at the Basilica of Saint Mary, Johan van Parys, Ph.D., explained during an introductory address to the congregation that to understand good liturgy, one might imagine being in a very beautiful place surrounded by a lush, thick, hedge that grows very high. Johan's voice became very soft as he provided imagery that allowed us to peek through the foliage to discover a magnificent glimpse of heaven! In unison, we realized he had transported us to another dimension with those few quiet words and gestures. That's good liturgy! Now when I worship, I anticipate that moment of transcendence. We Catholics are especially blessed when we are able to experience it through our liturgical ritual.

Nurture Acceptance

The word *family* no longer means the same thing to everyone sitting in the pews on Sunday morning. The stereotypical Catholic family of mother, father, and children in parochial school does not depict the way most of us live our lives. Prayers, petitions, and ongoing church activities must reflect the recognition of singles, couples without children, the elderly, solo parents, children who attend public schools, and the reality of families experiencing troubles. In my pastoral work, parishioners who are facing serious difficulties in their relationships repeatedly tell me that they feel like such failures because "everyone else looks so all together." One woman expressed embarrassment that she had come to mass with a very heavy heart and was terribly embarrassed when she could not hold back tears. "I felt so alone," she said, "and wished I had the courage to just ask the woman next to me for a hug."

Even in the wealthiest communities there are hundreds of people experiencing a spectrum of life's realities: job loss, chemical dependency, marriage problems, health problems, children's problems, relationships that are strained, domestic violence, verbal and emotional abuse. The list can be long, and the statistics tell us without doubt that none of these are unusual happenings in the lives of our families. Yet many parishes perpetrate a mode of denial that drives these people away and prevents others from addressing their problems in healthy ways. These experiences of brokenness may be the catalyst to deepened faith for individuals and community, but only if they are addressed openly, without judgment.

Community Education

The thirst for spiritual nourishment is powerfully strong in our adult population, and seems to be growing deeper. Edwina Gately, during a recent visit to Minneapolis, described it as a "hunger in the belly" that has become epidemic in American culture. I asked a friend of mine who has been a psychotherapist for 30 years if she has noticed it, wondering if perhaps this is just "church lady paranoia." "No," she answered somberly, "I have never seen anything like this hunger in all my years of counseling."

Traditionally, the Catholic Church has vested itself in the education of its children, but the time has come for us to address this spiritual hunger in adults. People who are already too busy do not want meaningless activity; they want time and space to journey inward, to reflect, and to use a biblical word I have come to love, *ponder.* Seekers are attracted to parishes that honor this spiritual need. Elaborate programs and expensive speakers are not required. Quiet gatherings where faith is explored and life stories are shared require little effort. Our tradition is steeped in spirituality and it is what people are looking for. We need to take a second look at the parish paradigm consumed with meetings and events that have little to do with building the kingdom.

Reconciling Pastoral Staff

Before beginning any outreach to inactive Catholics, it is imperative that your pastor and pastoral staff are actively involved in the planning and preparation. Their role is key in the development of a welcoming attitude among the community. It is likely that there will be parishioners who feel insecure or threatened by the idea of including *everyone* in your welcoming message. It takes sensitive, compassionate ministry to help these skeptical parishioners reach a point of acceptance. We must be careful that in our zeal to welcome some, we are not callously alienating others.

We urge those who are contemplating a ministry to inactive Catholics to schedule a candid discussion with the entire staff about the way each member responds to people who are struggling with church and faith issues. During a meeting with one staff, we were stunned to hear the pastoral minister state defiantly, "These people [seekers] need to accept the fact that the rules are good for them!" Another time we heard a pastor deny any need for listening or for free discussion, determining that all the seekers need is "more education." Still another parish priest insisted that there be no mention of the word *divorce* in any parish evangelization activity! It is essential that the pastoral team present a unified concern for the seekers and a shared commitment to accepting people where they are. Our ministry model would not be a good fit otherwise.

The staff also has to have time for seekers who need to draw on the community for support, comfort, and direction. These pastoral services should be easily accessible and available to everyone, regardless of membership. If your parish has these support services in place, people need to know that they exist and how they can plug into them. As our parishes grow larger, disseminating information becomes more and more of a challenge. And as the role of the priest is adjusted to meet the critical shortage of them, they are less and less accessible to the laity. In or out of the church, Catholics are still somewhat confused about how lay ministers fit into this changing church. It can't be assumed that people know what is available unless the information is widely circulated.

Obviously not every parish has the financial ability to provide programs that meet every need. It may be time to look seriously at inter-parish cooperation so that human and economic resources can be used more efficiently. Parishioners should be invited and encouraged to attend programs and events at other churches. As Catholics, our local parish experience sometimes belies the universal character of our faith by an unspoken rivalry that may exist between neighboring parishes.

Attitudes of isolation and superiority do not present an inviting atmosphere to newcomers and they impede the mission of the church.

Lay Ministries

Parishes that call forth the gifts of all parishioners, assist in the discernment of gifts and talents, and provide opportunities for ongoing adult catechesis will present a vital network of good ministry to both the churched and unchurched. Inherent in this process is the opportunity for the lay minister to engage in reflective introspection and dialogue with other ministers. It is not enough to provide the mechanics of what to say, where to stand, or when to be there. The whole sense of reciprocal relationship between minister and the one ministered to needs to be fostered, developed and nurtured on an ongoing basis. We have come a long way from warm bodies filling task-oriented slots. Ministry is first and foremost something we feel called to do because of our baptism, because we belong, and because we believe we are essential to the Body of Christ.

Freedom to Choose

Forced attendance at a parish determined by geographic boundaries must not be a condition imposed on returning Catholics. Fortunately many bishops have already removed this arbitrary means of assigning parish membership. As Catholics become more enlightened about our faith, its history, and its call to each of us to share our gifts with the community, we become less willing to worship in a parish where we are neither nourished nor spiritually challenged. Essential to those reconciling with the church is a parish community that invites them to a particular sense of belonging, where their gifts will be welcomed and received, their questions will be respected, and dialogue encouraged.

Welcoming New Members

As our understanding of parish as community develops, the way we extend hospitality to new members becomes critical. When the church was perceived solely as the means to salvation, very little attention was addressed to this welcoming concept of hospitality. As we deepen our understanding of parishes as gospel communities, we must look at how we invite new members to make their spiritual home with us. Active parishioners are often surprised when they take a good look at the welcoming procedure in place in their parishes. It may be something that developed over time with little or no attention directed toward its current effectiveness. Recently I learned of a large suburban parish with very small-town roots that had established a program for welcoming decades earlier. Parishioners would make home visits and get to know the new folks. While excellent in theory, when the parish membership erupted into thousands of families, many of whom rotated in and out according to corporate assignments, the effort became totally ineffective. The welcomers became cynical and resentful of the newcomers who didn't return their phone calls and rejected their offers to visit them. Their small numbers were waning as burnout took hold among their ranks. Rather than evaluating the whole welcoming picture, the process was patched up by mailing out packets of materials, resulting in new members receiving large doses of unrequested information at considerable cost to the parish. More important, the new parishioner received no human contact. When we looked further at the welcoming procedure in this parish, we discovered that the pastor had for years been sending form letters to newcomers, inundating them with information about the parish's busyness, the need to get involved, and the first-rate status of everything that went on there. The burden to establish relationship was placed on the newcomer and the message was that the parish was very busy, perhaps even too busy to make personal contact with new people.

But that wasn't all! The parish administrator also had a list of new people and quickly sent them their collection envelopes, another lengthy summation of the excellence and busyness in that parish, and a request for their stewardship pledge.

These practices had evolved over the years and were carried out with good intentions. The problem was that no one had put all the pieces together and asked if it was working. Newcomers, on the other hand, rarely became active in parish ministries. The same people continued to function in the same roles, giving an impression of an *in* group and an *out* group. (I call this the *Little Theater Syndrome:* a small percentage of parishioners rotate in the various liturgical ministries while everyone else watches, Sunday after Sunday.) When it was discovered through perusal of parish demographics that more than half of the people in that parish had been there less than five years, it was evident things had to change! There were many new voices to be heard.

I don't think this scenario is uncommon today. The priest shortage has resulted in large parish communities that almost defy any attempt to create a feeling of belonging and inclusiveness. Further complicating this problem is the reality that Americans are suffering from a poverty of time. Young families are stressed almost to the breaking point with the norm being two working parents. Single parents who must cover all the bases for their children and their jobs have little time and few resources beyond what is required for daily survival. Family support from grandparents and relatives is no longer the norm. Jobs take people far from those networks that used to ease the burdens of raising a family. The result is that people resist taking on more obligations. Secular, commercial welcoming companies have discovered that newcomers no longer want them to come and visit, basket of goodies or not. They are just too busy.

Moving into a new parish, particularly for those who have also moved from a different city, brings with it many unspoken demands. Life is not easy for some time after one is uprooted and transplanted. Great amounts of energy must be invested in finding new doctors, new schools, new friends. New parishioners tell me of their emotional exhaustion, that they just want their new church to be a place where they can find some quiet, some respite, a spiritual oasis in their lives. They are made to feel uncomfortable by intimations that they must get active, get busy, and above all, *do* something for their new parish!

Each parish is different and it is important that welcoming programs be developed according to the reality that exists. One parish where I worked welcomed newcomers to a wine and cheese evening. While the concept seemed fine to me, I was stunned by the fact that once the newcomers arrived, they were asked to sit down and listen to a dozen parishioners tell them about their heavy involvement in the parish. I was new there myself and wondered how all these people could spend so much time at church! When the litanies were completed, the pastor thanked everyone for coming and encouraged the newcomers to become active too. The next morning the parish receptionist referred two phone calls to me, folks who said in essence they felt more alone after that experience than they did before! Good ministry has to meet established needs. Had those new people been given time to share their stories in small groups facilitated by *listening* parishioners, there could have been interaction and discovery on both sides. These discussions should focus on what the newcomers have missed most since leaving their previous home and parish, and validation of their sense of loss, then move on to the gifts they enjoyed sharing with their former communities. Such conversations lead to discovery of new ideas, new ways of doing things, new people to do them. Too often, events are run by the same people year in and year out. I have heard a variety of accounts from newcomers who have tried to volunteer at parish activities only to be told, "We don't need you because we do this every year."

Effective welcoming of new members has to fit the parish; while monthly dinners may work for some, semiannual events may be a better solution for others. Still others introduce new members at weekend liturgies, or at coffee and donuts after Mass. What must be kept in focus is not the activity, but the possibilities for building relationships. At the basilica, we welcome new parishioners by invitation to a monthly dinner. It is a very simple meal, served on paper plates, and followed by a tour of the building provided by parishioners who are docent ministers. During the meal and during the tour, there is ample opportunity for free-flowing conversation.

Welcome Home Events

If your parish is already a welcoming community, you may want to sponsor a Welcome Home event, opening your doors to the community. This is an open house, where everyone is invited! It should include the necessary ingredients of hospitality: greeters, food (hospitality always includes food!), and lots of parishioners to serve as hosts. It is a time for friendliness and hospitality, and an opportunity to invite the curious to explore the church facility. There should be small-group tours, with informed parishioners as guides who are able to explain a little of the church's history and the purpose of the various parts of the church itself. In one parish, a highlight of this event is the sacristy, where the priest actually vests, explaining the symbolism of his attire. Few Catholics have had opportunities to see or learn about the church in which they worship every week; those outside the church may have only a vague sense of mystery about what goes on inside those Catholic doors.

I recently conducted a church tour with a seeker who had been away from the church for 12 years. I could feel her tense up when we entered the reconciliation room, so I invited her to sit down and visit with me for a while. We spent about fifteen minutes there, while she told me more of her story. It included a not-uncommon recollection of the black box, or confessional; indeed it was one reason she had stayed away from the church for so long. She could not imagine talking face-to-face with anyone; there was just too much shame in her life. I suggested that she had just done that very thing with me and she burst into tears. As she reflected on this, she said it would have been awkward for her to talk to me from behind the screen. I encouraged her to think about it and promised her that if and when she felt ready, I would ask Father Mark to celebrate reconciliation with her, assuring her that he would be compassionate and understanding.

The last stop on our tour was the Blessed Sacrament Chapel. She had never known anything like it existed in the Catholic Church, a quiet, out of the way place to simply be with God. "Do you mean even I could come in here?" she asked, adding that it seemed safer to her than the large sanctuary. I noted in the weeks that followed that she visited the chapel two or three times. Then she called and said she not only wanted to celebrate reconciliation, but was eager to do so. "I am ready to come back!" Father Mark eased her through the celebration of the sacrament, commenting later on the mutual blessing in the experience. A simple tour of the church was the catalyst for this woman's return.

Phone Access

In *A User Friendly Parish,* Judith Kollar asks if the following sounds familiar: "You have reached St. Augustine Parish. No one is available to take your call, but if you leave a message, someone will get back to you as soon as possible. If you have a touch tone phone, press one now; for Father Brown, press two; for the parish secretary, press three; for Deacon Charles, press four; all other calls, press zero. If this is a pastoral emergency, call our pager number, 367-9978."[3]

While voice mail is here to stay, we need to look at the impression our mechanical answering systems are giving to parish callers. While I was on staff at a large parish, I frequently received messages on my voice mail that began with, "My God, it took forever to get through to you." As Kollar points out in her book, there are advantages to voice mail, but we must choose a phone system wisely and monitor it to make sure it is providing appropriate responses to callers.

At a recent workshop on welcoming and reconciliation in the Archdiocese of Saint Paul and Minneapolis, the following checklist was developed. Perhaps it will help you take inventory of your parish.

The Welcoming Parish Checklist

Outreach

_____ Local papers (or other media) are used to publicize times of liturgies, educational programs, and parish services, including RCIA Inquiry Nights.

_____ Mailings are sent to surrounding neighborhoods about the mission and services of the parish.

_____ News about the parish is sent to inactive households.

_____ Gatherings, coffees, or information sessions are scheduled for new parishioners.

Outdoors

_____ Signs are set up to guide people to the location of the parish.

_____ The name of the parish is clearly visible, along with a message indicating that all are welcome.

_____ Grounds are well maintained within parish resources.

_____ Snow and ice are removed promptly.

_____ The building (roof, gutters, windows, etc.) is well maintained and attractive.

_____ There is adequate parking, well lit and well marked.

_____ There is adequate handicapped parking and access.

First Contact

_____ Parish offices are easy to find and accessible; hours are clearly posted.

_____ Parish offices are open some evenings or weekends for people who work during the day.

_____ Telephone contacts are personable and friendly.

____ Parish office staff is welcoming and friendly.

____ Mass times are available by phone.

____ Bulletin boards are attractive, useful, and up-to-date.

Church

____ People are stationed outdoors by the steps and heavy doors to assist those who need help.

____ Greeters welcome people.

____ All are clearly welcome: all ages, races, cultures.

____ The space is handicapped accessible.

____ Ushers have been trained to help people with disabilities.

____ Ushers have been trained to deal with emergency situations.

____ Large print liturgy guides are available.

____ Assistive listening devices (ALDs) are available.

____ The entry or gathering space is attractive and warm, clean and uncluttered.

____ Coat racks are available.

____ Washrooms are easy to find, accessible, and unlocked.

____ Washrooms are clean and well stocked with supplies.

____ Ushers help people find seating.

____ There is enough seating.

____ People who come early are encouraged to move to the middle of the row to leave room for latecomers.

____ Nave and sanctuary are clean and uncluttered.

____ All areas are well lit, not dreary.

Worship

____ Liturgy guides are provided for newcomers, especially containing items the community knows by heart.

____ The sound system works well.

____ Sight-lines to ambo, altar, chair, and font are unobstructed.

____ Aisles are roomy enough for processions.

____ There are enough hymnals or liturgy guides available.

____ All liturgical ministers are welcoming.

_____ People are invited to sing.

_____ The Word is proclaimed with skill and clarity.

_____ The homily is inspiring and challenging.

_____ Communion is offered under both forms.

_____ Signs and symbols are used richly.

_____ Most people come early or on time; few leave early.

_____ Refreshments are offered after Mass on a regular basis.

Other

_____ Thank you notes are sent whenever appropriate.

_____ Gatherings outside of worship that involve food are scheduled.

_____ "Time and Talent" sign-up sheets are provided with prompt follow-up.

_____ Child care is available when appropriate.

_____ Bulletin information is available to those with sight disabilities.

2. Forming a Team

If your parish is ready to begin serious outreach to inactive Catholics, it will be necessary to form a nucleus of committed, faith-filled people who will work and pray together. The invitation to learn more about forming a team or beginning this ministry should be a public one, extended through usual parish communication channels, including verbal announcements after all liturgies. It should be stressed that the team will be selected through a process of discernment. You may want to schedule an open, informational meeting simply to discuss the issue of inactive Catholics in your parish area. Those who attend will be likely candidates for team membership. Personal invitations from staff members would also be helpful. Often those most qualified for this ministry are unable to see their own gifts until they are affirmed by someone else.

The same kind of open, honest sharing you will offer to the seekers should be a part of your team's selection and preparation. Include prayerful reflection and sharing, with time to consider how their personal experiences of doubt and questioning have affected their relationship with the church. Through this process, some will determine for themselves that they would be more comfortable in another type of ministry. Sometimes, however, it is necessary to suggest that someone may not be ready to work directly with the seekers, but might be better suited for other areas of support. It is important that there be enough open, honest revelation in this phase of formation to allow such a gentle confrontation to take place. We cannot expect the seekers to be open with us if we are unable to be equally open among ourselves. A deep level of trust among team members is essential.

Team formation includes discussions about listening and boundaries. The team's purpose is to provide friendship, support, and appropriate resources. Confidentially is a given. Those of us who are blessed to welcome the seekers into our lives know only too well that we walk on sacred ground during those sessions. It would be unthinkable to betray the sincerity and trust placed in us.

The most significant credentials for this ministry are freedom from certitude and the ability to live with the tensions that divide our church today. The minister needs to be grounded in a sense of hope-filled faith in spite of those tensions, able to see the vision beyond the division. This ministry is not a vehicle through which the minister works out his or her own alienation, family problems, chemical dependency, codependency, gender issues, or unresolved church experiences. Nor is it a platform for preaching rules, regulations, and righteousness.

It is important that team members be given a clear estimate of the time commitment required, and that those who are going to work directly with the seekers during the sessions are able to commit themselves for an entire series. This allows the seekers to form relationships and develop trust in people whom they will feel free to call on as their reconciliation journeys continue.

A team should consist of men and women of varying ages and should represent married, single, and divorced constituencies. Remember, for the seekers, the team will be a first encounter with the church. It is important that it reflect the diversity of lived experiences within your parish. Too much church professionalism is not likely to result in a comfort level with the seekers.

WHO IS CALLED? Ten years ago, we thought it was essential to have a priest on the team. However, the reality of the priest shortage makes that something of an ideal. It is not necessary as long as the primary facilitator has a strong grounding in Catholic theology and church history. The seekers love it when a priest stops in to say hello, or listen for a while, or even participate in a whole session. We do ask them not to wear their clerics, however, particularly during a first visit. Remember that the priest is symbolic of the church; for many, the black suit and white collar make it difficult to get past the baggage of mistrust and discomfort they associate with the official church. The priests who have met with us over the years have steeped their visits in mutuality, sharing with the seekers some of their own struggles and their hopes for the church. I love to watch the body language during these discussions; the seekers are somewhat cool or distant at first and then literally lean in to participate and share more deeply.

We invite a priest to join us on the evening we discuss reconciliation, inviting a seeker to role play a confession. I give the seeker who volunteers a very general, safe script and establish with the entire group that it is role playing. Yet in nearly every instance, the seeker gradually moves into his own experience and the interchange becomes powerfully open and honest! Tears flow freely, from the penitent and observers. Afterward, the seekers explain that they are overcome by the priest's gentleness, compassion, and acceptance. Most begin to see the beauty in this much-maligned sacrament during this experience. When a priest cannot be present, any team member can play the role of confessor. What is important is that the experience of reconciliation be presented as one of healing and forgiveness.

Minimally, the seekers need to know that the pastor or priest supports what is happening. There will be some who feel a need to work through specific issues with an ordained priest, although the preponderance of well-trained lay ministers has changed this perception significantly in the past 10 years. Priests who invest time and energy in this ministry tell us the rewards far outnumber the sacrifices. Some say it is a powerful validation of their priesthood. It is impossible to work so intimately with people struggling through faith conversion without reaching new depths in our own journeys, whether we are ordained or not.

Wounded Healers

Called especially to this ministry are people who have acknowledged imperfection in their own lives. Note that we call these people *wounded healers,* not *the walking wounded.* There is a vast difference between people who have survived and grown through hardship and grief, and those who are painfully struggling to survive or those who cling to their victimization. We do no service to the seekers, nor to ourselves, when we try to minister to others while we are still feeling broken and uncertain about our own lives. But how do we know when we have healed? Perhaps the following reflection will help: (1) Do we feel stronger for having lived through the experience (illness, divorce, death, job loss, chemical dependency, etc.)? Or do we still feel vulnerable because of it? (2) Do we understand ourselves and our God better because of our experience? Do we recognize new strengths and gifts in ourselves that have resulted in our healing and recovery? (3) Are we past the need to go over and over the details? (Remember, this is a *listening* ministry.) (4) Do we feel a renewed sense of joy and lightheartedness, a hopefulness that we can share with others, or have we become angry and embittered?

Wounded healers rarely fall into the trap of becoming fixers who simply take over and tell a seeker how to resolve his or her faith difficulties. Having learned firsthand the value of working through their own issues, wounded healers are more apt to see the merit of a seeker's search as well.

COMMITTED CHURCH STRUGGLERS Those who have the most struggles with the church are often the ones who love it the most. Love that is never tested, questioned, betrayed, or forgiven invites complacency. If, however, love survives honest struggle, if we can still see sacredness and hope in the church, if we are in touch with its innate goodness and its historical and global centrality, we will do well in this ministry. It may be impossible for those who have never questioned the church to relate to the questioning of the seekers. Our entire team at the basilica consists of former seekers who identify with the new seekers' doubts, questions, and anger, but have come to accept the church as a human institution, capable of human frailty. They have wrestled through the process of healing and reconciliation, thus redefining their individual relationships with the church. They are faith-filled people who believe their baptism has called them to do more than sit in the pews on Sunday. This is the kind of faith maturation that frees us to accept our own imperfections, to be both cognizant and tolerant of the church's failures as well. Culmination of this experience is a firm commitment to the vision that Jesus espouses through the gospels. It goes far beyond parish membership!

It is not likely that those who have given up on church or who are embittered by it can help seekers move past their own anger. This is a ministry of reconciliation. Effective team members need to have resolved their differences with the church, to have put them into a perspective that allows their church commitment to grow while still working for change. This can be an awesome demand and at times even the most committed team members may need to step away from the ministry in order to reassess their own experience of church. We serve best in this ministry when we truly believe the church is growing closer to its mission of carrying out the vision of Jesus Christ. We cannot offer others a hope that we have lost.

Personal Relationship with Jesus

Team members need to minister out of their own lived relationship with Jesus. It is this relationship that sustains us in this ministry, and also speaks to the seekers at the very root of their faith journeys. While the church is a means of expressing and celebrating that faith relationship, faith rests primarily in Jesus, not in the institutional church. Many of the seekers have acquired a personal relationship with Jesus during their time away from church. They need to discuss this part of their lives with Catholics who live out such a commitment within the church. Our syllabus is really a journey toward discipleship revealed in the gospel. It is a blessing to work with team members who take their own discipleship seriously.

CURRENT THEOLOGY Obviously not every team member will be steeped in theology. Team formation should include overview discussions that allow for an understanding of Catholic doctrines and teachings. Especially vital is a clear understanding of Vatican II and how it has affected the church. Many seekers have had years of Catholic schooling, some have theology degrees. In order to have credibility, the team must have some theological depth. If you have a theologically educated person on your team—cleric or lay—that person may serve as the resource person for these issues.

CHURCH HISTORY It is essential to understand the history of a changing church and its ability to adapt across time and geographic boundaries. The minister should be able to find home in the confusion and open disagreement so prevalent in our church today, hope in a church that is alive and growing, finding its way into a new millennium. A historical perspective allows one to ponder past church crises, the people who lived through them, and the church that emerged from them. It is helpful to understand, for instance, the history that surrounds papal infallibility, celibacy, the Reformation, and marriage laws in order to consider the human contribution to the evolution of these teachings. Team members need to acknowledge those parts of church history that have not been holy, without feeling defensive or minimizing their existence.

SCRIPTURE Team members should understand the manner in which the Bible is revered by the church. If we clearly state the church's position on the Bible, we will not have to indulge in defensive debates with fundamentalists (Catholic and Protestant) over the literal meaning and intent of individual passages. Such interchange is usually fruitless and distracts from the overall group dynamic. We establish that Catholics Coming Home is a Catholic ministry, steeped in Catholic teaching; therefore, we do not read scriptures literally. It is an essential strength of our faith for which we need offer no apologies.

SUMMARY Definitely not called to this ministry are Catholics who measure one's goodness by absolute obedience to church authority. Most seekers are looking for honest faith exploration; they cannot change what they believe by being told they are wrong and what they must believe instead. People who value introspection and ongoing personal growth are best suited for this work. We need to be comfortable enough with our own limitations to feel unthreatened by the seekers. When we find ourselves arguing, defending, and persuading, we are probably not exercising good ministry. Convincing is done by the Spirit; our job is simply to facilitate the flow of information and nurture an environment of sincere welcome. If we feel responsible for whether or not it is accepted, we may be trying too hard to accomplish our own goals.

As a team, you will need to remind yourselves constantly that there are no success/failure records in this ministry. The Spirit is responsible for any progress the seekers make. We need to accept those who reject everything just as much as we do those who cooperate and participate. It is not unusual for seekers to come a second and even a third time through our series before they are able to let down their defenses. Others call me years later, asking if they can meet with me to discuss faith issues or life issues. We plant the seeds but we have no control over the harvest!

The intimate sharing that takes place in our sessions can be burdensome and, at times, overwhelming. Without a team closely bonded in prayer and friendship, you may find yourselves unable to process or let go of some of these experiences. Team members need to know that within the team itself they can seek counsel and comfort in a prayerful, supportive encounter without jeopardizing the sacred space shared with the seekers. Boundaries need to be clear and respected between the seekers and the team members. As in any ministry experience, burnout is common among those who do not avail themselves of sound spiritual grounding and support.

The following exercises will be helpful in team discernment, or in any consideration of fitness for this ministry. Used individually or collectively, they also provide opportunity for faith exploration and growth among active Catholics who may for the first time be confronting their own doubts and issues with the church.

Catholics Coming Home
Exploring My Own Attitudes About Inactive Catholics
(Circle one answer, or indicate by question mark if you are undecided.)

1. People who don't go to church are less Christian than those who do.

   Agree   Disagree

2. Inactive Catholics should not be allowed the "services" of the church, i.e., baptism, marrying, burying, pastoral care.   **Agree   Disagree**

3. People who break the rules should settle for a "non-Eucharistic" membership in the church. They can participate in everything else.

   Agree   Disagree

4. No one has an excuse to miss Mass unless they are physically disabled.

   Agree   Disagree

5. Jesus would be scandalized by people living in second marriages without annulments who receive Eucharist.   **Agree   Disagree**

6. Some Catholics need to be inactive; it may be the best solution for them.

   Agree   Disagree

7. Catholics who do not believe everything the church teaches are not really Catholics. They should leave the church.   **Agree   Disagree**

8. We should concentrate more on bringing in new members and forget about those who decided to leave.   **Agree   Disagree**

9. The best way to contact inactive Catholics is by anonymous mailings.

   Agree   Disagree

10. The parish I belong to would be a good place for a seeker to begin the journey of reconciliation with the Catholic Church.   **Agree   Disagree**

11. Sometimes Catholics don't belong at a particular church and should find a different Catholic church.   **Agree   Disagree**

12. I resent it when inactive Catholics crowd our church at Easter and Christmas liturgies.   **Agree   Disagree**

13. I am willing to ask forgiveness on behalf of the church for its offense against someone.   **Agree   Disagree**

14. The church is human. No one has a right to leave just because of bad advice or a bad experience. We have to learn to live with that.

    Agree   Disagree

15. I am very concerned about all the baptized Catholics in my parish who do not feel they can receive the Eucharist.   **Agree   Disagree**

Catholics Coming Home
Team Ministry Discernment

1. What were the major events in my life that led me to this place and time?

2. Who are the people who have ministered to me during my life?

3. What did they do for me?

4. What is my greatest strength for ministry to inactive Catholics?

5. What is my growing edge? My bias?

6. What is my biggest fear about working with the seekers?

7. Who will be the most help to me in this ministry?

8. Who am I the most concerned about working with? Why?

9. What am I willing to do about people who have concerns about working with me?

10. Is God calling me to continue in this ministry? If I have doubts, am I willing to consult the team? Am I open to team members giving me honest feedback about "my call"?

11. Why am I a Catholic?

Catholics Coming Home
Alienation Worksheet

1. As I reflect on my own life in the church, my personal alienation has been the result of the following: (Please list.)

2. Do areas of alienation still exist? Or has healing, forgiveness, and reconciliation occurred?

3. If alienation has been resolved, was there a contributing factor or person that was critical to the reconciliation process? Describe.

4. If I have unresolved issues of alienation, what has stopped reconciliation from taking place? Can anyone help in the healing process? What must happen in order to achieve reconciliation?

Catholics Coming Home
Feed My Lambs

*When they had eaten their meal, Jesus said to Simon Peter,
"Simon, son of John, do you love me more than these?" "Yes,
Lord," he said, "you know that I love you." At which point,
Jesus said, "Feed my lambs."*

John 21:15

1. How has the issue of Catholics who feel they cannot receive the
    Eucharist affected you or someone you know?

2. What does the Eucharist mean to you?

3. Who is unworthy to receive the Eucharist?

4. What would happen if the following was inserted regularly in your
    parish bulletin?

    *Welcome! We are glad you are here. If you are a baptized
    Catholic who does not receive the Eucharist but would like
    to, please call (name and number of parish staff member) so
    we can talk. We miss you at the table!*

Catholics Coming Home
Seeker Case Study (A Role Play)

The group observes as two volunteers role play the following script. Encourage them to make notes on their scripts as they listen. Group discussion follows, using reflection questions.

Mary has been attending Catholics Coming Home for several weeks. After the last session, she asked a team member for an appointment for a private visit.

1. **Mary:**   Thanks for seeing me today.

1. **Team Member:**   No problem. That's our job, you know. (Chit-chat is exchanged for some time. Mary seems very uneasy.)

2. **Mary:**   Some of those people in our group are weird.

2. **Team Member:**   They say you judge a good church by whether or not people on the *fringe* show up!

3. **Mary:**   I guess that's true.

3. **Team Member:**   Mary, is there something you especially want to discuss with me today?

4. **Mary:**   I just don't buy some of that God stuff; I mean I can't talk to God as though he was a loving father, whatever that means.

4. **Team Member:**   To you, God is...?

5. **Mary:**   Cold, demanding, mean...a kind of *thing* that I can't talk to at all.

5. **Team Member:**   I'm sorry you feel that way, Mary.

6. **Mary:**   (Angry) Maybe you see him as this warm, loving person, but I don't. Every time I reach out to God I get punished. You don't understand the real world.

6. **Team Member:**   O, come on now; you don't mean that.

7. **Mary:**   Who says I don't?

7. **Team Member:**   I used to feel that way but I have such a different concept of God now. It's hard for me to understand how you feel.

8. **Mary:**	See what I mean? It's easy for you...
8. **Team Member:**	(Interrupting) But, Mary, God is good and loving. Look at what God has done for you in your life. You're pretty, intelligent, I can tell from the group that people like you. We need to count our blessings.
9. **Mary:**	God has never done anything for me...not really.
9. **Team Member:**	Perhaps you would like to talk to Father Tom or Father John. They're good at this.
10. **Mary:**	Oh, no, not any more of those guys. They just listen for a while and then dismiss me with something like, "Oh, you don't mean that." Kind of like God in a way.
10. **Team Member:**	How is that?
11. **Mary:**	He's just like the priests: cold, authoritarian. Just waiting for a chance to punish me...just waiting for a slip-up! If I don't live by the rules, I'll get it, either from the priest or I'll burn in hell!
11. **Team Member:**	When have bad things really happened to you, Mary? You've never been hungry or homeless, you have a family and friends.
12. **Mary:**	You're wrong!
12. **Team Member:**	Do you want to talk about it?
13. **Mary:**	No, I'm wasting your time.
13. **Team Member:**	Mary, I wish I could share my faith with you. It is rooted so deeply inside me, keeping me going. I will pray that you will see God in a more positive way.

The visit comes to a friendly conclusion.

Catholics Coming Home
Case Study Reflection

(After role play, allow time to go over these questions alone before beginning discussion.)

1. What is your overall impression of this visit?

2. How would you rate the team member's welcoming attitude toward Mary? Explain.

3. How do you think Mary is feeling about this visit? Why do you think that?

4. In what ways does the team member open up discussion with Mary?

5. How do you feel about the team member's answer in Paragraph 5? Explain.

6. Any observations about Mary's response in Paragraph 6?

7. Any observations about the team member's response in Paragraph 6?

8. What is happening in Paragraphs 7 and 8?
   - With the team member?
   - With Mary?

9. What message does the team member give to Mary in Paragraph 9?

10. What are your feelings/observations about the outcome of this visit?

11. Explain whether you think Mary accomplished what she needed from this visit and why.

12. What seems to be Mary's issue from this conversation?

13. Do you sense any "hidden issues" from this conversation? Explain your answer.

After Group Discussion:

14. Any group conclusions, observations, comments as a result of our discussion?

3. Getting the Word Out

Getting your invitation out is probably the easiest part of this ministry. We use the local media, parish bulletins, preaching, mailings, and personal invitations, even web pages. We do not, however, go door to door, nor do we advocate spending lots of team hours on parish census or related projects. To understand why such outreach projects are seldom long-lasting, you have only to recall your own reaction the last time someone from another denomination knocked on your door. Were we not convinced that the Spirit will bring to our gatherings those who are ready to embark on a faith journey, our ministry would not have endured beyond the first year. Without the Spirit's leading, we cannot force people to subject themselves to spiritual introspection. It is an indication to us that we are doing the Lord's work when we are energized and exhilarated by our efforts, rather than exhausted and embittered.

MEDIA It is news in the secular world when a Catholic church opens its doors to everyone. Sadly, our public image still isn't very good in this area, so the public is interested in what we are doing. Local newspaper stories have brought many people to Catholics Coming Home; they have also identified parishes in which this ministry is offered as welcoming parishes. The primary invitation to our series is issued through ads placed in our metropolitan newspapers. Most often it is the only Catholic invitation among numerous invitations from Protestant churches. If you advertise this way, include phone numbers of people available to minister to those who respond. It is equally important that your parish receptionist and office personnel are fully informed of all details so they can field inquiries in a professional manner. Recently, during a series at the Cathedral of Saint Paul, an elderly seeker who had been away for more than 40 years said it was the welcoming phone response from the parish receptionist that encouraged him to risk coming the first night.

We hear touching stories from the seekers about the newspaper invitations or ads. It is not unusual for them to pull ads out of their wallets that they have been carrying for months, even years, before finding the courage to contact us or come to a series. An elderly couple gave us our ads, yellowed and frayed, from two papers. Each of them had secretly cut it out and tucked it away, not daring to confide in the other. They kept those ads for three years before they called us. When we asked why they waited so long, they replied, "You were our last hope; neither of us could face losing that hope."

PARISH BULLETINS We have been blessed with strong support and response from the pastors in the Archdiocese of Saint Paul and Minneapolis throughout our years in this ministry. Each time we schedule another series of sessions, we write to them, requesting that they place our invitation in their parish bulletins. At every session we meet seekers who learned about us through these bulletin announcements. They may have read it themselves. More often a Catholic friend, coworker, family member, or neighbor has shared the bulletin announcement with them.

PREACHING AND PRAYERS As discussed earlier, your pastor's support is essential to any evangelization effort in your parish. Some pastors devote homily space to this ministry; others write letters to their parishioners asking for their prayers and support. Every effort communicates to the community your parish's concern for inactive Catholics.

MAILINGS When it is practical, low-cost bulk mailings are also a good way to invite. Seekers tell us they receive mailings like this from Protestant churches all the time. New parishioners tell me they received them in their first batches of mail at their new addresses. Our experience indicates that it is better to send two or three mailings, stressing a similar theme and logo, than to put all your dollars into one high-cost mailing. If you use mailings, remember that the message has to be simple, nonthreatening, and inviting. Like the newspaper ads themselves, they serve only as gentle invitations.

PERSONAL INVITATIONS Many inactive Catholics are simply waiting for an invitation to consider coming back to the church. Don't be afraid to extend a personal invitation. Sometimes we underestimate the effectiveness of personal invitation extended by a trusted family member or friend. You may be surprised at the results of personal invitations. Extend them with no expectation or attempt at persuasion.

Please do not solicit names of inactive Catholics and send anonymous invitations. I will let the following letter speak for the many who have told us about this approach, always with the same reaction to it:

> I was one of those anonymously invited to this series. Apparently [name of church] had a campaign to ask the parishioners to offer names of "lapsed" Catholics that they might contact, without ever mentioning who it was that offered their name. I went out of curiosity. The anonymity of the person who reported me intrigues me; I'm offended that someone who apparently does not know me well enough to discuss spirituality openly with me thinks that my spiritual journey is off-track or nonexistent and is convinced enough to notify a church official. The session went from uncomfortable and uncertain to disastrous. In particular, I learned that going to the same pew when I attend Mass every Sunday would acquaint me with others who habitually come to the same pews and that stopping for donuts after Mass was a rewarding technique for building community. I am writing this with regret because I suspect these people were trying and that they are very good people. Suffice to say that your sessions were a real blessing and I've just realized it in a different way than before.

Whatever form of invitation you use, be sure your message is honest, gentle, and appealing, without any demands on the seekers to phone ahead, make reservations, or pay fees.

At last, you are ready to begin. Your parish has become a house of welcome and prayerful support for your ministry, you've formed a team that can pray and work together, and you've extended your invitation into the secular community. This is a time to wait, pray, and trust the Spirit to carry that message to those who are looking for it.

Confused Catholic?
Inactive Catholic?
Alienated Catholic?

A Christmas Invitation

If you've been away from the church, or are drifting away from it; if you've been hurt by the church or are confused or angry because of your Catholic experience, please consider this invitation to come and talk with us.

...perhaps you can come home for Christmas!

MONDAY, November 9 at 7:00 P.M.
(Continuing for six Monday evenings)

BASILICA OF SAINT MARY
Sixteenth at Hennepin, Minneapolis

Please come to the Cowley Center on Sixteenth Street,
located on the east side of the church,
across from the parking ramp.

Carrie Kemp: (Phone Number)   (Staff Member and Phone Number)

Confused Catholic?
Inactive Catholic?
Alienated Catholic?

An Easter Invitation

If you've been away from the church, or are drifting away from it; if you've been hurt by the church or are confused or angry because of your Catholic experience, please consider this invitation to come and talk with us.

Perhaps this Easter can be a time of resurrected hope in your faith journey.

TUESDAY, February 24 at 7:00 P.M.
(Continuing for six Tuesday evenings)

BASILICA OF SAINT MARY
Sixteenth at Hennepin, Minneapolis

Please come to the Cowley Center on Sixteenth Street,
located on the east side of the church,
across from the parking ramp.

Carrie Kemp: (Phone Number)   (Staff Member and Phone Number)

Confused Catholic?
Inactive Catholic?
Alienated Catholic?

An Invitation to Consider

COMING HOME AGAIN

(We've missed you.)

If you've been away from the church or are drifting away from it,
if you've been hurt by the church,
or are confused or angry
because of your Catholic experience,
please consider our invitation
to come and talk with us.

Six week series begins:

Tuesday, September __, 2000
7:00 until 9:00 P.M.

BASILICA OF SAINT MARY
Sixteenth at Hennepin, Minneapolis

Please come to the Cowley Center on Sixteenth Street,
located on the east side of the church, across from the parking ramp.

Carrie Kemp (Phone Number)   (Staff Member and Phone Number)

Chapter 4

The Reflection Journey

Statement of Purpose

Welcome to Catholics Coming Home! We're glad you're here. We invite you to join in our process of reflection on your relationship with the church. It is not intended to pull you back into the church, but to invite you to consider that possibility. We begin with the assumption that God meets us wherever we are on our faith journeys. And we assume that the word *catholic* defines us as the setting for all who want to celebrate their Christianity within our faith community. We are eager to know what brought you here and will devote this first session to that discovery. Throughout the six-week series, you are invited to share your thoughts and reflections as they relate to the group's focus.

Based on input from thousands who have participated in this ministry over the years, we have put together a curriculum in an adult format that we feel will help you reassess your own spirituality and the teachings of the church. Feedback from most who attend indicates that this information is both enlightening and helpful. Many feel they can return to active participation in the church; others who are regularly attending Mass feel they understand more clearly what it means to be Catholic.

People are drawn to Catholics Coming Home for many reasons. Some are simply wanting to update their understanding of their faith, while others have very serious issues that may even be painful to discuss. Some have been wounded by their church experience, yet find the courage to reach out for new understanding of what it means to be Catholic. We try to respect all viewpoints and ask participants to do the same.

We do not have answers for all questions, nor can we undo hurt that has occurred. We can only offer the hope and information, along with acceptance and reassurance, that may assist you in the journey back to the church—or the decision that you have a right to "go in peace." We are not a support group and cannot facilitate a healing process for those whose issues deserve that. We can, however, provide individual meetings and resources that may be helpful in those cases. All of our ministry is steeped in respect and confidentiality.

It is our endeavor to honor the group focus and to conduct our time together in a Christian manner. If you have particular issues with a particular individual, it is preferable that names not be mentioned in the group. If you choose to schedule a private meeting with the facilitator, priest, or member of the team, you are free to divulge this information at that time.

If, during the series or afterward, you feel a need for a private meeting, please see one of us and we will help you arrange that. It is our primary hope that this connection with the church, for whatever reason brings you here, will result in an increased awareness of God's love for you.

We have found this statement of purpose a great help in establishing boundaries for the series of sessions to follow. It also gives nervous arrivals something to read while they are waiting to begin. We can usually identify the seekers as they arrive. Parishioners who are coming for other parish activities hurry in, give a short greeting and hang up their coats in a common foyer. The seekers, though, are apprehensive and uncertain, may avoid eye contact, and seem to be embarrassed about being there. Some prefer to keep their coats with them as if in anticipation of a quick exit. "Is this the right place for...?" Their voices drift off and we reassure them it is. This is the place for people who want to talk about their problems with the church. Immediately, they seem relieved. We said what they hardly dared speak in a Catholic environment.

Team members direct them to the registration table and assist them in filling out a name tag, assuring them that it's all right to use first names only. And most do just that, preferring to stay anonymous while they check out their comfort level. They are guided to the gathering space where team members continue light conversation and project a sense of hospitality. We're fortunate in Minnesota because we can always talk about the weather during this time! In addition to the purpose statement, we give each seeker a syllabus, providing more reassurance about what we'll be discussing in the coming weeks. This early information not only raises their comfort level, but helps them understand that we do have purpose and intent, and we are going to do just what the invitation promised, discuss issues about their faith.

Our syllabus has developed over the past 15 years, always in response to two considerations: the most frequent concerns expressed by the seekers, and information about our faith that will help them broaden their understanding of what it means to be Catholic. Even the order in which we address the issues has been carefully determined. Catholics Coming Home is a ministry of adult reflection that provides opportunities to listen and reflect, information, and community experience. Our hope is to develop a new context of church in which the seekers can process new information. We address any church news that may break in the media during the time we meet with the seekers. And because we usually conduct our basilica ministry during Advent and Lent, we include prayers and meditations that link personal faith journeys to the liturgical seasons. It is often the first time seekers have understood these rich seasons of the church in a way that touches their personal lives. We are committed to the process of personal reflection and seek to facilitate their spiritual journey throughout our contact with them. I believe this has been the key to the return of so many and the very low attrition rate. In essence, we are acting on what we believe about the beauty and sacredness of our faith, trusting that given the opportunity, information, and encouragement, the seekers will respond to that sacred beauty.

We know some of the people who come the first night will not return and the reasons become apparent during the first session's process. Some want to state their opinion and having done that, have no interest in returning. They are not interested in pursuing reconciliation with the church. Occasionally there are those who decide not to come again once they read our purpose statement. They are not looking for growth and new discovery. They appear to want only validation of their particular position. Others may be very active in the church but at odds with almost everything going on there. The rest usually express enthusiasm about coming back, and may bring friends or relatives with them. The group remains surprisingly constant after that first night, with seekers letting us know if they won't be there the next time, making sure a team member saves handouts, and asking, "What will I miss?" Some have come through another entire series because they've missed what they believed to be key sessions. During an Advent series we debated about whether to cancel the session scheduled for Thanksgiving Eve. The seekers said no, and only two, who were going out of town, weren't able to be there. The others laughed about planning their holiday preparation around their priority of being together for that session. Their almost childlike enthusiasm warmed my heart and I told them no one would think of scheduling an event the night before Thanksgiving for even the most active Catholics! Once they begin the journey of reflection most seekers become very serious about their commitment. The marvel in all of this is that we have established no expectations, no rules about attendance, and no sense of obligation. Yet, for most of them, church has already begun to happen and they feel a sense of belonging. It is a soul-stirring observation for the ministers who have done little but accept, affirm, and inform.

For the sake of clarity, I will divide our syllabus into six sessions. It is the sequence that is significant to our ministry. The group's response or participation determines whether we need to table a topic until the following week. Frequently, energetic discussions flowing from new insights on the previous week's material will begin a new session. These insights are often the result of the seekers' interaction with coworkers, friends, or family members about what they've been learning at Catholics Coming Home. These people are discussing their faith out in the world! I love the energy in these conversations, the evidence of community already seeping through their church disconnection, the result of their newfound sense of belonging. And the humor! No longer awkward and insecure, the seekers learn quickly to laugh at themselves. The emotional bonding resulting from shared tears and shared laughter is pure gift to all of us.

It is the facilitator's job to be mindful of the entire curriculum in guiding the group's movement. Early in each session I let the group know what I have prepared for the evening's presentation, and I ask them to choose whether they want to continue discussions or go on to something new. Nearly always, they want more.

When I am invited to parishes or diocesan gatherings to talk about our experience, the questions are many and very specific. The phone calls I receive from all over the United States indicate that people are looking for fairly succinct concepts in the beginning phases of this ministry. In an attempt to honor that need for specificity, I do not assume that we have all the answers, or the only way to conduct this ministry. It is important that the charisms of the community, of the ministers, and of the seekers be considered in every situation.

Catholics Coming Home
SYLLABUS

WHAT'S WRONG WITH THE CHURCH?

CONCEPTS OF GOD AND JESUS

WHAT IS CHURCH ANYWAY?

HOW DO CATHOLICS USE THE BIBLE?

FAITH/RELIGION: Is There a Difference?

WHAT DOES CONVERSION MEAN TO A CATHOLIC?

CATHOLIC VALUES? What Are They?

VATICAN II: What Difference Does It Make?

CONSCIENCE: Do You Mean, "Do What You're Told"?

DO CATHOLICS SIN ANYMORE?

SACRAMENTS

    CONFESSION (Reconciliation)

    EUCHARIST

    MARRIAGE:

        DIVORCE

        ANNULMENT

        REMARRIAGE

Session One

Hospitality is crucial to this ministry, particularly at this session. The facilitator has key responsibility for continuing the atmosphere of a welcoming and nonthreatening environment throughout the evening. It is also the facilitator's job to: (1) Enable group discussion, tempering those who dominate the conversation and encouraging those who may be quiet or too apprehensive to raise their issues. (2) Keep order and honor the purpose statement. Creating an open atmosphere where seekers can share feelings about God and church can lead to volatile debates or arguments, particularly on the first evening. The facilitator must keep order in a way that is respectful to all, and does not hinder discussion. (3) Honor the time commitment.

The team's function is: (1) Assist in all the above by welcoming and mingling with the seekers when they arrive. (2) Assist with registration, handouts, seating, refreshments. (3) Listen, observe, and offer support to the seekers. (4) Serve as recorders and small group leaders when necessary.

Team prayer before and after each session is invaluable. When we join together in prayer, we empty ourselves of any expectations for the session. The nervousness and anxiety over how many seekers will come or concern about potential confrontations lessens as we ask God's Spirit to guide us throughout the evening. It is important to remember that many of the seekers will be uncomfortable about being in a Catholic church after a long time away. We must be present to them in the most natural way possible. This is not a ministry of formality or protocol, just being friendly!

We deliberately do not begin the first session with prayer. It is important for the introduction to this process to be as nonthreatening as possible for everyone who attends, and to make no assumptions about where people are on their faith journeys. Some may feel compromised if they are forced into prayer situations while they are still harboring resentment, anger, and confusion about their church relationship.

At the designated starting time, a team member officially welcomes the seekers who have gathered, and gives housekeeping information about restrooms and the like. The importance of confidentiality is stressed, asking the seekers to respect one another's views and to consider the evening as sacred space: whatever is said there will not be taken outside the gathering. We promise our own respect for confidentiality. We clearly state when the session will end and the amount of time the team will remain afterward, explaining that the team needs to excuse itself for prayer at a particular time. We have learned that without these time boundaries, the seekers would continue discussing issues for hours!

As a warm-up exercise, we give personal introductions, beginning with the facilitator. We ask the seekers to introduce themselves, tell us how they learned about Catholics Coming Home, and how they feel about being there. Team members acknowledge their role, offering a sentence or two that explains why they are participating in this ministry. This nonthreatening introduction serves a dual purpose. We learn which advertising efforts are bringing the most response and which parishes are placing our invitations in their bulletins.

Then the fun begins. The facilitator invites the seekers to reflect on the following statement: "What I *dislike* most about the Catholic Church is..." Nervous laughter often follows, calling the facilitator to reassure them that we are actually inviting them to state their grievances openly. In any relationship, divisive issues must be acknowledged before reconciliation can even be considered. These negative issues brought them here and are the reasons for their church estrangement. We can't expect them to put those issues on hold while we present our own agenda. Trust begins to build the minute seekers realize we mean what our invitation said: we will listen to whatever they have to say, no matter how unpleasant. It is common for the group to become very silent, even after this reassurance, and you can feel the tension in the room as the seekers nervously look at one another or stare at the floor. In retrospect they tell us that their silence meant they still could not believe anyone representing the Catholic Church would propose such an opportunity.

It is important that they understand that the objective of this exercise is to compile *a list of dislikes,* not engage in discussion about any of them. One by one, the issues are offered at random, a team member writing them down, and the group pulling together to help with the wording. It's fun to watch this group of strangers as they weave the strands of their common Catholic experience. Although this is no time to force anyone to say anything, it is the facilitator's job to encourage everyone to participate. The higher the comfort level and sense of hospitality within the group, the easier this is to do. This exercise sometimes lasts a long time, with even the most reticent members contributing to the list eventually. Although it is important not to allow any one person to monopolize the process, we allow a free flow of contributions, listing them on tear sheets that we post around the room.

When they finish, we invite them to generate a second list. This time we ask them to reflect for a minute on this statement, "What I *like* about the Catholic Church." More nervous giggles and bantering between the seekers. The process for this list is the same, but do not be surprised if you find this list to be much shorter!

This second list is used for several purposes. First, it points out very quickly that the two lists overlap, with some of the *dislikes* showing up on the *likes* list. This illustrates the diversity of the church and of the group that is gathered. We have different spiritual needs and life experiences. We have experienced church in many different ways and have conceptualized church according to our experience. We encourage the seekers to listen, support, and try to understand one another without debating the merits or pitfalls of any particular issue on either list. The following list was compiled during a recent Catholics Coming Home series:

DISLIKES	LIKES
Exclusive: Shut out women, gays, etc.	Appeals to intellect
Pyramid: Pope at the top;	Music
people at bottom	Liturgies
Traditions	Generous
Suppression	Social justice: the poor
Jesus lost in human authority	Core theology
Humorless	Lineage and continuity
Hypocritical	Global
Nonrelational clergy, hierarchy	Earthy
Rigid	Eucharist
Confession: the box!	Reconciliation and forgivenes
Use sacraments to control,	Reverence for God and human life
judge worthiness	Saints
Law more important than gospel	Scriptures
Too receptive to change	Prayers
Birth control	Higher education

DISLIKES	LIKES
Cold, impersonal parishes	Family oriented
Inconsistencies	Capacity to change
Emphasis on money	Vatican II
Unequal role of women	Sacredness of art and music
Takes too long to change	Pope John XXIII
Annulment process: phony	The Mass
Repetitious liturgies: boring	Sacraments
Position on sexual issues:	
Homosexuality	
Masturbation	
Premarital intercourse	
Celibacy	
Rewards blind obedience:	
Don't think!	
Papal authority	
Rituals	
Judgmental and nonforgiving	
Cater to rich; forget the poor	
Old-fashioned definition of family	
Suspicious of intellect	
Need more rules	
Priesthood becoming elitist group	
Confusion about Mary	
Catholic school stories	

Although the lists change from group to group, the issues raised are usually similar. It is interesting to observe the group members move from their frustration, anger, and confusion during the *Dislike* List to a mood of camaraderie as they draw from one another experiences that support the *Like* List. It is equally interesting to observe that within each group, there are conflicting issues on both lists. Yet, somehow, this exercise demonstrates clearly the common Catholic identity prevailing among them. I like to post these lists at every session. They are often referred to throughout the series and become an important part of our final wrap-up. When new people join us, they are invited to add to the lists.

Not until the group is unable to come up with anything more for either list do we open the discussion, inviting anyone to select something from the Dislike List. They are warmed up now, more comfortable with one another and with us, and eager to speak. Obviously, some seekers will be more energetic than others at this point. It's important for the team to note the quiet ones, those whose body language and facial expressions say more than their voices. And it is important for the facilitator not to allow any one person to dominate the discussion. The more relaxed and comfortable everyone feels by this time, the easier it is for the facilitator to suggest it's time for someone else to speak.

During this discussion, the team's primary function is to *listen* to the seekers and observe the process taking place as they support the seekers. While this support may include acknowledging a similar feeling or experience, the focus remains on the seeker, not on the team member. Our job is to encourage the dialogue, affirm the seekers' goodness, validate their experience, and weave throughout the conversation the sense of a God who calls them beloved. The seekers are assured that in the weeks that follow they will be given opportunity to consider their issues, and to consider information that will help them resolve their conflicts. Also, that each of them is welcome to schedule time with the facilitator or a team member to discuss issues privately. For most, coming was an act of courage. Many tell us they haven't discussed their church problems even with their closest family members! They seem reassured to know that at last someone is going to listen to them.

We do make it very clear, however, that we don't have all the answers, that we have many questions of our own—and always will, and that faith is about living *with* questions, not about having other people define all our answers. We validate the sacredness evidenced by their presence and ask with humor, "Is this the kind of thing you do normally, come to something like this to discuss topics this way?" That's when we hear the wonderful stories about why they decided to come, their fears and apprehensions, and the way some of them create cover stories for family members concerning their whereabouts. One woman in her 70s confessed to the group, "I told my adult children that I joined a bowling team!"

Sometimes my statement about their sacredness evokes quiet tears, whispers of "I can't believe someone finally invited me to do this." For most, it is the first time anyone has suggested that their struggle with the church, their confusion about their own relationship with God, and their lived experience are all part of a vital spirituality.

Occasionally, a seeker's pent-up anger or hurt explodes; it is as if once detonated, the blast cannot be stopped! It is important to allow that person to say whatever is necessary in order to release that anger. Giving seekers space and permission to vent their frustration is an essential ingredient of this ministry. This may be a part of the bonding process for the entire group. Many are able to personally identify with what is being said and with the emotions being expressed. It is touching to observe these strangers reaching out to one another with support and encouragement.

This is not a time to explain, placate, or excuse. An appropriate response to an emotional outburst, whether it is anger, crying, or the revelation of raw pain, is silence. It is a good time for silent prayer. After a moment of silence, I often feel compelled to say "I'm sorry," acknowledging that I am grieved by the pain the church has caused. There is no prescription for these moments. We have learned to trust our hearts for a response that is genuine and appropriate. It is important that neither the facilitator nor the team take these outbursts personally. We cannot take responsibility for their pain; we can only validate it. Following the session good team processing is helpful, sometimes essential, in restoring everyone's sense of perspective.

Less frequently, you may encounter another difficult situation: former Catholics who have become fundamentalist Christians, convinced they have the whole truth and determined to impose that on the group. We've learned to spot them as they arrive: they come with their Bibles in hand. They may come to accuse the church of its sins, using literal interpretation of scripture to make judgments, and to argue. As our process has evolved into a journey of reflection and invitation to come home again, we have responded differently to this group. In the beginning our invitation was to come and talk about what they didn't like about the church, so we felt an obligation to let them speak. However, in every instance, it became disruptive to the entire group process, with the other seekers growing resentful and irritated by the accusers. Such defensiveness is not beneficial to spiritual journey ministry. Our approach is different now.

I acknowledge the evangelicals' strong faith commitment and thank them for coming, but refer to our purpose statement, reminding them that this is a process developed to assist those who want to explore the Catholic faith. I also invite them to schedule private time with me if they desire it, and invite them to let the group know how to reach them if anyone wants to dialogue further with them. I also ask them to respect my relationship with Jesus and our common heritage of discipleship. The result is much more peaceable, less upsetting, and allows everyone to retain a sense of dignity. They rarely come back a second time and I have never had a call to meet with any of them individually. One of them waited till all the seekers had left one night to tell me he was shocked to hear a Catholic woman profess a relationship with Jesus, inviting me to come to his church. "It is the *true* church," he explained.

Traditional, or pre-Vatican II, Catholics in the midst of a more progressive group can also cause uneasiness. Since most seekers are struggling to discover a more personal, less institutional experience of church, the more traditional seeker may feel out of place. Gentle reminders to the entire group will help preserve the atmosphere of respect for one another's issues and viewpoints.

Catholics Coming Home is not a support group. Because we gather with neither commitment nor expectation, we cannot impose a support-group dynamic on the seekers. Occasionally people come solely to vent, ranting that first evening on one experience over and over. They are not interested in shared discussion, only their agenda. It may be apparent that they deserve professional help. I returned home late one evening after an encounter like this, to find two messages on my voice mail from seekers asking me to please find a way to quiet "that woman." They wanted to be sure we got on with our syllabus the following week. These are the kinds of experiences that prompted our purpose statement, giving us a platform from which to speak to the individuals privately and explain that we won't be able to help them. Again, we always offer options for them to consider regarding a more personal approach to their problem.

Most often, however, these first sessions are filled with good, positive energy. The mood changes dramatically from beginning to end, along with the seekers' comfort level.

Toward the end of the evening, we go over the syllabus with them, promising to provide lots of information for them to consider. It is an underlying premise in all of my ministry that people are busy, overburdened with tasks, with too much to do. If we are going to schedule an event at church, there has to be meat! The seekers are hungry for substance.

Inevitably, seekers will ask if they can bring someone to the next session. My response is always, "Yes!" But I ask them to be sure the new person understands what happened that evening. Those who join afterward will not have that same *venting* opportunity and we want them to understand how we arrived at the issues that will be posted. When we welcome new people, we always invite them to add their issues to both lists.

Although we try very hard to convey a sense of freedom and anonymity, we do live in Minnesota and our weather forces us on occasion to cancel events. For this reason only, we pass around a sign-in sheet that first evening, asking those who plan to return to give their names, addresses, and phone numbers. As newcomers join us through the series, we invite them to add their names to our list. Our purpose for the list is made very clear, although anyone who lives in Minnesota readily understands. Very few people leave that first night without signing in. In ten years of this ministry, we have only canceled once. Seekers have driven through impossible blizzards to attend these sessions! On occasion, I've left my parish job where everything has been canceled because of the weather, to find seekers at the basilica already sharing horror stories of blinding snow and gridlocked freeways. They laugh at their determination, in spite of the weather, to get to....*church!*

An expression of appreciation, an acknowledgment of our having been church together that evening, and an invitation to close with the Lord's Prayer *for those who feel comfortable doing* so brings closure to the evening. There is quite a bit of conversational spillover as they leave. Some will want to talk to someone individually so it is important that the team members make themselves available.

Team processing and shared prayer is a vital component of this ministry. Sessions can be very draining, particularly these first nights. It is helpful to share observations, the result of heart listening. Scattered throughout the group, each team member has a unique perspective of response and participation among the members. Finally, in prayer, we turn all the pain and hurt shared that evening over to the Lord. We place the seekers' lives during the coming week in God's care and ask the Spirit to comfort and guide them. These evenings are unusually intense experiences of church; it is important to leave with a sense of peace in our own hearts.

In the weeks that follow, there will be some attrition, but we are encouraged by the high percentage that do return for the entire series.

Some come to the first session out of curiosity and others may see it as an opportunity to vent. Still others are not ready to embrace the process yet, but may be at another time. Seekers have come to first nights two or three times before finally deciding to go through the series. Numbers in this ministry are not important. What matters is our response to those who *are* ready to reconsider their concepts of church. Those who come back for the second session are likely to attend the entire series. Some even bring friends back for another entire series!

Session Two

I have come to prefer circular or rectangular table arrangements for our gatherings. The tables provide a bit of emotional safety and allow the seekers to take notes or use the worksheets. Of course, they also allow us to keep the cookies and coffee close at hand! Welcoming, name tags, and appreciation for their return are conveyed as the seekers arrive.

Except for the first evening, we begin all of our sessions with prayer, providing the seekers with a variety of prayer experiences, drawing from scripture, prayers of the liturgical season, and extemporaneous prayer acknowledging the significance of our journey together. Psalms that acknowledge the aching desire for God so familiar to the seekers, passages that emphasize God's love, forgiveness, and healing, and published prayers that relate to a concept of faith journey all help reinforce a sense of relationship with a God who cares and loves—regardless of where we are in our faith journey.

After prayer, we invite the seekers to tell us about their week. Some tell us they've had dreams (good and bad) as a result of that first session, others have done lots of reminiscing, some have wept, some have shared the experience with their active Catholic friends and family. And, of course, some are still wary, having told no one what they're doing and seeming somewhat surprised that they are back.

We acknowledge once again the Spirit of God at work in their lives and assure those who have anger issues that we don't expect them to be past the anger in one week. I like to remind them that anger is a gift of God, signaling a conflict between me and something that compromises me (the me God created!). It is important to lean into that anger and follow it to its root cause, to discover the other, perhaps more vulnerable, feelings that may be camouflaged. We also remind them that unresolved anger, especially about faith/church issues, affects all relationships, that anger can lead us to reconciliation or repairing a relationship, even with the church! Believing that anger can be evidence of God's Spirit working in the lives of all who search for truth, we assure the seekers that we're relying on that belief as we proceed. This is a good time to openly address doubt and questioning as steps toward mature faith rather than as symptoms of a lack of faith. This kind of reassurance is met with surprised pleasure by the seekers.

The focus for the rest of the series is on moving the seeker beyond the pain and anger surrounding specific issues. As one seeker put it, "Thanks for helping me get unstuck!" We are evangelizing, offering hope that there is more to their faith journey, that there is purpose to their conflicts, and that there is much that is life-giving in the church for us to explore together. A sensitive balance must be maintained between the need to pursue painful issues and the effort to move forward in presenting positive realities of our God and our faith.

Concepts of God and Jesus

We begin with concepts of God and Jesus, the bedrock of any Christian's faith. We facilitate these discussions with a handout, giving them time to go over it alone before breaking into small groups led by team members. Even those who choose to remain silent in the groups seem to participate in this introspective process of jotting down notes about their concepts. Newly discovered thoughts and feelings become less threatening to verbalize once they have written them down. Some tuck their worksheets away in order to devote more time to them in the quiet of their homes. It is through the lens of their perceptions of God and Jesus that the seekers tell their stories, which are too often powerful revelations of people in fear of a vengeful God. Those who taught them about God showed them little evidence of God's loving care. It is difficult to develop a concept of a God of love when one is raised in a loveless home, so we will often nudge a little, "Was there *anyone* whose eyes lit up when they saw you?" Most often, the answer is my grandmother, or my grandfather, bringing joy to this grandmother's soul. This ministry has convinced me that God is more like a loving grandparent than a parent. Those of us blessed with grandkids know how unconditionally we love them. Gone is the parental stress of doing the

right thing at the right time, and the economic worries that go with raising a family. We know that childhood is measured in minutes and that
children's love is one of life's greatest treasures.

During these God/Jesus discussions we hear tragic stories of
harsh, disciplinary authority figures in families and church experience,
people who invoked shame and damnation, searing the spirits of the
very children Jesus called us to welcome into our hearts. One seeker
acknowledged that her childhood image was that God was very distant
and demanding and that she understood little of what she was taught
about God in parochial school.

Many indicate that their prayer life and their comfort level with
God waned seriously during their teenage years. "Because of sex," they
point out, drawing nods from nearly everyone in the room. Since hell
seemed to be the destination for anyone who had a sexual thought or
did anything even close to a sex sin, adolescence was one roller coaster
of sin and confession, with a large reserve of shame accumulated in the
process. The similarity of stories from all over the United States would
indicate that many confessors knew little about healthy sexual development in the days before Vatican II. Nor did our parents or teachers.
When it came to sex, it was simply bad. Many quit going to church
because they had nowhere to go with all the conflicting feelings, the
shame, and the futility of denying the changes and yearnings that were
occurring in their bodies. These seekers are at first shocked and then
pleased that we talk about sexuality so freely within the group. "Never
thought I'd hear anything good about sex in a Catholic church" is a frequent response to these discussions.

The reflection on Jesus is also revealing. Many Catholics are
uncertain where Jesus fits in their faith life. Some say they are so confused that they pray to God and eliminate Jesus altogether. Many connect Jesus' suffering with human sinfulness but haven't connected it to
the joy of resurrection! Others are stuck with a historical figure who has
little impact on their daily lives.

When everyone who wants to has had an opportunity to share
within the small groups, we bring the group together to share stories
and observations. The seekers are amazed at their common experiences. We talk about how the people who teach us about God influence
our image of God, stressing that Jesus is an example of God's love and
desire for relationship with us. We hope the seekers begin to realize that

God wants only our happiness, and that the scriptures are filled with that promise. We remind them that Jesus' admonishment to love our neighbors isn't a threat, but a prescription for a way of life that brings inner peace. And we introduce the concept that loving is natural for us because we are created in God's image, created with a thirst to grow closer to God and other people. While this may seem elementary to Catholics who have seriously reflected on these issues, the seekers respond as if they are seeing life in color for the first time.

Helpful in these God/Jesus discussions is the user-friendly book, *Good Goats, Healing our Image of God.* Under the heading "Good Old Uncle George," we meet the fire and brimstone God in language that the seekers relate to wholeheartedly. And in "God's Twenty-Thousand-Year Pout," we are treated to an imaginary insight into the damnation/ salvation theology that dominated church teaching since the eleventh century. This joyfully illustrated little book is an eye opener for the seekers. It is helpful in laying the groundwork for the concept of Jesus calling us to discipleship, living in and among us, building the kingdom through us. In less than 100 pages, and in big print, the reader is moved into a whole new realm of understanding God.[1]

What Is the Church?

Time permitting, we close this session with a discussion about church, referring to the many dislikes—we refer to those lists during every session so the seekers know we haven't dismissed their issues— that put the idea of church in a category of *they* and *them* or *the hierarchy.* The dislikes reveal church as an institution that makes and imposes rules. It is startling for the seekers to hear that the church is us, the people of God, always growing and changing. They begin to realize that the church has always been *in process* just as they are, and to understand why the church is capable of human error: it consists of human beings! We present Catholicism as a way of living modeled by Jesus, described in the New Testament, and in the experience of the early church. We point out that the pope and clergy have roles in the church but they are not *the* church, but fellow members of the church, with us. We are all called to discipleship, to bring about the reign of God's peace, love, and forgiveness on this earth.

In this context, the church becomes a road map, giving us directions for the journey, providing relationships that encourage, support, and celebrate life with us through sacraments and liturgical celebrations. In a sense, *church* is a verb, what we do, what we say, the way we acknowledge God's presence in every moment of our lives, not just on Sunday mornings. We see new faces of God every day, in every experience, in every person we meet. Always growing and changing, the people of God create a church that cannot do otherwise.

This simple message is powerfully moving to the seekers. They are beginning to see themselves as vital to a church that is vital to the world. Conversion begins.

We close this session with a promise of what we'll discuss the following week and with the Lord's Prayer, reminding them that we are praying together as church, a reality that is beginning to take on new meaning for these good people.

Catholics Coming Home
WHAT IS MY IMAGE OF GOD?

In the boxes below, please describe your image of God at the various stages of your life.

CHILDHOOD	TEEN YEARS	YOUNG ADULT	PRESENT

REFLECTION QUESTIONS:

1. Who taught me about God?

2. How did these teachers influence my concepts of God?

3. What kinds of images do I have of God?

    ____ Cop in the sky

    ____ CPA who keeps track of my sins (heavenly bean-counter)

    ____ Judge

    ____ Mother

    ____ Puppet master (God pulls the strings)

    ____ Old man with a beard

    ____ Voice deep inside me

    ____ Loving parent

    ____ The Tester! (God only gives me what I can handle.)

    ____ Other (Explain)

4. What has caused my concepts of God to change?

5. When did I last talk to God?

6. Did God hear me?

Catholics Coming Home
WHO IS JESUS?

Then Jesus and his disciples set out for the villages around Caesarea Philippi. On the way, he asked his disciples this question: *"Who do people say that I am?"* They replied, "Some say John the Baptizer, others say Elijah, still others say you are one of the prophets." *"And you,"* he went on to ask, *"who do you say that I am?"*

7. Who do you say Jesus is?

8. What does Jesus mean to your everyday life?

9. Why did Jesus die?

10. Why is Jesus important to the church?

11. What difference does Jesus make in the world today?

12. What was your concept of or relationship to Jesus:

    When you were a child?

    When you were a teenager?

    As a young adult?

    As an adult?

13. What has caused your concepts of Jesus to change or not to change?

Catholics Coming Home
WHO IS THE

C H U R C H?

YOU ARE!

YOU AND I: WE ARE THE CHURCH!

YOU AND I, THE PEOPLE OF GOD, are an unfinished, changing, growing, broken, forgiven, loved, and healed people. We are called through our baptism to be ministers of the gospel, to be the hands and feet and heart of Jesus in this life.

REFLECTION QUESTIONS:

1. How would you respond to the suggestion that *church* is a verb?

2. Why do we need church buildings?

3. How is the church defined by *they* and *them,* different from a church described as *us*?

4. Why doesn't the church stay the same?

5. How does the church change?

6. What is the mission of the church?

Session Three

An invitation to address any leftover comments from the week before leads into this session's agenda: (1) Faith vs. Religion; (2) How Catholics View Scripture; (3) Catholic Conversion; (4) Catholic Moral Values. Any one of these topics could take the entire evening. We make no claim to a thorough study of any issue we present. Because of the variety of backgrounds and purposes among the seekers, we try to offer a range of reflection topics that will unlock preconceptions and open new ways of considering their faith journeys.

Faith vs. Religion

One of the greatest gifts of the Catholic faith is the rich spiritual nourishment that has been the core of who we are as a faith community since the very beginning. We seem to have lost its emphasis in the elaborate defining and law-making process that followed the Reformation, resulting in a people who may be doing the right thing, but have no idea why. Nor do they find in their religious experience the kind of internal spiritual nourishment essential to fulfillment as human beings. Religion that does not include deepened spiritual awareness becomes a mechanical way of living inspired by external influences.

In his book, *Redemptive Intimacy,* Dick Westley lists the following effects of religion:

> Relating to God out of fear; Feeling the need to appease an angry God; Relating to God out of self-interest, i.e., attempting to get God to do our will; Considering ourselves as little and unworthy in God's sight; Belief in two worlds, one in which we live, and another in which God dwells; Belief that some things in the world, e.g., sex, pleasure, material goods, etc., are in themselves evil; and Violating the freedom and personhood of another by doing physical or psychological harm to her "in the name of the Lord."[2]

The seekers readily identify with this list, declaring that many of these characteristics describe their belief experience. The concept that faith is more than religion, that it is far more than a list of rules and obligations, opens a new dimension for many. Rather than blind obedience, faith is a way of living in close relationship with God, finding God not only within our hearts, but in all of creation, in all people. Faith is the moment-by-moment discovery of life's sacredness, our belovedness. While religion gives shape and substance and continuity to a community's faith, it is not a substitute for this personal, intimate connection with all of creation.

Westley states, "Whenever we find ourselves cowering in the presence of God, it is a sure sign that we have lost our consciousness of faith and have returned to the reflex action of religion....A fear-filled people can never truly be Church, for they can never truly be sign. Fear makes us incapable of witnessing either the presence of God or the Kingdom that is coming. Faith empowers us to do both."[3]

Discussion on this subject begins to loosen imbedded concepts that have defined the seekers' Catholic identity. This opens them to new ways of thinking about their relationship with God and church.

Catholics and Scripture

We have added to our series of reflections a brief insight into the way Catholics approach the Bible. The rationale is twofold: First, many seekers learned little about the Bible in their Catholic education and therefore assume that the church's teachings are not rooted in scripture. Others are confused by fundamentalist claims that scriptures form the entire basis of salvation, and that they are to be taken literally. Without apologizing for the fact that we do not read scripture literally, we clarify that this is a difference between Catholics and Evangelicals in particular. Ours is a means of embracing truths much larger than the words on the page, truths fluid enough to handle new issues that are only beginning to challenge scientific, sociological, and biological assumptions we've lived with for most of the last millennium. The varying literary styles in the Bible—historical, poetic, narrative, legal, liturgical, prophetic—are not lost on the seekers, nor is the reality of cultural and language distortion of meaning over centuries. It is helpful to provide each seeker with a copy of *Exploring the Sunday Readings,*[4] challenging them to set aside time during the week to reflect on Sunday's readings, whether or not they plan to attend Mass. For people who have seldom held a Bible, it is a user-friendly introduction to a whole new way of living and praying as a Catholic. Many parishes include the daily reading references in their bulletins, another welcome resource for the seekers.

How Catholics View Conversion

Presenting a concept of church as subject to ongoing growth and discovery requires an understanding of conversion from a Catholic perspective. If we invite the seekers on a journey of reflection and reconciliation, they will need to understand their own conversion process in the light of Catholic teaching. Just as we ask the church to be open to change, we must be willing to incorporate renewal into our own lives. The process of reconciliation demands that one be willing to consider new ways of thinking. Throughout the scriptures, Jesus shares a message of conversion. Being his disciples and embracing our Catholic faith is more than understanding its tenets; it requires a sense of ongoing conversion in many areas of our lived experience and acquired knowledge. The good news of Jesus is definitely an invitation to continuous conversion.

It's important to point out during these discussions with seekers that there is no wrong stage of conversion. The handout at the end of this section, on page 125, is only meant to be a guide for reflection, a means to focus on where we are and where we want to be headed, the areas in which we want to grow. I like to introduce the subject of certitude into these discussions, asking where it belongs in a faith journey. When have we reached that point of knowing all there is to know or defining something for all time? We encourage reflection on *life* as our teacher, stressing our Catholic belief in sacred truth emanating from tradition, the church's presence in the lived experience of the people of God throughout the centuries. The threads of belonging, understanding, regard for the sacred in creation and history, for life itself, begin to weave together in these discussions, leading to deeper awareness of God's love for us. A sense of Jesus as the human face of that love, sharing our struggles and our goodness, our deaths and resurrections, our ongoing quest for relationship with Abba, begins to take form in the seekers. And the need for the church to sustain, support, guide, and nurture this new way of living in relationship with God and one another becomes more and more evident.

Catholic Values

A journey of reconciliation will seldom lead us to a destination of *doing what we're told.* Faith reflection will lead one deeper into the sacred space within, where the answers must find peace with the soul's reality. A seeker who has been reconciled with the church for some time called me late one evening because he had just begun reading a book on Catholic morality that astounded him. The book's purpose is "to paint a different picture of morality, one rooted in the Catholic tradition, which sees morality as a positive, creative capacity that helps us know not only what we should do, but what kinds of persons we want to be...not as chafing under obligations of the law, but as *a process of discovering happiness and real human fulfillment*."[5] (Italics mine.)

Joe had already called Catholic friends to ask them if they ever thought Catholic morality had anything to do with an attempt to be happy. Answers were equally and incredulously negative. So he called me. "Carrie, can this be true?...If it is, why did it always feel like Catholic morality was something we had to have shoved at us under penalty of damnation? Where were books like this when I was in college?"

Inherent in Catholic teaching is the sense of human sacredness. We are the beloved of God. Not only Catholics or Christians, but every human being who ever lived has this mark of sacredness within their soul. (This is a far cry from the pagan baby theology so many of the seekers recount with humor.) Living out of our values is more about integrity than about laws.

Jesus never gave rules or one-size-fits-all answers. He lived from a value system that assumed sacredness in the human condition and the human need to live in close relationship with one another. He called us to live this way not in lieu of damnation, but in order that we may have full, happy lives! His way isn't about *shoulds* or obligations, but about a way to life that is consistent with the God-center within us. Our Catholic values call us to a countercultural way of life, particularly here in America where the values of individualism are deeply ingrained in our society. It is this undergirding of Catholic values that gives us confidence that we can make a difference in the world, we can bring about the reign of God on this earth. When we live out of these basic Catholic values, we create peace, bringing us closer to being the kind of people God loves us into being.

Like Joe, the seekers ask, "Why weren't we ever taught any of this stuff?" It's on nights like this that the minister can feel very good about what the church has to offer: an alternative to a lifestyle characterized by too many possessions, too much competition, too little time, and too little caring. It's impossible to choose the alternative without community support, spiritual nourishment, and ongoing discovery. Again, a reason for the church! But the seekers are already figuring that out for themselves.

The value chart in this section, page 126, is not intended to be a good/bad dichotomy, an either/or choice. Certainly American individualism allows people to choose to do things that are good. The difference is that we believe our gospel values are the intrinsic core of a sacramental people. Creation is permeated by a loving God who invites us to participate, minute by minute, in the ongoing discovery of the glory and mystery of God in our midst. Ours is not a *do what feels good* value system, but a conviction that all life is sacredly infused with hopefulness and potential. It is up to us, the Body of Christ we call church, to reveal this presence to one another, celebrate the wonder of it all, and buoy one another up when spiritual darkness prevents us from experiencing God's love. There is something very joyful and expansive about a faith that opens a single human being up to a sense of belonging to all of creation, of connection to all of history, and to the promise of the future. Ours is a theology of hope: We can change the world. As church, we can make a difference.

Occasionally, seekers will balk at these values, defending the values of the American individualism as the basis of our free enterprise system, our capitalistic economy, and our affluence. Without a doubt, there is truth in this defense. This reflection is not about right and wrong; it is about being called to live in discipleship. We are all affected by the values that prevail within our culture, in varying degrees. A culture without a common value base will discover its values according to the media. At no time in history has a population been so invaded by media; the effects are evident everywhere. Without clear options, we find ourselves caught up in the prevailing values of the day. Even those who strictly follow church rules will be pulled into decisions and behaviors more indicative of the culture than the gospel. Our job is not to judge others, but to get in touch with who we are, the beloved of God. Discipleship calls us to make our decisions accordingly.

The discussions on conversion and values inevitably lead to discussions about change and how it affects the church. The church becomes more relevant to the seekers as they contemplate the role of prophets in the church and consider who today's prophets might be—

the people who call the church to purify itself. Pope John XXIII, in opening Vatican Council II, "called for a study and exposition of doctrine that would employ the literary forms of modern thought," and stated that, "the substance of the ancient doctrine is one thing and the way in which it is presented is another."[6] Modern theologians continue to challenge all of us to examine ancient teachings in light of history's gift to us, a new understanding of reality. It is through this ongoing scrutiny that our faith remains alive, relevant, and truthful. The seekers discover dignity in their own questioning once they realize that Catholic history is filled with faithful women and men, some now regarded as saints and more whose names we will never know, who questioned and challenged church teachings while remaining faithfully committed to the central teachings and values of the church. They did not dissent because they desired to undermine the church, but because they believed sincerely that God was calling them to a different understanding of truth. Now aware that dissension from within has historically resulted in positive consequences for the church, the seekers are free to contemplate constructive ways in which they too can effect change.

Catholics Coming Home
HOW CATHOLICS APPROACH SCRIPTURE

The Catholic approach to scripture is very different from that of fundamentalist believers who insist that every word be taken literally. Scripture scholarship is ongoing, revealing more and more about the origins of the books in the Bible, the cultures in which they were written, and the root meanings of words that have been passed down to us through a number of translations.

None of this diminishes our regard for sacred scripture; in fact, it enhances it. Ours is not a superstitious need to mold scripture to fit our needs and our truths. The Bible is an inspired chronicle of the struggle of human beings throughout the ages to understand themselves and their God, to learn from the stories of others who have journeyed before, the hopefulness that comes from listening for God's voice in all of our daily activities and relationships.

There is a decided difference between the Hebrew Scriptures (Old Testament) and the New Testament. That difference is Jesus. Jesus' message was purely one of love: God loves us, God wants to be in relationship with us, and through Jesus, God dwells in each one of us. We are holy, our lives are sacred.

Therefore Catholics consider scriptures from three aspects:

1. Historical Setting and Context: Who were the people receiving the message? Who was sending it? What issue was being addressed? What was the context of the issue in the time in which it was written?

2. Message/Revelation from Writer to That Community: How does the message to that community call us to move forward as a community (church) in this time and this culture? How does it help us to learn more about ourselves, to incorporate this discovery into our faith journey as church?

3. What Does All This Say to Me...in the Circumstances of My Life...Today? How does it affect my decisions? How does it affect my actions?

Catholics Coming Home
HOW CATHOLICS UNDERSTAND CONVERSION[7]

TYPE	FROM	TO
Affective Conversion	Blockage of feelings. Just give me the facts and the rules. I want certitude!	Incorporation of feelings in faith life, decisions, actions, etc. May result in struggle and ambiguity.
Intellectual Conversion	Knowledge as facts...I can define everything by the facts if I get enough of them!	Knowledge as meaning (wisdom). Life/experience also teach me.
Moral Conversion	Satisfaction of law is criteria for my choices.	Values are criteria of choices.
Religious Conversion	Life is series of problems and/or achievements. No deeper sense of meaning or purpose.	Life is mystery and gift. It is a journey with and toward God and all of creation.
God Conversion	God is force out there.	Personal relationship with God.
Christian Conversion	Historical Jesus—we have to believe to be saved.	God's love for me evidenced by the risen Christ who dwells within.
Church Conversion	Church as *they,* the institution.	Church as *we*, a community.

REFLECTION: *Where am I on this journey of conversion? When do we get to the end of the journey? Where do I want to be? How do I get there?*

Catholics Coming Home
VALUES: Differing Views of the Human Person

Catholic Christian Values	American Individualism Values[8]
All life, all creation is originated by God. God has infused human life with God's love through Jesus, the Emmanuel *(God with us)*.	The human person is completely autonomous, independent of others, of our environment, of any sense of global community.
Each of us is connected to the rest of humankind, to the rest of creation, through this God-presence within us.	My connection, social ties, or responsibilities to others result only from freely-chosen contracts or agreements.
Because we share God's life with all human beings, we have co-responsibility for human dignity, suffering, freedom, etc.	We are naturally and morally independent of one another. I am not affected by the plight of others unless I choose to be.
Value Center: Relationship with God and others	Value Center: Self as individual
Other values derived from my relationships with God, other people, and creation	My moral values reflect my private choices and preferences
My private moral values affect my choices and actions not only in my home, but in the public/work sector as well. There is a consistency in my behaviors based on my inner beliefs.	My private, moral values apply to my personal life only. The marketplace is a different matter where different rules may apply. It is basically for the pursuit of self-interest.

REFLECTION

1. Which value system is closer to mine?

2. How does one exist in a culture dominated by values that do not define what I believe?

3. What does any of this have to do with my spirituality?

Session Four: Keystone Session

The image of keystone is a powerful one for me. During liturgies at the Basilica of Saint Mary, my eyes are often lifted to the main arch and its keystone. Set in the very center, the keystone is a wedge-shaped piece that supports the two sides of an arch. Tremendous pressure must come to bear on that stone if all that comes before it is to bear the weight of the building blocks that follow that vital link. This session is like that. It provides the link between the seeker's deepening awareness of his or her own faith concepts and their relationship to the church. It makes sense of a church that has existed for centuries, yet is adaptable enough to move into the new millennium. The block that makes sense of the changes and challenges in the church is Vatican II. It is not necessary to give lengthy, detailed information about the council itself or its documents. What is most helpful to the seekers is information that provides a historical perspective of church, events that brought us to this point, and how those events still affect our experience and understanding of church. The seeker is beginning to see the church as a pilgrim body, constantly growing and changing, rather than a static organization focused on rigidity and rules. Continuity is based on our ongoing discovery of who we are as disciples of Christ.

Seekers identify with the defensive stance assumed by the Council of Trent (1545–1563) after the Reformation. It is a common human tendency to defend what is attacked. Confronted with radical opposition, church authorities rallied the troops and circled the wagons in order to protect and preserve everything that defined church for them. Any form of questioning or suggestion of reform was looked on with suspicion. Those in authority were fearful of change. The sixteenth-century imposition of a rigid faith expression resulted more from its opposition to Protestant reforms than from revelation found in scripture or tradition.

We wonder together what would have happened if Martin Luther had access to a fax machine or E-mail, or if the Catholic laity had been as involved and educated as it is today, as aware of its rightful ownership of the church. Dialogue can neither change the reality of church history nor relieve the suffering it has caused. It does provide rational understanding through which the seekers can begin to assume personal responsibility for reconciling the reality of their life circumstances with church teachings. The seekers appreciate discussions that reveal the church's errors, and even its changed position on critical issues. Open exploration of the historical context in which some of these decisions were made often leads seekers to the point of forgiveness as well. And the forgiving begins with themselves. Too many seekers have heaped hot coals of shame upon their heads for years because of their inability to live in absolute obedience to all church laws. Before they can ever forgive the church, they need to forgive themselves. When they begin to identify with Catholics throughout the ages who have wrestled with these same kinds of conflicts, they are able to resolve their church differences in a much wider, healthier arena. Helpful resources for both seekers and team members who are interested in learning more about these events are *Time Capsules of the Church* by Mitch Finley (Our Sunday Visitor); *A Concise History of the Catholic Church* by Thomas Bokenkotter (Image Books/Doubleday); and *Catholic Update No. C0393* (St. Anthony Messenger Press).

Our discussion on Vatican II begins with a brief background of the political and religious situation in Europe during and after the Reformation. Providing light-hearted context to the historical facts surrounding the Reformation, Mitch Finley notes, "...the seeds of the Protestant Reformation were in the ground before Luther was born."[9] Obviously, Martin Luther's criticisms of the church were not a figment of his imagination. It took nearly three decades for the church to officially respond to the 95 theses Luther sent to local bishops on October 31, 1517. Finley points out that the legendary account of Luther nailing his theses to the church doors in Wittenburg is probably not accurate, adding, "...even if he had, it would have been no big deal, as people did that sort of thing all the time. The doors of the local church were used as a kind of community theological bulletin board."[10] This imagery provides intriguing insight to the church climate of the day. Even the most apathetic church-goer was drawn into the controversy!

In its attempt to restore order and address the abuses cited by Luther, the Council of Trent seemed instead to seal the fate of the schism. The result was a heavy dose of legalism that would permeate Catholic life for centuries.

By the end of the nineteenth century, the Spirit was well at work within the church body, that is, if one considers conflict, intense dialogue, and involvement as signs of the Spirit! Pius IX called a council called Vatican I in December 1869 to address mounting dissension within the church. The number of participants reveals that the world was a smaller place; fewer than 800 bishops attended, most from Europe. Vatican I reaffirmed edicts declared by the Council of Trent, insisting that the church remain in defense against worldly influences that were challenging the core of public thinking. Emerging concepts of democracy, freedom of the press, and the developing disciplines of psychology, medicine, and science were all seen as threats to the church's stronghold on truth.

While all of this may seem like ancient history to the seekers, these events directly influenced the church as we knew it for the first sixty years of the twentieth century. This was the period that also saw the exodus of immigrants from Europe, their hopes and dreams resting on freedom and the abundance of opportunity promised in America. My own Italian Catholic grandparents came to this country during this period, bringing with them their Catholic faith as they knew it, including deep suspicion of the Protestantism they had been taught was diluting their faith. Also arriving just a short time before were my Danish Lutheran grandparents, convinced their very salvation rested on disassociation from the pope and all his followers. The personal effects of this period of history on my life are dramatic. The twain did not meet between my parents' families; there was no common ground, and the reason was religion.

So went the patterns of immigration in America. Catholics built their own schools, their own hospitals, and their own communities around their church. Protestants felt some sense of safety in the prevailing separation of church and state and relied less heavily on building their own brick and mortar fortresses. However, their church communities provided a nucleus of certitude and conviction that Catholics were suspect. Unexposed to the light of reality, these biases remain imbedded in our culture. I am often challenged by fundamentalist Protestants who question my salvation because I am a Roman Catholic. They are convinced it is impossible for us to walk with Jesus.

When the church closes us off from the world around us, the intent of Vatican I, the result is a dichotomized existence of walking in two worlds, one presented by our culture and the other professed by our church. During this same period of time, women were considered chattel, bigotry was the norm, and there was to be no mention of politics or religion in any social setting. Denominationally, we isolated ourselves, Protestants and Catholics judging each other on beliefs inherited from a bygone era. Being right was more important than being together. Salvation was only possible through the "right religion." This was our common American religious experience.

Vatican II

The world would wake from all this religious antagonism in a totally unexpected way. A grandfatherly Angelo Giuseppe Roncalli was elected pope on October 28, 1958—John XXIII, the pope most Catholics today recall with love and affection. In only a matter of days, he began to speak of the need to bring the church into the twentieth century. (Nearly 40 years later, Pope John Paul II would declare Vatican Council II "The Advent Liturgy of the New Millennium.")[11] Church insiders were aghast, convinced this peasant-like man could not possibly lead the church. Many church leaders were convinced the authority established by Vatican I was the end of open discussion for all time. Why stir things up again when everything had been put in its place?

Vatican II was convened on October 22, 1962, and for this council 2500 bishops participated. It is doubtful that any of them, not even John XXIII himself, had any idea that what they were about to begin would change not only very important aspects of Catholicism, but its influence on the entire world. This new pope challenged those who claimed that history has nothing to teach us.

It is not our intent to present a study of church history either in this book or for the seekers. I am forever indebted to church scholars, theologians, and writers who have gifted us with a rich legacy of written material, some easily understood by the average lay reader. What is important is to provide the seekers with a context in which to interpret the church as it exists today. The issue of papal infallibility, for instance, is usually met with surprise. Seekers represent the prevailing assumption among pew Catholics as well, that papal infallibility is somehow connected to Jesus giving the keys to Peter. For pre-Vatican II Catholics, this may be a consoling concept, but to the average seeker, it is not believable. When they come to understand that the teaching does not imply the pope himself is infallible, but rather that papal teachings under specifically qualifying circumstances are considered to be without error, the issue is nearly mooted. Placed in its historical context, however briefly, we again see the church evolving, responding, and changing on a continuum.

In an article titled "Vatican II, Thirty Years on the Road from Rome," Jim Castelli presents brief but thorough information, including a brief list of the major documents.[12] Also included is a key, listing the general principles of Vatican II:

- The Church is a mystery, or sacrament, and not primarily a means of salvation.

- The Church is the whole People of God, not just the hierarchy.

- The whole People of God participates in the mission of Christ, and not just in the mission of the hierarchy.

- The mission of the Church includes service to those in need, and not just preaching of the Gospel or the celebration of the sacraments.

- The Church is truly present at the local level as well as at the universal level. A diocese or parish is not just an administrative division of the Church universal.

- The Church includes Orthodox, Anglicans, and Protestants.

- The mission of the Church includes proclamation of the Word, celebration of the sacraments, witnessing to the Gospel individually and institutionally, and providing service to those in need.

- All authority is for service, not domination.

- Religious truth is to be found outside the Church as well. No one is to be coerced to embrace the Christian or the Catholic faith.

- The Church is always for the sake of the Kingdom of God and is not itself the Kingdom.[13]

Short, succinct, and powerfully profound, this key gives the seekers a rich point of reference within which to understand the essence of Vatican II. Our reflection sheet entitled Changing Concepts of God and Church helps them process their own changing views. It is never our intent to simply tell them what to believe or where they need to be on the journey, but to provide a process through which they can integrate their own experience and their changing awareness of church.

Another helpful Vatican II resource that is both user friendly and economical is *Vatican II: The Vision Lives On!*[14]

Catholics Coming Home
CHANGING CONCEPTS OF GOD AND CHURCH

Prior to Vatican II: **After Vatican II:**

DESCRIPTION OF GOD:

Prior to Vatican II	After Vatican II
Punished sin	Forgives sin
Is distant, out there somewhere	Is near, within me
Male	Above/Beyond gender images
Judge	Friend
Hostile, angry	Compassionate, loving

DESCRIPTION OF CHURCH:

Prior to Vatican II	After Vatican II
Them: hierarchy, pope, clergy	Us: We are the People of God
Tradition	Tradition and scripture
Only source of salvation	Set of values modeled by gospel/Jesus
Possesses unambiguous truth about everything	Questions are not incapable with faith
Universal	Local, relationships
Structured, rigid, unchanging	Adaptable, responsive, always changing
Rules to obey	Informed conscience
Condemning sin(ners)	Forgiving sin(ners)
Dogma, law is the bottom line	Human person is most important

MY PERSONAL CONCEPTS

_____   _____
_____   _____
_____   _____
_____   _____
_____   _____
_____

Conscience

Development of a mature conscience is essential to an authentic faith experience. We deliberately wait until this point in the process to present this material. Taken out of context it could easily be construed as a quick fix, a rationalization of a prevalent *do your own thing* value system. It is neither. At the heart of our Catholic value system is the essence of the sacred soul that defines each human being. Yet many Catholics have accustomed themselves to doing what they are told, or assuming that their inability to do so renders them excluded from the church. A faith reflection process must include mutual challenge. By now we are ready to challenge the seekers to take adult responsibility to live out of the God center within each one of them. They may need support and we need to make sure that our message is understood. The alternative is for them to perceive a church that stands for nothing. Discipleship is demanding; the measuring rod is our intimate relationship with God, not what we do out of resentful obedience.

While proclaiming January 1, 1991, World Peace Day, Pope John Paul II proclaimed its theme, "If You Want Peace, Respect Everyone's Conscience." The Vatican announcement included the following: "There are always violent consequences when individual consciences are not respected, especially in their thirst for God. Any sort of violent oppression of the conscience provokes equally violent reactions, and this is true for individuals as for communities and peoples....An important and primary place ought to be given to the rights of conscience and to the duties which correspond to them."[15]

The seekers are now at a crossroad. Even the pope is telling them they must think for themselves, take responsibility for their decisions! In a sense, it's time to shuck the mantel of victimization and be counted as a healthy human being. Of course, this realization must be approached gently. I have ministered to victims of domestic violence, victims of sexual and racial discrimination, victims of unjust employment practices, and victims of spiritual abuse. Victims in all these categories have taught me to own my own victim tendencies, to live assertively and with dignity. I offer their invaluable lesson to the seekers. The Dislike List is up at every session, but now I ask them to take a good look at it as I ask, "How much of what is on this list really has power over your daily walk with God and the faith community?"

It is through a mature, informed conscience that we begin to retract our sense of harmony and peace in our church relationship. We have discovered that the church will never be without struggle, without conflict. It is made up of flesh and blood, human weakness, and human brilliance. How did we ever become cookie-cutter Catholics?

To further support the church's insistence on the dignity of conscience, we quote from the Vatican II document Church in the Modern World *(Gaudium et Spes)*, Chap. 1, Para. 16–17:

> Deep within their consciences men and women discover a law which they have not laid upon themselves and which they must obey....Their dignity rests in observing this law and by it they will be judged. Their conscience is people's most secret core, and their sanctuary. There they are alone with God whose voice echoes in their depths. By conscience, in a wonderful way, that law is made known which is fulfilled in the love of God and of one's neighbor....Yet it often happens that conscience goes astray through ignorance which it is unable to avoid, without thereby losing its dignity. It is, however, only in freedom that people can turn themselves toward what is good. The people of our time prize freedom very highly and strive eagerly for it....Yet they often cherish it improperly, as if it gave them leave to do anything they like, even when it is evil. But genuine freedom is an exceptional sign of the image of God in humanity....Their dignity therefore requires them to act out of conscious and free choice, as moved and drawn in a personal way from within, and not by their own blind impulse or by external constraint.[16]

Armed with a foundation firmly establishing not only the freedom but the right to follow conscience, we now address the responsibility that goes with the freedom, using the Conscience reflection sheet. The discussion is energetic and intense. There is often laughter as the seekers read the descriptions of immature and mature conscience, most agreeing readily they have been planted firmly on the first list since grade school.

A focus on conscience will inevitably lead to a discussion on sin. In an effort to help the seekers move beyond the "grocery list" mentality familiar to pre-Vatican II Catholics, we consider excerpts from *A Spirituality of Wholeness*. In part, Bill Huebsch addresses sin this way:

> The "letter of the law" approach to sin and grace has gotten us into some trouble. We've forgotten to seek authenticity which is more

difficult than keeping the letter of the law. But it would not be possible for you to show me in Scripture where it was ever suggested, even remotely, that keeping the letter of the law would somehow be enough for the followers of Jesus....the very opposite is true: the law is a guide and can sometimes be helpful but it is by no means all there is. By no means. There is much more.[17]

Now it is the "much more" that sparks conversation. Living according to a well-informed conscience doesn't mean life is easier by any means. Discipleship is not about controlled behaviors, but living in loving relationships, requiring continuous commitment to our own sacred identities and the recognition of God's unrelenting love. For many, this is unexplored territory and begs more prayer and reflection. Seekers whose religious upbringing printed indelible messages about right and wrong behaviors with little or no regard for the internal development, capability, or wounding of the sinner have the most difficult time grappling with this new concept. "Why should I be good if someone else is going to get off without punishment?" More discussion follows about heaven, hell, and why we need to feel that some people will go to hell! Salvation-driven religion may seem more secure than the call to walk closely with Jesus, building the kingdom in the here and now. In spite of our 2000-year history, we have a hard time believing in the power of God's love.

Finally, we tease them a bit with the "sin quiz." I love their reactions to it: "I could have answered these easily before I came here; now I'm not sure." "Does this mean if I do it or someone else does it?" "Whoa, kinda stops us from judging, doesn't it?" And so on. The crosstalk, banter, support, and humor are clear evidence that change is occurring.

This is a powerful evening, filled with new self-awareness and conversion. We select a gentle closing prayer, one that reassures us of God's love and participation in our struggles and triumphs. We've come a long way during our four sessions and begin to realize we have very little time left together. The realization is as painful for the ministers as it is for the seekers. This hard work, honesty, openness to change, and laughter are soul food. I wish everyone who ministers in the church, ordained or not, could experience a steady diet of this nourishment.

Catholics Coming Home
CONSCIENCE

Immature Conscience	Mature Conscience
Legalistic collection of rules: Do this—Don't do that!	My conscience is who I am, and is only as good as who I am.
Trained behaviors taught by others, formed by teaching rules.	My behaviors are not who I am. What I stand for and what I believe in are who I am.
My primary motivation is obedience and fear of being punished or caught.	Forming my conscience uses all of myself: my intellect, my emotions, my spirituality, my regard for the sacredness of others, the sacredness of myself!
	I know I cannot make mature, moral decisions without reflection and prayer.
Without rules, decisions are difficult and inconsistent.	Sometimes my decisions cause great pain and rejection from others.
Requires approval of authority.	My decisions have to include effects on others as well as myself.
It's not my fault; I followed the rules.	I can admit mistakes I have made.
Approval of others is reward. Behaviors are affected by response from others.	I try to keep learning, growing. I admit I do not have all the answers.

MATURE CONSCIENCE REQUIRES "HOMEWORK"

Reflection - Sense of others - Sense of values - Church's position (although we may be at odds with the church) - Prayer - Effort to discover what is right.

REFLECTION

1. Which type of conscience results in anger at outside forces for "controlling my life"?

2. How will my behavior be affected if my primary value is obedience rather than living out of my conscience?

3. Is there a difference between feeling guilty because "I broke the rules and got caught" and feeling guilty because "I violated my conscience"?

4. Where does church teaching fit into my conscience formation?

Catholics Coming Home
SIN QUIZ

Read each of the statements below. Then make a decision. Is the situation described a sin? If you think it is, circle S. If you do not think it is a sin, circle N. If you are undecided, or "it depends," circle D.

S   N   D   Killing a human being

S   N   D   Missing Mass on Sunday

S   N   D   Sexual intercourse outside of marriage

S   N   D   Abortion when mother's life is at risk

S   N   D   Drinking alcohol

S   N   D   Using cocaine

S   N   D   Being a homosexual

S   N   D   Failing to vote in state/national elections

S   N   D   Obeying dishonest corporate policy at the workplace

S   N   D   Wasting food

S   N   D   Refusing to give to the poor

S   N   D   Investing in companies that disregard human dignity

S   N   D   Exceeding speed limit on highway

S   N   D   Smoking cigarettes

S   N   D   Buying pull tabs

S   N   D   Refusing to forgive someone who has hurt you

S   N   D   Disrespect for our environment

S   N   D   Discrimination based on gender, color, religion, economic status

Session Five

Sacraments

I like to begin this evening with a question: "Anyone remember what a sacrament is?" Surprisingly, many have the Baltimore Catechism answer down pat: "A sacrament is an outward sign instituted by Christ to give grace." The baby boomers, however, haven't a clue. When I ask those who know the answer to tell me what it means, the entire group ends up laughing because no one has any idea what the words mean. A common image of sacrament is a magical zapping, in which the priest gets God to do something to us. This concept also keeps us in the role of spectator on our spiritual journey, passive and helpless. It's up to the priest and God to do it.

And so we begin to fill in the gaps. It's important for them to know that the sacraments have evolved. The Protestants are right when they say Jesus didn't specifically originate them all. But we are right when we say they are the result of early Christians trying to preserve the presence of Jesus in their midst. Like us! We live in a culture that is counter to our spiritual values and beliefs. Jesus calls us to live in a radically different way, yet one that brings us peace and serenity at day's end. In order to do that, we need a sense of belonging to community, and rituals to reinforce what we believe. We need to be reminded constantly that God is in our midst.

Like the early Christians, we need rituals that say more than the words. Rituals are necessary for healthy cultures. Unhealthy cultures will also produce rituals, but they are too often divisive and do not provide the sense of relationship and belonging we all need. The number of sacraments isn't as important as the fact that they exist. There have been as many as 30 and as few as five throughout the centuries. Not until the twelfth century were they fixed at seven, with the addition of marriage, the last sacrament to be added to our current list. In the beginning, baptism, confirmation, and Eucharist were one sacrament, called the sacrament of initiation. And at one time, confession, now called the sacrament of reconciliation, was only celebrated once in a lifetime, setting the stage for death-bed confessions, still common.

Sacraments help us remember and take note of the presence of the risen Christ in our midst. They don't cause this to happen, but they stop us in our spiritual tracks so we pay attention to what is happening! Throughout church history, there has been an ebb and flow of sacramental understanding, and correctives have been required, particularly when the focus is on the ritual rather than the revealed presence of Christ. When the bread and wine become objects of adoration apart from the reality of Christ's presence, we lose sight of what Eucharist is, and we may minimize our role in the sacramental relationship. A confession steeped in fear, condemnation, and judgment can hardly bring to mind the presence of a forgiving Christ to even the most devout among us. And when we participate in sacraments by going through motions without meaning, neither understanding nor taking personal responsibility for intent, we miss the whole purpose. Eventually, meaningless ritual becomes empty or worse, exploitive.

Sacraments are not the cause of God's presence in our lives, but the reassurance of God's everlasting love and participation, moment by moment, throughout all our days. How could we possibly hold on to this awareness without something more than words? The seven sacraments—baptism, reconciliation, Eucharist, confirmation, matrimony, holy orders, and anointing of the sick—are the church's official reminders of the ongoing relationship between the recipient, the community, and Jesus, with God's grace abundantly flowing through all three. The community is called not only to witness the sacramental reality in marriage, or baptism, or any sacrament, but also to provide a sense of belonging. In a particular way, the community and the sacramental recipient bond themselves to one another in a covenant relationship.

Sacramental belonging calls to mind not only those present when the sacrament is celebrated, but all who have journeyed before and all whose lives are connected to ours throughout the worldwide faith community. Wow! In a world where more and more people are feeling disconnected and isolated, sacrament is a powerful gift. As the concept of sacrament develops, the seekers quickly note that there are many more sacramental experiences than seven. Life is filled with moments, and people, and events so powerfully sacred they can only be described as sacramental. We don't need a church declaration to believe in the sacramentality that defines us differently than the rest of Christendom. Once realized, even mundane experiences take on new meaning for the Catholic. I recall the Sunday we took our first grandchild to Mass.

Although only days old, Gary and I felt some primeval, mutual need to bring Krystal to that holy place. We had shared very few words about our motivation for taking her, but this tiny babe had moved into our souls more powerfully than our human experience could articulate. During the Consecration Prayer, our eyes met and Gary whispered "sacrament," as he nodded toward the precious child cuddled in his arms. Not bad for a converted Methodist! Of course, our relationship with Krystal was not about that day, but that day said everything about our relationship. We are connected, the Lord, this child, and us, and will be every day of our lives, with a kind of love that can only be God's gift.

When we ask the seekers to search their lives for sacramental signs, they have no trouble coming up with an unexpected kindness observed, a sunset, a coincidence, life-changing events, even the event of death. With this new understanding of sacrament, the seekers are ready to look at some of them specifically. Usually, we focus on Eucharist, reconciliation, and marriage. Our placement of marriage/divorce/annulment issues this far into the series is intentional. By now, the seekers are at a very different place and have a context within which they can reflect on often painful, confusing issues.

Sacrament of Eucharist The early Christians' efforts to remember Jesus evolved into small gatherings in one another's homes. There they shared stories of their lives and retold the stories of Jesus, what he said, events of his life, his death and the resurrection. Unfortunately, according to Paul in 1 Corinthians 11:17–22, some of these rituals lost their focus on Jesus and drifted into unsuitable gatherings. Paul felt a need to address this issue with the newly forming community: "When you meet in one place...it is not to eat the Lord's supper, for in eating, each one goes ahead with his own supper, and one goes hungry while another gets drunk. Do you not have houses in which you can eat and drink? Or do you show contempt for the church of God and make those who have nothing feel ashamed?"

Even in the early church, we had to learn that coming together to celebrate, to give thanks and praise meant little if anyone among us was left out in the process. Note that Paul didn't criticize who was doing the blessing, what kind of bread they were using, or the songs and prayers, but the attitudes in the hearts of the believers. It is this heart attitude we need to check when we embrace this sacrament.

As time evolved, clergy began to preside over the ritual of Eucharist, perhaps in response to all the chaos troubling Paul. Eventually, the priest presided and we watched, his back to us in private ritual. Bells rang at the sacred moments during which the bread and wine was changing into the body and blood, pulling our focus on the "magic" and away from our deep involvement in this sacrament of unity.

Vatican II restored our sense of Eucharist as an experience during which we gather in thanksgiving to remember Jesus' life and death, his presence in the gathered community, and our ongoing call to *be* the Body of Christ to one another. The cycle of relationship finds its fullest expression in Eucharist, the core of our faith. It defines us as part of the community, individually and collectively graced as the beloved of God. It is the essential spiritual nourishment.

Sacrament of Reconciliation It's still the black box to most seekers! Horror stories abound at every series. The reconciliation role play I described in an earlier chapter invites them to reconsider their dread of this sacrament, and to take responsibility for finding confessors who are pastoral and compassionate. That this sacrament, too, is a celebration of what God is already doing, for example, forgiving us, may be a difficult concept for some to grasp. We have found it helpful to discuss the Prodigal Son with the seekers, giving them a reflection sheet on which the entire parable is presented, along with reflection questions.

Catholics Coming Home
PRODIGAL SON
(Luke 15:11–32)

After reading these verses from Luke, reflect on the following questions.

1. What does the son's request for his share of his father's estate say about his relationship with his father? His father's relationship with him?

2. What was the son's motivation to return home?

3. Who initiated the reconciliation? How?

4. At what point did the son express his sorrow?

5. What did the father want to celebrate?

6. Have you ever felt like the older son? Why?

7. What does the older son's reaction say about his motivation for staying home?

8. What do we learn about love, forgiveness, and relationship with God from this story?

Most of us find it easier to identify with the resentment of the elder son than with the unconditional love experienced by the prodigal. And it doesn't seem fair. In a prayerful reflection on this parable, Henry Nouwen notes: "Outwardly, the elder son was faultless. But when confronted by his father's joy at the return of his younger brother a dark power erupts in him and boils to the surface. Suddenly, there becomes glaringly visible a resentful, proud, unkind, selfish person, one that had remained deeply hidden, even though it had been growing stronger and more powerful over the years."[18]

Reconciliation and forgiveness are the heart of this ministry; for that reason, we purposefully schedule our Catholics Coming Home series to end the week before our parish community celebrates this sacrament communally. Having observed the individual role play, it is an opportunity to invite the seekers to observe another way of celebrating the sacrament. We always invite them to observe or participate only to the degree to which they are comfortable. Afterward, we spend some time together, processing their experience. It is always the same. They are moved by the gentleness, the freedom with which the community acknowledges its sinfulness and the assurance of God's forgiveness. "Not what I remember confession being like," is a common response.

Sacrament of Marriage We begin this discussion by asking the seekers what marriage is celebrating, referring to the relationship cycle that characterizes sacrament. Clearly, sacramental marriage is lived out on a daily basis, is freely chosen on good days and bad days, by both parties. That was not, however, the early understanding of this sacrament. During the Council of Trent, when the church determined marriage to be a sacrament, the prevailing perception was that the woman was property, marriage was basically the way of procreation, and any marriage witnessed by a priest and members of the community was sacramental. We've come a long way. With new understanding of the human condition, relationships, sexuality, and psychology, we realize that a sacramental marriage can hardly be defined so sparsely. Procreation is no longer the sole criterion by which marriage is seen as being "lifegiving"; the whole life of each partner must be reverenced by the other. The life of the relationship itself must be open to the growth of each. We will discuss this further in Chapter 5. What is most important is that the seekers understand that annulment is not a declaration that a marriage didn't exist, only that the existing marriage was not sacramental.

I prefer to discuss privately with the seekers their individual situations and concerns. They deserve the dignity of a pastoral visit, allowing time and attention to their problems. An article I wrote for the Paulist National Catholic Evangelization Association, "Divorce and Remarriage in the Catholic Church,"[19] addresses sacramental marriage and annulment in a brief, easy-to-read format. It has been helpful not only to seekers, but to the hundreds of Catholics who have invited me to serve as their advocate in the annulment process.

It is important that the seekers understand that there are different kinds of annulments: External Forum, the public process we hear about most often; Lack of Form, required when a baptized Catholic has been married in a ceremony outside the Catholic community; and Internal Forum, perhaps the best kept secret in the church. All are addressed in Chapter 5.

Except for specific questions, we usually don't have time to go through all the sacraments during this discussion with the seekers. Once they understand the general concept of sacramental relationship, they make their own application to the others. If a sacramental encounter has been particularly painful for any of them, we invite them to schedule a time when they can address it in private.

Prior to closing prayer, we remind them that we have only one meeting left, and that we will use that time to wrap up their experience. At the basilica, we have been combining this final time together with a meal provided by the parish. It becomes eucharist with a small 'e'!

Session Six

This final gathering has become a very poignant experience. Attitudes have changed, even the most reticent have joined in the humor and serious revelation that characterized each week's session. Referring to the Dislikes List, posted for the last time, I ask them to reflect back on their first night, recalling the conversation that resulted from our list. The list has taken on an entirely different significance. Usually we agree that we resolved very few of the issues. However, new information and understanding makes it possible to see beyond the church's imperfections to the beauty of its vision. Somehow, discipleship means making room for everyone, letting go of our personal need to judge and condemn, as we open our hearts to receive God's limitless love and forgiveness in our own lives.

I invite them to give us feedback on what we could do differently, what we could add. Always they ask for more. It is sad, for me, that I cannot journey longer with them. I recommend to all parishes beginning this ministry to consider something that will pick up where this series ends. Spiritual appetites have been whetted and the joy and fullness of Catholic life that so many take for granted is shiny and new to these folks. Minimally, these reconnected seekers need to be invited to full community participation. Part of our job is to help them find parish communities that meet their needs, either according to location, or specific preference. Some may want to be part of a small, community-based parish while others like the larger, more impersonal parishes. Some want to belong to parishes that have inclusivity as a goal and that seem to live the gospel rather than just provide programs and activities. Most want good liturgies and all have gifts to share. By the end of the series we come to know the seekers well enough to suggest several parishes they might want to "check out" in their search for a spiritual home.

We close the session and the series with a healing liturgy, simple and quiet. As always, we make it clear that they are free to participate or not. If a priest joins us, this liturgy becomes the sacrament of anointing, with the seekers drawing from deep within their own hearts the mental, physical, emotional, and spiritual healing that has begun during our time together. If a priest is unavailable, we clarify that the ritual is not a sacrament. In either case, it is an opportunity to use oils, to reflect on our journey, and to acknowledge that the Spirit of God has been with us throughout our time together. After they are anointed, each seeker stands before team members who declare with hands placed on their shoulders, "John (Mary), through baptism you are my brother (sister) in Christ. I ask your forgiveness for any wrong the church has done to you." The responses are touching. Tears flow freely. Over and over, forgiveness is granted without hesitation.

There is something very powerful about this simple liturgy. A seeker reflected on that healing celebration not long ago, from her new vantage point of full participation in the church. "You explained that it would not be a sacrament, Carrie, because a priest wouldn't be there.

But now that I understand sacrament, I know that for me, it was sacrament. It was the most important liturgy of my life."

The absence of a public closing ritual of reconciliation with the church is deliberate. The seekers are at different places and will be returning to different parishes. Some are not ready to return, needing more time, more reflection, and more pastoral care. A few will never be able to return but find this process a way of letting go, freeing them to get on with their spiritual lives. We must be very sensitive at this point to the individual preferences among the seekers. This process has brought us all very close. Needs are expressed freely about how and when they want to return. For many, it begins with an appointment to celebrate the sacrament of reconciliation, their ritual of return. Others want to attend the Eucharist at other parishes, gleaning a flavor of church diversity before committing themselves to a particular parish.

For those struggling with whether or not they are worthy to receive Eucharist, we give no directives, only a promise to work with them individually as they resolve this dilemma. I have walked too many painful miles with Catholics whose hearts have been craving the very nourishment we believe essential to our spiritual survival. My faith, my conscience will not allow me to tell anyone they should not participate in this sacrament. On the other hand, to arbitrarily tell seekers to return to the table at this point would, I think, be an injustice to the sacred journey we've shared. Yet my heart is heavy whenever Catholics feel compelled to sit in the pew while the rest of us receive. I know my worthiness is no greater than theirs. I believe fear is at the root of this painfully embarrassing reality in our church, and I would like us to address this fear openly so we can lance the wound and begin healing our injury as a faith community. How can we celebrate this wonder of all wonders with full joy and thanksgiving when we know our brothers and sisters have been rejected for any reason?

In a short, powerful book, *Becoming Human,* Jean Vanier addresses communion, essential to the human sense of belonging, in this way:

> Communion is the to-and-fro of love. It is the trust that bonds us
> together....Trust is continually called to grow and to deepen, or it
> is wounded and diminishes. It is a trust that the other will not pos-
> sess or crush you but rejoices in your gifts and calls you to growth

and to freedom. One who is weak, who lives in true communion with another, will not see his own weakness as something to be judged, as something negative; he will sense that he is appreciated, that he has a place.[20]

What a beautiful description of what we Catholics have known all along about the sacrament we lovingly addressed as communion for centuries. How can this beautiful sense of belonging be enhanced for any of us if we deny a place to those who want to participate in the "to-and-fro of love"? Eucharist has been defined for me by the searing pain of those who are refused a place at our table.

Our perception of reconciliation with the church includes full participation. For those who seek unity with the Catholic community, the call to the table is one they have a right to choose freely. As the Vatican II document Declaration on Religious Liberty *(Dignitatis Humanae)* Chap. 1, Para. 3 states:

All are bound to follow their conscience faithfully...so that they may come to God....Therefore, the individual must not be forced to act against conscience nor be prevented from acting according to conscience, especially in religious matters...the practice of religion of its very nature consists primarily of those voluntary and free internal acts by which human beings direct themselves to God. Acts of this kind cannot be commanded or forbidden by any merely human authority.[21]

In their beautiful, prophetic document, *Go and Make Disciples,* the bishops of the United States remind us, "Evangelization inevitably involves the parish community for, ultimately, we are inviting people to our Eucharist, to the table of the Lord. When an individual evangelizes, one to one, he or she should have the Good News and the Eucharistic table as the ultimate focus."[22]

Amen!

Chapter 5
The Issues That Separate

While Catholics Coming Home has been developed to help seekers take responsibility for resolving their conflicting issues of faith, the ministry does call us to look carefully at issues that cause the greatest problem for the most people. Seekers point to concerns that present difficulty for active Catholics as well, issues that would surface in every parish if open dialogue was encouraged among church-going Catholics. To be Catholic is to live with tension; the church is a living, growing, developing organism composed of human beings. A marriage without tension hardly speaks to the world of God's commitment and love. If both partners are growing, being true to themselves, and responding to each other with soul-searching honesty, there will be tension. To ignore or ward off tension within any covenant relationship destroys intimacy, trust, and sense of belonging. The reality of a church that belongs to everyone is that its members will at times be frustrated by teachings, practices, or inaction.

The "law and order" concept of church embraced by so many is not without foundation. For several centuries, up to and including the middle of the twentieth century, pastoral care consisted mostly of diagnosing sinfulness, specifying degrees of severity based on the deeds of sinners. Ordained ministers prepared for their priesthood by diligently studying copious manuals that meted out prescribed punishments for specific sins. The rigidity of the manuals evolved from ancient teachings influenced by Aristotle, Aquinas, and Augustine. Assuming the role of spiritual parent, the church defined God as judge and controller of individual actions. Morality was defined objectively, with the sub-liminal implication that "God said it was so." In practice, religion became separated from lived experience and the church became a place where the powerful (ordained) ruled the powerless (laity).

Vatican II changed the concept of moral theology and with it our concept of church. No longer called to a primary focus on sin, moral theology was to focus on charity.[1] From a pastoral perspective, the shift in the church was from law enforcer to a compassionate befriender. The goal of the pastoral minister is to awaken the seeker to his or her own goodness, thereby empowering the call to participation in the Body of Christ. The pastoral minister begins not with the law of God or of the church, but with the lived reality of the seeker. The more we can know about that reality, the more effectively we serve as catalyst to new aware-ness of God in their lives.

In a response to the United States bishops' pastoral letter *Always Our Children,* Michael Bayly had this to say about pastoral theology:

> All theologies seek to point to the nearness of God....Pastoral the-ology...says that to know God, to be near God, we must be close to, and open to, the experiences of others and ourselves, including those experiences that are challenging, disconcerting, and unpleasant—those experiences in other words, that encompass not only joy and comfort, but uncertainty, loss, and suffering. It is in these experiences that the image of the loving, guiding, and watchful shepherd who gently tends to—indeed lives with—his flock of sheep out in the pastures is readily conjured.[2]

My favorite image of the Good Shepherd hangs on the wall in my office. In a photograph taken during the war we called Desert Storm in 1991, amid tanks, artillery, bunkers, and blowing sand, a shepherd cra-dles a bleeding lamb in his arms. A fierce wind is proclaimed by the bent desert palms in the background and by the folds of his robe pressed tightly against the shepherd's legs. In all of that human chaos, this shepherd of the Mideast sees only the plight of the wounded lamb. The lamb's blood drips through a crude bandage onto the shepherd's hand. Feet exposed through his sandals, the shepherd has to navigate through thorny bramble tossed about by the wind. There is desolation every-where in this picture, but the shepherd's face is distant, serene, almost hauntingly reassured. I take this picture off my wall often to look more closely at that face. To me it has become the face of Jesus. Unaffected by worldly events, his focus is on the lost, the straying, and the wounded.

Not a scholarly definition of pastoral theology, this image does define my ministry and helps me center myself when worldly distractions and church controversy cause me to lose my primary focus, the lambs. But it is not just about them, just as the shepherd's focus was not just about the lamb. It is a mutual journey of life and love and belonging, a call to fullness and wholeness of life for both. In ours, or any ministry effort, there must be room for this pastoral approach. Again and again, the minister will be called to reflect further into her own lived experience, to challenge her own biases. The pastoral minister's task cannot be defined solely by reading rules and dogmas, nor by defending "the system."

The following issues represent the most commonly experienced trouble spots for inactive Catholics. Validating their experience requires us to let their words stand on their own. We will present the church's perspective and the pastoral perspective in response. There will be gaps in these perceptions, the painful reality of the church today and always. Faith is not about knowing answers, but about living with questions, struggling, accepting others where they are, reveling in God's love for all. Our greatest challenge as church is to be a haven where people can bring their burdens, their doubts, and their triumphs. Parishes that celebrate or acknowledge only the triumphs will not be blessed by the seekers' journeys.

Pope, Hierarchy, Clergy

Seekers' Perspective

- "The church is the pope and all those in power in Rome. They make all kinds of declarations and rules without understanding anything about us or our lives."

- "Celibacy seems to detach those men from close, healthy relationships."

- "The sincerity of our faith is completely discounted. Our opinions, our life experience are of no value to church leaders. They respond to human problems with rules and edicts."

- "We are tired of having men we know nothing about discern God's will for us. We want to participate in the life of the church, we want leaders who care enough to listen to us, who are willing to listen to us. We're tired of top-down communication from Rome that seems more intent on preserving institutional traditions than trusting the Holy Spirit. If we are the church, where is our voice?"

- "I cannot be an active part of the Catholic Church as long as the hierarchy continues to cause pain for so many and appears to be disenfranchising those who challenge their teachings."

- "I've been fairly active in the church all my life. Honestly, I feel fear when I think of the power they have to dismiss me and my life's circumstances. How can that be of God?"

- "Whatever happened to compassion and understanding? I find more of that in other Christian denominations."

- "I'm tired of all these middle men between me and God. I prefer a personal, Bible-centered Christianity without all the corporate structure and outside authority telling me what I have to believe and do to be saved."

- "Why doesn't the hierarchy quit worrying about our sex life and start focusing on issues that threaten all of us as a human species?"

- "This business about not ordaining women is ridiculous. Where would the church be without them?"

- "Money and who you are seem too important to church leaders."

- "Why can't we vote for bishops?"

Church's Perspective

At this point in the history of the church, the reality is that we are a hierarchical church. It is not a democratic institution. For Americans, this is a hard fact to grasp. There is widespread disagreement on many levels on church teachings. Also, some church teachings are of greater significance than others. Bishop Raymond Lucker, Diocese of New Ulm, explains the levels of teaching in the Catholic Church:

(1) Divinely revealed truths are those beliefs that Catholics must believe....they include truths such as the trinity, incarnation, resur-

rection, immaculate conception, and sacraments. (2) Non-revealed truths, including principles of natural law, such as "love one another," teachings based on human dignity and the immortality of human beings. (3) Authoritative Level. Examples include artificial birth control, in-vitro fertilization, sacramental procedures, and the ordination of women. Those teachings could be changed, like the former teaching that the sun rose and set, which Galileo disproved with his theory that the earth rotated around the sun. There is a long list of teachings that have changed. In fact, there have been more changes in the church during the past thirty years than during the previous five hundred years. (4) Disciplinary rules, such as those on fasting, feast days, celibacy of clergy, and others. These can change with church practice. (5) Theological opinions. These can be disputed because they are, in fact, opinion. (6) Pious practices and devotions, such as praying the rosary, saying novenas, or wearing medals. Catholics may choose to use those practices, but if they choose not to, that doesn't make them non-Catholic.[3]

Few Catholics seriously reflect on the origin of church teachings. Generally, there is an assumption that the truths are without context, imposed at whim by church fathers over the centuries. In reality, teaching reflects the truths revealed in the lives and hearts of Christians throughout our history. The essence of church teaching is that God loves us and is always calling us to live in closer relationship with one another and our Creator. In the span of 2000 years, there has been a tremendous amount of focus and discovery on that basic truth, resulting in laws, rules, and traditions in numbers far beyond the ability of any one Catholic to know and embrace.

While there have been periods throughout our church history when change has been very little and very slow, change is guaranteed nonetheless. In the Vatican II document Dogmatic Constitution on Divine Revelation *(Dei Verbum)* Chap. 2, Para. 8, upholds, in part, the teaching of an evolving faith:

> The tradition that comes from the apostles makes progress in the church, with the help of the Holy Spirit. There is a growth in insight into the realities and words that are being passed on. This comes about through the contemplation and study of believers who ponder these things in their hearts (see Luke 2:19, 51). It comes from the

intimate sense of spiritual realities which they experience. And it comes from the preaching of those who, on succeeding to the office of bishop, have received the sure charism of truth. Thus, as the centuries go by, the church is always advancing towards the plenitude of divine truth, until eventually the words of God are fulfilled in it.[4]

Pastoral Perspective

Once seekers know that *we* are the church, and that *we* have a right and obligation to live out of our informed conscience, they seem less intent on combat with church authorities. The seekers become aware of changes that have occurred since they left the church, and that change is the result of Catholics changing the way we experience our faith, not because the hierarchy has proposed a new organizational flow chart. The challenge to all of us, then, is to assume our sacred membership as equals in the Body of Christ. As the laity moves away from its spectator stance into full participation and contribution, the church will reflect that change, regardless of its structure.

It is helpful to remind the seekers that not all documents emanating from Rome are infallible. Most are surprised, as are active Catholics, to learn that pastoral letters are theological reflections on issues of pastoral concern in an attempt to raise discussion and reflection. Few Catholics avail themselves of the rich opportunity to inform, encourage, and understand Catholic teaching found in these pastoral letters, assuming they are documents of specific concern to church leaders. Because the contents of these letters are open to discussion and theological development, they are not infallible.

We make every effort to help the seekers place papal infallibility in perspective, reminding them that this privilege has only been exercised twice, both times defining issues regarding Mary, her immaculate conception and her assumption. These aspects of Mary's life had been a part of oral church history for centuries, reflected in paintings and literature dating back to the very early Christian communities. The infallible declarations were set in a context of accepted belief and mythology, not from a startling revelation of truth that the pope alone experienced. Attentive, respectful discussion on this issue reveals that it is not as significant as the seekers believed in the beginning. The pope simply will not wake up one morning and begin speaking infallibly about issues that will constrict our lives.

It may also be helpful to explain that bishops are really teachers, offering moral guidelines and focusing attention on issues that can be helpful in examining our Christian faith. We emphasize the values underlying the various controversial teachings and invite discussions on those values (see Chapter 4). Many times seekers will find themselves in complete accord with the root values of these statements, thus enabling them to see their differences with church teaching as one of degree. To offset the impression that the bishops are simply branch managers for the pope, we quote Cardinal Francis George of Chicago, who in an address to presidents of United States Catholic Colleges said in part: "A bishop has no right to impose his own proclivities or his own theology on the faith community. He has only the obligation before God to see that the Catholic faith in its integrity is taught and handed on. What is a faithful Catholic is not up to the individual bishop. It's up to the church herself, and within that there's a lot of wiggle room."[5]

The seekers are comforted by this assurance of "wiggle room," particularly those who have not been active in the church since Vatican II. The realization that the church is all of us coming together as the Body of Christ, all of us with significant roles to play, is very reassuring to them. To make sure this message hits heart-home with the seekers, I ask throughout the series, "Who is the church?" In the beginning, their response is muffled and unsure; by the last session, they literally shout "We are!" and then break into light-hearted laughter. As resentment gives way to an appreciation for this new, inclusive concept of church, it becomes possible for the seekers to cite advantages in a church structure that has allowed it to transcend time, geographical, and political boundaries for 2000 years.

Preaching

Seekers' Perspective

- "Homilies are long and boring and have nothing to do with my life."

- "Father sounds like he needs to get a life. He never includes his own experience, his own doubts and struggles. How can I relate to him?"

- "I need to hear more about what Christianity is about in my daily life, things I can apply to my relationships, my family, the hard decisions I have to face."

- "Why doesn't the priest ever explain all these changes and new teachings to us when we are at Mass? How about a sermon on sexuality?"

- "It's pretty hard to believe I've lived this long and had to come to Catholics Coming Home to find out I am the beloved of God. Why wasn't I ever told that in church on Sunday?"

- "We're too busy to go to all kinds of classes and parish activities. We come to church on Sundays, starved for something that will last throughout the week, and get boring trivia from a boring speaker."

- "If we are the church, how come the priest is the only one who can preach?"

Church's Perspective

Since Vatican II, great emphasis has been placed on the homily. It is to be rooted in the scripture readings for that day and have application to the daily experience of being a Catholic Christian. Homilies should offer encouragement and insights that the community can take with them when they leave. More and more parishes are making concerted efforts to improve the caliber of preaching. Priests and seminarians now have at their disposal all kinds of resources to help them with both content and delivery. Some dioceses are offering training programs for lay preachers, men and women who feel called to preach in their local parishes. Preaching has been an area of marked improvement over the past ten years, as the homily time becomes regarded as sacred, time to reflect together on the scriptures and their message for our lives.

Pastoral Perspective

If this is a major concern for a seeker, we encourage them to seek out a parish that places a high priority on preaching. There is little to be gained by attending Mass at a parish week after week, only to experience frustration and disappointment from the homily.

Education

Seekers' Perspective

- "The God I learned about in Catholic schools was not a loving God!"

- "The sisters never encouraged us to question anything. We were told to accept what they taught."

- "We learned bigotry in Catholic schools; there was one way to get to heaven and that was the Catholic way."

- "I can't imagine allowing someone to hit my children, but our parents never said anything when the sisters hit us."

- "Why all that money to educate children? What about adults?"

- "Our parish is nothing more than a school with a Mass schedule. If you weren't involved with the school, you were an outsider."

- "I picked up a lot of guilt in Catholic schools; it has messed up my life."

Church's Perspective

Historically, the church school played a vital role in preserving religious and cultural identity for immigrant Catholics who came to this country. Often poor and lacking social and financial position, European Catholic immigrants found comfort in the structure of their local parish communities. As taught in many of those schools, religion did not contribute toward a healthy understanding of one's own faith or relationship with God—and certainly not an appreciation for individual differences and respect for other denominations and cultures. Protestants of the same era were equally intent on maintaining their separate identity. Catholics seem to bear deeper scars, however, because our vast school system separated Catholic children from the rest of society. Many of the issues and concerns that separate Catholics from their church are rooted in these childhood misconceptions of the Catholic faith. Fortunately, we are becoming more and more aware of the need to educate our adults. One of the biggest challenges faced by any parish, however, is trying to get the adult population to respond to programs that will enable them to sort out their faith and life issues.

While parochial schools have declined in large numbers, there is a recent resurgence of interest in providing Catholic schools. For some, it is a means of providing their children with a private education; for others, it is a desire to protect their children from the secular influences in the public schools. Unfortunately, most of the inner-city parochial schools, almost mission outposts, have had to close for financial reasons. Others are being kept open by dedicated pastors and laity who are determined to offer far more than education to the children in their locality, Catholic or not. Father Michael O'Connell, rector of the Basilica of Saint Mary, is breaking ground in this area, adding to his basilica position the pastorate of an inner-city parish with a school that educates children of all faiths, 80 percent of whom are not Catholic. Children growing up in poverty, from fractured families with little opportunity for hope to spiral them out of this kind of life, are nurtured and loved in that school. Without those ingredients, education really can't take place. Schools like this become powerful witnesses for the kingdom and have the capacity to change the lives of the children they welcome.

Pastoral Perspective

For Catholics who grew up in America, the school experience is the major common denominator. The sameness of the stories has been a revelation to us. It is important that their stories—many are amusing, some are gruesome—are told. The value in encouraging the stories to be told, especially the deep, painful memories of childhood, lies in the reexamination of those incidents from an adult viewpoint. Through this process, not only do seekers, who rarely recall their parents coming to their defense, have an opportunity to vocalize their pain and name the injustices; they also have their painful experiences validated by the group. We, as team members, facilitators, and ministers, often ask for forgiveness for what amounted to emotional and psychological abuse for some Catholic children.

I like to share with the seekers one of my favorite Catholic school stories. I spent a beautiful fall day at a local retreat house. The woods were bursts of oranges and red and yellow, nearly lighting up the walking paths throughout the grounds. As I strolled in that sun-lit sanctuary, I repeatedly encountered a very old sister. Finally, we introduced ourselves and when I asked her what brought her there that day, she responded:

> I come here often now that I am retired. I taught school for 40 years and I did so much damage to so many children. I had no idea God was gentle and loving then. I'm afraid I made it difficult for my children to believe God loves them. So, I spend a day on each class, remembering each face as they sat, row by row, and ask God to heal each child from any damage I may have caused. I'm amazed at how easy it is for me to remember their faces. I'm nearly half way and they are all still with me, here in my heart.

Ironically, many of these same people who complain about their childhood education are now begging for more education now that they are adults. They want to know about the whys of what they were taught and how that fits into the broad picture of church. They want a fresh look at Bible stories, a deeper understanding of scripture. Seekers at this point of their journey have crossed a major hurdle; directing them to appropriate church education programs may be all the further motivation they need.

Community and Parish Life

Seekers' Perspective

- "I don't feel like I belong, even though I have gone to the same church my whole life."

- "I tried to go back to church after being away for a while, but I felt so isolated and lonely."

- "Catholic churches seem so cold, lifeless, uncaring. How can I belong to a church that does such a poor job of reflecting Christ's love?"

- "The parishes are getting too big; thousands of members with only one priest. No personal recognition, no contact with the priest, no sense of belonging."

- "Father looks so burned out I don't feel like bothering him with my troubles. But who does a Catholic turn to when we have trouble?"

- "My parish favors families that have been there a long time, those neat little two-parent families with kids in the parish school. There isn't anything going on for single people, young adults, widows, or solo parents!"

- "I joined a Protestant church after my wife died. No one showed up from our parish, but those folks were all there right away. I feel welcome at that church."

- "Most of what goes on in our parish is self-sustaining; they are always doing things to raise money so they can keep doing them. Everything is same old, same old."

- "I feel out of place; most of the people in our parish are wealthy and well educated. They don't seem to notice me or my kids. It really hurts."

Church's Perspective

In the past, Catholics belonged to the parish defined by the geographic area in which they lived or by the nationality of its members. That usually meant a church close to home and included the Catholic school where most of the neighborhood Catholic children were educated. It may even have included a cemetery for parishioners only. The same people came and went to Mass and the sacraments for years. Families watched other families grow up, knowing little about their private worlds of sorrow and joy, success and failure. Worship was a private matter and church was there for the dispensation of sacraments and salvation.

Vatican II brought new life and meaning to the concept of Catholic community. It is ironic that at this point in our history, the priest shortage is resulting in enormous parishes at the same time we are emphasizing the need for Christian community. One of the biggest challenges we face as church today is whether or not one can truly experience community in sprawling parishes that provide weekend liturgies for thousands. There is an ongoing effort by clergy and laity to foster a sense of belonging in even the largest parishes. Clusters of small groups offering opportunities to share faith experiences and Christian fellowship are becoming the norm in many Catholic parishes. Lay ministry abounds, resulting in increasing numbers of Catholics ministering to one another within the larger parish structure. The Body of Christ is about belonging, about relationship. This newfound sense of who we are as a people of God has brought new power and vitality to Eucharist and its call to each of us to be church for others. It is the basis for our longing for the return of the seekers, whose absence lessens the sense of community for all of us.

Pastoral Perspective

It is important to remember that what may be a hoped-for ideal for one group of seekers can be a threatening obstacle for others. Some complain that they don't like all of this new friendliness in church. Even the sign of peace is a source of anger and resentment for Catholics raised during a time when church was a private matter and people left you alone. It is sometimes tempting to become impatient or judgmental with folks who seem so unwilling to open their hearts to others. Instead, we try, through gentle listening and affirming, to build a trust level with them. Often their closed attitude is the result of feeling inferior, even bewildered about what has happened to their church and why.

For most, community is a positive experience and our message to those who have not found it in their local parish is very definite: *Find a parish community that not only meets your needs but also one in which you can participate, share your gifts, and grow.* Given an opportunity to discuss this, the solution usually becomes obvious. Seekers can hardly blame the church for all of the Sunday-morning anxiety when they haven't even tried to find a different parish community. This diversity within the church is one of our greatest strengths!

I don't like using labels, but no Catholic can avoid church jargon that places people and parishes in "conservative" and "liberal" camps. Once a label is embraced by a particular parish community, it may exclude all those who do not relate to that identity. Rather than hanging in and fighting for acceptance, we suggest the seekers find a community where they can worship in comfort.

This is a caution to all of us who remain in the church: to reflect on the kind of image presented by our parish community. We need to make room in all of our parishes for all people, regardless of where they are in their faith journeys.

Jesus

Seekers' Perspective

- "The Catholic Church doesn't encourage us to have a personal relationship with Jesus Christ. I never heard anything like that when I was growing up."

- "I feel cheated, robbed, that I wasted all those years trying to obey man-made rules in order to be saved."

- "Catholic discipleship seems to be based more on the hierarchy than on Jesus."

- "I felt so responsible for everything bad that happened to Jesus when I was a kid. But I don't recall having a sense of personal celebration about the resurrection."

- "He only suffered three days. My whole life has been a living hell."

Church's Perspective

Perhaps the seekers who are most surprised by our ministry are those who left the church because of attitudes like these about Jesus. They soon discover that our sessions are conducted in a faith environment deeply influenced by Jesus. As one young man said, "I was shocked to hear people here talking about their own personal faith in Jesus; I didn't think Catholics ever did that." Except for those who have been deeply entrenched in fundamentalist concepts of Bible study, these seekers, bonded in Jesus, may be the easiest to help move through the reconciliation process. The current emphasis on Bible scholarship and scripture-based liturgies, discipleship, and empowerment of baptized laity are marvels they had no idea coexisted with being Catholic.

Pastoral Perspective

It is helpful to explore various theological concepts of Jesus that encourage deepened understanding and reflection of who Jesus is, what his mission was, and how that connects with church. Moving beyond the one-dimensional perception of Jesus as savior calls forth a whole new way of perceiving relationship with him. Accepting his call to build the reign of God in this life provides a new perception of faith. We want the seekers to know they are invited to live in an ongoing relationship with Jesus, an ever deepening awareness of his vision for the kingdom here on earth, and his human modeling of inclusiveness, intimacy, and forgiveness. Reflection on Jesus as the human face of God stirs energy and vitality beyond theological statements about the incarnation. We do not take responsibility for defining Jesus for the seekers; they are encouraged to redefine him for themselves, to look for his face in others, to see his goodness in their own lives.

Very recently, a seeker who realized that along with his faith journey he had another journey to embrace said to me, "You saw God in me, you reminded me that Jesus walks with me even when I'm ugly....Finally I am able to admit that I have a serious problem with alcohol." He can finally believe in a higher power that has a name and a face and a presence in his heart. That discovery has opened him up to new dimensions of his own creativity and strength; it is calling him to healing and sobriety. We never know where the Spirit will lead the seekers if we get out of the way.

Divorce, Annulment, and Remarriage

Seekers' Perspective

- "My kids don't want me to get an annulment because it will make them illegitimate."

- "Why should I pay the church in order to get a Catholic divorce?"

- "[A famous person] got an annulment because he knew the right people."

- "I know someone who paid $2000 so the priest would get them a quick annulment."

- "I won't get an annulment because I don't want to fight with my 'ex' again. The civil divorce was traumatic. I just can't go through that again."

- "My divorce wasn't a sin! It was the only healthy alternative I had. I don't need a piece of paper from the church to know I'm okay with God."

- "I've never been married or divorced but my Protestant fiancé was. Why does the church make *him* get an annulment in order to marry me in *my* church?"

- "What does a celibate hierarchy know about the devastation that comes with a broken relationship, or an abusive one?"

- "My kids lives are ruined; they grew up in a horrible family environment filled with abuse and alcohol. Yet Father refused to give me permission to get a divorce. My kids all blame me for staying in the marriage, but I feel like the church made me. It was either hell on this earth or hell for all eternity. What kind of choice was that?"

- "I was a lector in the parish I had belonged to all my life when my marriage ended. Father told me I couldn't lector anymore; it would cause scandal. My ex-wife joined another parish where she is a Eucharistic Minister!"

- "How can this be allowed in a church that is supposed to present Christ's forgiveness unconditionally? Why, in the entire realm of human failure, is this one area allowed to remain outside the redemptive power of Jesus?"

- "What right does the church have to give my (wife/husband) an annulment, declaring we were never married? We were married!"

- "It's ridiculous; I don't even want to bother with it. And it has no effect on my relationship with the church whatever. It's nobody's business whether I've had an annulment or not."

- "I was divorced years ago, knew little about annulments, and no one invited me to talk about them. I married outside the church five years ago...a really good marriage. Now we belong to a parish where the pastoral minister invited me to talk about having our marriage 'blessed.' We talked about annulments and it makes sense to me now, so she helped me fill out an application to begin the process. All of this has involved a lot of conscience struggle. I have learned a lot about the church, and sacraments, and what marriage is supposed to be. My desire for the Eucharist is so great that I have been receiving, especially since I became pregnant with our first child seven months ago. When I went home to visit my parents, back to my old church, the priest humiliated me by turning me away from the Eucharist in the most horrible manner. I just can't get his rage and contemptuous comments out of my mind. Of all people, he knew the full details of my first marriage, the abuse, the unfaithfulness, all of it. Who is he to say I am not worthy?"

• "I just don't understand it. I know people who have horrid marriages; cheating on each other, verbally abusive, no kindness at all. But no one tells them they are not worthy to receive."

Church's Perspective

It's about Eucharist. It always comes down to that if we listen long enough. In one way or another, these same comments are expressed every time this issue is raised. It is heartbreaking to me that in the fifteen years we have been offering this ministry, I have seen little attempt by parishes and churches to address this issue openly. Support groups for separated and divorced Catholics are common, but rarely do the people who attend feel equal to their counterparts in the faith community. I was recently invited to give a Sunday afternoon retreat for one of these groups in a large suburban parish. When I arrived, I noted signs of healthy parish life everywhere, lots of activity, people coming and going in the parking lot, through the halls of their large complex. When I found the room reserved for our retreat, it had been preempted by a recent request from another parish organization. A very nice man took me to the pastor who was vesting for an afternoon liturgy. Father met me with his usual open candor, and asked someone to take me to a room he thought we could use. It was in total disarray. Desks haphazardly filled the only available gathering space. Chalkboards were scribbled with graffiti. The pastoral minister in charge of this group arrived, out of breath from her room-search pilgrimage, shortly after I did and the two of us frantically moved desks, straightened up the room, and avoided eye-contact. The message was too much to acknowledge at the moment and we had wounded people to prepare for, to minister to. The retreatants ambled in, confused about whether or not they had finally found the right place, while others left to track down participants they knew would be lost out there in the maze of hallways and activity. When we finally quieted ourselves and reaffirmed our place together in the church, the afternoon was fruitful. But that unspoken message so obvious to Sister and me must have penetrated the awareness of participants. We made excuses for the busyness, and such, but the reality we all knew in our hearts was that this wounded group was far down on the hierarchical list of parish activities.

This happened in a parish that is considered open to healing and reconciliation; the pastor is a wonderful man who does too much, and he does it better than any priest I know. He is compassionate and caring to all and spends 24 hours a day ministering to his flock and the larger community, resulting in a great amount of kingdom work. Yet the unspoken message given to divorced people in Catholic churches all over the country prevailed: "Somehow, you are not as worthy."

Healing and growth groups, retreats for the separated and divorced at Catholic retreat centers, and dedicated ministry to those experiencing broken relationships contribute to a changing awareness, but we have a long way to go. The only way Catholics learn about issues faced by those suffering through a broken marriage is to encounter the experience themselves. Getting through the menial tasks of the day can be almost an impossible fete when our lives, our children, our sense of who we are is being catapulted into black clouds of fear and grief.

Whenever I've been invited to talk about these issues with active Catholics, the response has been very receptive, inviting. Catholics are concerned about their children, their siblings, their parents, their grandchildren, their friends going through divorce. They don't know what to say because they don't know exactly what the church teaches and they feel uncomfortable about wading into waters filled with questions about Eucharist, excommunication, and the like. Consequently, family members are often unable to provide the kind of support so desperately needed by anyone going through profound loss.

There is so much misinformation that needs to be clarified with affected seekers before we can begin to discuss reconciliation with the church. It is a jolt for many of them to realize they have been living with perceptions totally ungrounded in church teaching. False information is rampant in all areas of Catholic divorce experience.

It is still not uncommon for someone who is divorced and has never remarried to assume their excommunication. While that may surprise some church professionals, it is a reality I cannot ignore in my ministry. It happens too often and it grieves me every time I hear these stories. In fact, the Council of Baltimore in 1843 did place excommunication upon divorce, but 41 years later, seeing that this was far too severe, the Third Plenary Council of Baltimore of 1884 withdrew the censure.[6] The removal of this censure is still one of the church's best kept secrets!

"But," someone will inevitably reply, "if they remarry without annulment they are excommunicated." That excommunication was rescinded by the American bishops in 1977. The late Father James Young, C.S.P., clarified the relationship of remarried Catholics to the church in his now out-of-print book: "Catholics who marry a second time without the church's approval are told they're excommunicated. Nothing could be further from the truth. No matter what happens to the marriage of two Catholics, no matter how many times they get divorced or remarried, they remain Catholics."[7]

The church teaches that marriage is a sacrament, a lifetime covenant of fidelity and commitment, mirroring God's steadfast faithfulness to us. Implied in that teaching is the assumption that those who have divorced and remarried without annulment are unworthy to receive Eucharist. The phrase once used was *living in sin* and remarried Catholics are painfully aware that the label is still part of Catholic vocabularies. In 1981, Pope John Paul II stated, "I earnestly call upon pastors and the whole community of the faithful to help the divorced...to make sure that they do not consider themselves as separated from the church, for as baptized persons, they can, and indeed must, share in her life....Let the church pray for them, encourage them and show herself a merciful mother, and thus sustain them in faith and hope."[8]

Pastoral Perspective

While discussing these topics of divorce, annulment, and remarriage together, we need to consider them as individual incidents that occur in human lives. Each carries its own pain, isolation, anger, and shame. Lumped together in the life of one individual, the feelings are so many, so varied, and so painful that it becomes a major challenge just to sort them out. It is our job to assist in this process. Although my own divorce experience was more than twenty years ago, every encounter with a seeker who is working through these issues reconnects me with the anguish that engulfed my soul for months and years after my marriage ended, along with the miracle of resurrected, new life I have experienced since that time.

I am always moved by the amount of pain and the amount of goodness that I see in the eyes of the speaker who describes the weight of grief, guilt, and loneliness that accompanied their divorce experience, often infused by a nearly intolerable sense of shame and failure. To rebuild a life after a loss of such magnitude, betrayal, and shattered dreams takes great courage. That some are able to find that determination is an awesome revelation of God's grace. It is unlikely that that grace will be revealed without close relationships with people who care, who believe, and who have something to offer, *hope*. We begin by acknowledging that hope, by asking forgiveness for the pain heaped upon them by the church's insensitivity to their grief. This honest exchange needs to take place before the onset of any instructional activity.

Rather than offering a series of how-to loopholes and methods that will reconnect them to the church, we prefer to start with an understanding of what sacramental marriage is. Pastoral concern demands that we place information regarding annulment and remarriage within the context of a sacramental people, us, the church. To simply hand someone the paperwork needed to complete an annulment is a terrible disservice to them and to the church. How many people have found the annulment process a catalyst for their eventual return to active, meaningful participation with the faith community?

And after years of working with thousands of separated, divorced, and remarried Catholics, I am convinced that few marriages fail because the partners are bad or because they didn't try to make the relationship work. Most marriages fail because the life experience of one or both of them has rendered them incapable of a lasting, faithful relationship that is life-giving and energizing; in short, they are incapable of celebrating sacramental marriage. Gratefully, as a church and as a society, we are beginning to realize the effects of unresolved family issues on succeeding generations. I see those effects in the daily struggles of human beings who seem oblivious to the root of their failure to succeed in relationships. Promising to honor and obey does not create the capability for lifelong intimacy between two human beings. Intimacy, the very essence of sacramental marriage, is impossible to achieve for many who have been emotionally starved or abused as children if they have had no opportunity to heal. It is commonplace in my work with troubled marriages to see the effects of unhealed child abuse manifested in the inability to remain closely involved with a lifelong partner. I have sat with these victims while they wept in grief and bewilderment, wondering why they have pushed away the very person they wanted to be close to.

I have come to see unfaithfulness as an indicator of serious wounding that needs to be addressed before the marriage can heal, before the person can ever achieve lifelong intimacy in any relationship. But sacramental fidelity is much more than not having an affair! In a society prone to addictions on all fronts, the variety of extramarital affairs is legion. Anything given a higher priority than the primary bond or marriage relationship becomes a potential infidelity. Working too much, excessive investment in children, family, even volunteer and church activities can pull partners away from intimacy. When I work with married couples at Cana dinners or parish workshops, it is clear that many have long ago lost the ability to gaze into one another's eyes, to connect on a soul level. Busyness has prevailed and intimacy has been lost. But the human soul longs for intimacy and the hunger creates a loneliness that cries out for satiation. A marriage counselor told me recently of a survey that determined most intact American marriages can be described as a socioeconomic agreement lived out in parallel civility. Hardly a sacramental concept!

Since Vatican II, there has been a drastic evolution in our understanding of human behavior, human needs, sexuality, and relationships. This wealth of discovery about ourselves has to be considered when we consider the sacramental nature of marriage. Marriage is not a one-time "zapping" at the altar! It is an ongoing communion between two people and their God, always growing closer in their relationship to one another and in their response to the community around them...in and out of the church. It is a union characterized by cherishment, from God and between partners, a cherishment that fortifies and nurtures the couple's call to reach out to others, first within the family and beyond. This is the marriage that is likened to Jesus' love for his church, and a far cry from what the seekers have labeled, tongue-in-cheek, as a kind of "offer up, put up, and shut up" attitude all too prevalent in many marriages that don't end in divorce.

In this new understanding of sacramental marriage as a life-giving intimacy that flows between two people, nourished and fed by mutual trust in God's presence, the seekers begin to assess their marriage for what it really was. This new perspective helps them to forgive themselves and their former partners, to move beyond victimization, and address the areas within themselves that need healing and change. I see profound evidence of resurrection in my work with separated, divorced, and remarried Catholics. Finding solace in the church community often leads these wounded people through a process of healing, forgiveness, and growth that calls them to serve the brokenness of others. I have facilitated a number of retreats for the separated and divorced. To spend a weekend with 70 or 80 people whose lives are entrenched in grief and loss is a sacred experience. To journey with them through the pain toward new hope and reconnection with community is to walk on holy ground. Father Young described the process thus:

> The spirituality, the holiness, that we see emerging among separated, divorced, and remarried Catholics in the United States is...a spirituality, a holiness born of suffering, rejection, and pain, rooted in the real struggles of everyday life, yet reaching to God and finding him, coming to new life through that very suffering and those very struggles. Spirituality and holiness in the Christian community takes on many authentic shapes and styles, but the earthy style of the divorced is one the church needs today.[9]

Annulments

During our Catholics Coming Home series, the subject of annulment is discussed only after we have discussed those issues that give context to this misunderstood subject. Of course, the issue is always raised the first evening and we validate the seekers' concerns when it is. Our syllabus indicates that the group's discussion on this topic will take place toward the end of the series, after we have explored conscience and sacrament. When I am asked to explain annulment in any other area of ministry, in or outside the parish, I always begin with a discussion on sacramental marriage. Without understanding of the church's teachings about sacrament, marriage, and conscience, there is the risk that annulment is reduced to a legal process imposed on divorced people who want to marry in the church. I see it as much more than that.

Annulment has touched my life very directly from an assortment of perspectives. As a divorced, remarried Catholic woman, I have personally experienced the process. As a pastoral minister, I am confronted about this issue constantly, by active and inactive Catholics. As a Field Advocate for our local tribunal, I am privileged to facilitate the application process for petitioners on an ongoing basis. And, as a Catholic, I am continually asked to defend the existence of what seems to be the most misunderstood aspect of Catholicism. Stories and rumors abound, many unfounded, depicting the callousness of tribunals across the United States. A massive amount of misinformation, suspicion, and confusion abounds throughout our Catholic population, spilling over into the secular world. While we have yet to come up with a better word that provides clear understanding, the word *annulment* does not describe what occurs during this process. The church does not annul a marriage; it only has the power to rule on the evidence of its sacramentality. It is purely and solely a Catholic theological process, bearing no weight nor influence on the existence of the marriage itself.

Within the framework of sound information and grounded pastoral care, this subject becomes understandable and approachable. Without those ingredients, people refer to the process as loopholes imposed on people for control and punishment or one more way the church has weakened since Vatican II, convinced that an annulment is simply the church's approval of divorce. Nothing could be further from the truth.

If marriage is not automatically sacramental, it follows that the church would have a process to determine sacramental criteria. There is great value in looking objectively at a broken marriage not from a standpoint of right and wrong or good and bad, but in order to understand more clearly why the marriage failed, why it wasn't found to be sacramental. The time and introspection devoted to this reflection can be invaluable to healing, forgiving, and moving beyond the pain of divorce. There can be positive benefits. Seekers who are afforded this kind of experience through tribunals that stress the importance of sound, preliminary pastoral care tell of new insights they gain not only about themselves but about their former partners as well. For many, it is a welcome closure to a pain-filled part of their lives. The self-knowledge gained through the annulment process becomes invaluable to any future sacramental bond.

I am always grateful for the opportunity to dispel the myths listed earlier in this section, providing correct information in their place. It is almost amusing that so many of the same falsehoods are presented as absolute truth in nearly every region of the country! We try to lighten up a bit on this subject and gently challenge the sources. Group discussion often reveals the stories for what they are: hearsay, false, and misleading. Because there are two major misunderstandings that seem to create the most difficulty, I like to begin any conversation on annulment by making two points: (1) Annulment does not mean there wasn't a marriage. There was. The annulment process is purely a Catholic theological process, the sole purpose of which is to consider the sacramentality of a given marriage, as the church understands sacramentality. (2) Children are not made illegitimate by a declaration of nullity, because the marriage existed!

We also dispel the misconception that the annulment fee covers the purchase of a decree from Rome, making it clear that it is a justice issue involving reimbursement for expenses incurred by the process. I have yet to meet a seeker who resents contributing toward the salaries of those who work for the church in the tribunal offices. We need to make clear the financial policies within the local diocese, the amount requested, how payment is made, and whether or not there are considerations made for those who cannot afford the process. I do not have access to these policies in every tribunal in the United States, but I cannot imagine anyone being denied this right (it is not a privilege) because of an inability to pay. I like to provide as much information as possible about the financial aspects since there are so many stories out there about famous people who have paid thousands of dollars for a quick annulment, or priests who insist on a large up-front cut to intervene with the tribunal.

Another frequent point of contention occurs when a Protestant is asked to go through the annulment process prior to celebrating a sacramental marriage with a Catholic partner. When this situation occurs, I invite both parties to come in and talk. Always I begin by admitting to the non-Catholic that this must seem confusing and I apologize for the discomfort and misunderstanding. Then I reassure them with my two points and carefully explain how Catholics understand sacramental marriages, that we begin with the premise that all marriages are regarded as sacred, in and out of the church. To arbitrarily eliminate Protestant marriages from the same standards that apply to Catholic marriages would be tantamount to declaring Protestant marriage in some way less holy, less valid than our own. Therefore, we treat their marriage exactly as we would a Catholic marriage, using criteria established by their denomination. In nearly every instance, the Protestant partner has expressed relief at the new understanding, and out of respect for their Catholic's partner's faith, finds no problem with going forward.

I am concerned when relationships are stalemated on this issue by the adamant refusal of one party to seek a declaration of nullity in a prior bond when their partner wants to be married in the church. If it is important to the faith life of one partner to be married in the church, this standoff presents a fairly serious red flag about the relationship itself, one that I address from a spirituality perspective. I encourage both of them to consider what is best for their relationship and their future together. This kind of impasse is usually rooted in erroneous concepts about what an annulment is and what the process entails.

While I would hope that every encounter with the tribunal or any other church office would be a caring, supportive experience, it is not the job of the tribunal to provide pastoral care. It is our job to develop the kind of pastoral relationship with the seekers that will help them understand this process and what it will require of them. I have found my Field Advocate work to be some of the most powerful in my ministry experience. When I hear their stories, validate their goodness, and answer their doubts and questions, seekers come to a new experience of church. Often it is a deeper connection than they experienced before their divorces.

I am aware that there are dioceses in which the annulment process is impersonal and legalistic. And there are individual priests who refuse to assist anyone in the process, stating unequivocally that they don't believe in it. Seekers have brought valid, heartbreaking stories to our sessions about such encounters. In these cases, and in all cases where the wounding is deep and personal, I invite the seeker to schedule a private meeting where we can dignify their story with appropriate heart listening and pastoral care.

EXTERNAL FORUM The outward appearance of the marriage meets the criteria of a sacrament so the exploration must go deeper into the relationship itself to consider sacramentality. The marriage took place in accordance with Catholic teaching and was witnessed by a priest. In other words, it *looks like* a sacrament from the outside. These are the annulments we hear about most often. Guided by questions provided by the tribunal, the parties provide a written experience of growing up, the development of their relationship, the reasons they decided to marry, their understanding of marriage, and the mutual understanding shared by both parties regarding the sacredness of their commitment, the role of religion in the marriage, the effects of alcohol or addictive behaviors of any kind, including abuse, in the marriage, attempts made to save the marriage, and some understanding of how the divorce came about. The tribunal may even ask whether the petitioner sees the relationship as sacramental, asking for substantiating reasons. I am always touched by the significance of the seeker's written account of his or her faith journey. Even those who approach this process with grave apprehension seem to find some kind of spiritual discovery in the nonthreatening process of recalling the history of their marriage. Some tell me that it serves as a closure; others tell me it allowed them to see for the first time their own role in selecting the wrong person to marry!

LACK OF FORM OR DEFECT OF FORM Some call this the "short form" annulment. A seeker's question, "Why did my friend get an annulment in a week when mine took a year?" reveals the confusion between the different kinds of annulment processes. In the external forum the outward appearance of the marriage indicates sacramental presence. The tribunal has to extend its search for sacramentality or its absence. When a Catholic marries without the obvious external indications of sacrament, the proof lies in the official documents and papers. A baptism certificate establishes the petitioner or respondent was indeed a baptized Catholic and the marriage certification establishes that the marriage did not take place in a Catholic church, nor was a Catholic witness appointed to represent the faith community. Finally, the divorce decree establishes that the marriage has ended civilly. As in any other form of annulment, the tribunal will accept no request for Declaration of Nullity of sacramental marriage unless or until a civil divorce is completed. Supplying the evidential paperwork and a brief testimony from a petitioner that is substantiated by a witness results in the obvious declaration: this marriage was not celebrated sacramentally.

INTERNAL FORUM No discussion of annulments is complete without accurate information about the internal forum. The procedures we have been discussing involve the documentation of interaction with official representatives of the church, an external process. The church in its mercy and compassion must have an alternative for those who find the external forum to be inappropriate or impossible. Father Francisco Javier Urrutia, S.J., states, "The law of the Church has to bring forth and may never destroy the merciful character of the Church's mission. The Church may never turn away, in the name of any of her laws, a sinner who repents. The Lord himself never turned away a sinner but came precisely for their sake."[10]

Sometimes called "the good conscience decision," the internal forum relies on the good conscience of the individual in cooperation with a priest, mentor, or spiritual guide. As with the external forum, it is imperative that the petitioner understands and initiates the process. Deeply rooted in our church's tradition and history, it should be administered with charity, gentleness, and deep regard for the seeker's spiritual journey. Father Barry Brunsman explains: "The exercise of Internal Forum by either clergy or laity usually takes a deeper faith and more maturity than exercise of the External Forum. Because it is personal, the responsibility for exercising it is assumed by the individual and not by church hierarchy or law. The Internal Forum honors the personal conscience of an individual—his or her honest appreciation of a life situation."[11]

It is the pastoral responsibility of the minister to ground this process in the seeker's understanding of sacramental marriage, the church's role in the process, and the depth of responsibility that rests solely with the individual selecting this forum. To offer less is to diminish the dignity of the seeker and to risk directing them into situations that will only result in future confusion and guilt.

It is with deep, spiritual conviction that one should approach the internal forum. A problem may arise in finding a priest who is willing to participate in the forum with the same degree of commitment and conviction. Many are hesitant to participate at all; others feel it demands too much of their time. Still others consider it an invalid process or will admit they have been taught very little about it. I have provided solid documentation from our seminary library for more than one priest in the latter category! Because the opportunity for misunderstanding is so great on this issue, I recommend exceptional care in referring seekers to priests for assistance in the internal forum.

The internal forum is not some back-room escape for privileged Catholics as the dearth of information on the topic might indicate. It is the right of every Catholic, a very sacred right that should not be ignored or trivialized. The official church position is cited in a directive from the Congregation of the Doctrine of Faith, issued on April 11, 1973: "In regard to admission of sacraments, local bishops are asked on the one hand to stress observance of current discipline, and on the other hand to take care that pastors of souls exercise special care to seek out those who are living in an irregular union by applying to the solution of such cases, in addition to other rightful means, the church's approved practice in the Internal Forum."

Inherent in the responsibility of the petitioner and the priest or church representative in the application of internal forum is the avoidance of scandal. Since there is no public declaration regarding the sacramentality of a prior marriage, a future marriage cannot be celebrated in the church. The individual is considered a fully participating Catholic in every sense of the word, even if they marry in a civil or Protestant ceremony. In no way is a subsequent marriage to be considered invalid.

In any pastoral encounter regarding the internal or external forum, it is the minister's responsibility to explain the context, reasoning, and tradition in a way that respects the church's deep reverence for marriage and the seeker's right to prayerfully discern a proper course of direction. It is the seeker who selects the appropriate forum. All of this takes time and is most effectively handled on an individual basis. I consider these encounters to be evangelization opportunities.

Sexual Issues

While often accusing church leaders of preoccupation with matters related to sex, the seekers sometimes share this preoccupation, responding with rage, confusion, and dismay at their perceptions of church teaching on sex, which they regard as extremely judgmental or out of touch with human experience. Some claim that such pronouncements have caused notable scrupulosity and guilt. All of us who minister in the church hear the painful accounts of the psychological consequences—guilt and shame—that the church used to instill its moral teachings on young children. As adults now, many of them cannot forgive the church for its legacy of fragmented and unhealthy concepts of sexuality. Rather than being acknowledged as a sacred gift, sex is perceived as permeated with feelings of guilt, shame, and sin. Since scars from childhood and teenage wounds heal slowly, they feel there is great risk in looking to the church once again for direction in this vital area of their lives. Many have discerned through painful counseling and healing therapy that they dare not trust at all what the church has to say about sex, assuming it is all falsehood, even harmful.

While it is common for Catholics to say, "The church has no right to control or make judgments on how we are to express our sexuality," further discussion usually reveals that very few adult Catholics comprehend what the church really is saying about sex these days. Before we address specific issues, it will be helpful to consider what the church is teaching and why it teaches what it does about human sexuality. Clear understanding of the sacredness of sexuality as an integral part of our humanity is essential if the seeker is to move beyond acceptance or rejection of rules and restrictions. The conversion journey is a process through which the seeker discovers the wholeness of his or her life in relationship to God and others. Holiness is not about doing what we're told; it is about living in intimacy with God and with one another. Incorporating our sexuality into that process is an ongoing journey of discovery, especially if sex has been considered as something we *do* instead of who we *are*. When emphasis is placed on individual deeds and sins, the perspective of the whole, and with it, the moral values that underlie the church's teachings are lost. Unfortunately, all of this emphasis on sexual transgression has resulted in a narrowed concept of immorality, one perceived to rest solely on one's view of sex. Other transgressions or wrongdoing can be forgiven, even understood, but defying the church's rules pertaining to sex invokes an aura of damnation and elimination from the church community. Consider the immorality of racism, consumerism, discrimination, exploitation, child abuse, sexism, social injustice of all kinds. The list is endless. While the church does make pronouncements in these areas, few of us feel tainted or judged by the words. Fewer feel obligated to change by them. Many openly disagree, proclaiming their right to think for themselves, declaring the church has no right to interfere in these issues. This same attitude about sexual matters is rarely expressed—out loud. Even more rarely does the church invite dialogue on these issues that affect all of us. The very place where we should be learning about our sexuality, the church, is the one place where we don't dare address it!

It is a unique challenge to the minister both to be a catalyst for the seekers regarding the moral values that underlie centuries of distorted teaching practices, and at the same time assure them that in this area as in any other of their lives as Christians, it is normal to explore, to learn and grow in the discernment of God's will for them. It is our job to help the seekers understand that the church's teaching on sexuality is based on the premise that human sexuality touches every aspect of our existence. Young children, teenagers, adults, and senior citizens are affected by their sexuality. We are by our very nature, sexual beings; it is the gift God has given us that draws us toward one another. The process of understanding this gift, learning how to make healthy choices, and to respect the sacredness of this gift in others, is a lifetime journey. To the degree that we incorporate an awareness of this gift in ourselves and others, we will be able to sustain closeness and intimacy in our primary relationships. Sister Fran Ferder and Father John Heagle address this developing awareness in a book "that explores our emerging self-awareness, our growth toward responsibility in relationships, our capacity to be intimate, the challenge to integrate our sexual energy in healthy ways, and the deepening ability to love in a mutual, life-giving manner."[12]

A Catholic perspective on human sexuality will be different from a secular perspective. Our values, presented as ideals and based on the fulfillment of the Christian experience, are not the same as secular values. In every area of our lives, the values provide us with a goal, the epitome of life lived in harmony with God. It is naive to expect that any of us will achieve the ideal in any area during our lifetime. Still, the faith community holds up the ideals so that we may better understand what discipleship asks of us.

Church teaching suggests that the ultimate goal of human sexuality can be expressed to the fullest only in the sacramental union between husband and wife. Indeed, this is the example held up to us in the scriptures, the human experience most resemblant of God's intimacy with us. When a couple enters a sacramental marriage, this human love and union are given new depth and new meaning because they are placed in a spiritual context. Any sexual expression that is not open to the relational and procreational goals of human sexuality is considered incomplete, therefore wrong according to the church.

Loving relationships that are not open to the ideal goals of human sexuality, both relational and procreational, reject the sacramental essence of Christian love, for God and one another. Sexual intimacy outside the context of marriage is not wrong simply because of an arbitrary rule. Instead, according to the church, it is wrong because it violates the ideals of Christian living and in the end, diminishes the sacred dignity of one individual or the other. Even within marriage, sexual intimacy must occur within a context of a loving, caring relationship. Anything less becomes exploitive, even abusive, married or not.

In a comprehensive pastoral letter to the people of Baltimore, Archbishop William Borders explains that the church considers three important components in its teaching on human sexuality:

Biological: This dimension of our sexuality is what we have in common with all life forms: reproduction.

Psychological: This dimension of our sexuality stresses our capacity to know and to love another. The psychological brings the biological to a new and deeper meaning.

Spiritual: This dimension is the fullest level of our sexuality, for it places our sexuality in relationship with God. The knowing and loving of another is united with our knowing and loving God.[13]

The church teaches that these three distinct aspects of our sexuality must always be linked together. As Christians, we cannot fragment our sexual acts from the sacred gift of our sexuality. To emphasize only the psychological or biological, missing the reality of the spiritual dimension is to deprive the gift of its essence. Our lives develop into wholeness, holiness, only when we are able to integrate these ingredients into our actions and relationships. The church teaches that sin occurs when we attempt to view sexuality from only one dimension. Sexual activity that does not regard the sacredness of this life-giving gift, that is purely self-gratification, neither recognizes nor nourishes the spiritual and psychological dimensions of individuals or the relationship. With this discussion in mind, let's look at the sexual issues that are raised most often by the seekers.

Sex Before/Outside Marriage

Seekers' Perspective

- "I'm not ready to settle down and get married; I have to finish school, find a job. Sex is a natural part of life. What's the big deal?"

- "We've been engaged for over a year; sex has become a natural expression of our love for one another. We've already made a commitment which we intend to live out for the rest of our lives."

- "Our marriage has been empty for years. We just live together for the kids with no sharing or love between us. We stopped having sex years ago because it was empty and horrible for both of us. I can't live as a celibate and the church doesn't condone divorce and remarriage. I can only see two choices: break up my family or have these occasional affairs. The church says both are wrong, so how can I win?"

Church's Perspective

The church is clear on these issues: there must be a stable bond and permanent commitment (marriage) between a man and woman in order for sexual expression to be acceptable. Sexual expression void of true commitment does not offer protection for potential new life, nor for the two partners to encourage their mutual support, love, and growth for the rest of their lives. The church sees any sexual relationship that does not meet this criteria as one that reduces human sexuality to the biological dimension. The spiritual and perhaps even the psychological dimension has been cast aside, creating a fragmentation that falls short of the Christian ideal of wholeness.

Pastoral Perspective

Reality tells us that many people find it as impossible to live up to the ideal of sexuality as it is to live up to the ideal in any other area of their lives. Our challenge is to help the seekers understand the church's teachings and the values on which they rest, to go beyond the rules to an understanding of the sacred gift of human sexuality. It is often the first time the seekers hear what the church is *really* saying. They have a chance to stop and reflect on their lives and relationships. We invite discussion about the effects of sexual intimacy on a relationship, the tendency to shut down the development of other areas of intimacy and rely on sex to communicate unexpressed feelings and unspoken needs. Sexual activity outside the parameters of healthy sexuality seldom sustains intimacy; rarely does it substitute for the intimacy we all crave. While these discussions will not force everyone to accept church teaching, many begin to see their sexuality in a new light, give them new goals to consider. We stress that the church's requirement of openness to life requires more than the minimal concept of having babies. It is essential that our sexual relationships include the respect for the sacredness of the life of each partner—the health, wholeness, and dignity of each. This is the epitome of Christian sexual relationship, a far cry from sex for the sake of sex and a long way from society's currently pervasive concept of sexuality.

When we present this new way to frame their specific situations, the seekers can consider their lives and their decisions from a different stance, one of interior commitment rather than obedience to something that makes no sense to them. We continue to support, encourage, and guide them as they seek their own moral truths, guided by a new awareness of their personal convictions and the values that form the basis of church teaching.

Masturbation

Seekers' Perspective

- "I can't believe the church is really concerned about this anymore! It's a phase people go through."

- "As soon as I reached puberty I knew I was in trouble. I had to confess this over and over again. I felt ashamed and dirty and now I resent the church for making me feel that way about something that was so normal for an adolescent."

- "Are we supposed to believe that celibates don't masturbate? Why do we all have to feel so sneaky about this?"

- "Doesn't the church have something more to do than create nightmares for teenagers?"

- "If the church is open to learning from other disciplines, why don't they take seriously some of the research on this subject from the medical and psychological professions? We are not living in the dark ages...or are we?"

Church's Perspective

Officially, the church still considers masturbation a sin, particularly if it becomes a substitute for a healthy relationship. The church says that the act itself, lacking the relational and procreational goals of sexuality, has little true sexual meaning and is, therefore, usually associated with some degree of sexual immaturity. It falls short of the ideal.

Pastoral Perspective

Many seekers have resolved this issue for themselves, during their own process of maturity. But the scars left from all that judgment without any positive guidance or teaching during early sexual development are deep. It is often surprising how candid these discussions are, long repressed feelings shared and experiences evaluated from a new perspective. Exposed to this kind of scrutiny, childhood nightmares can be replaced with increased self-awareness and compassion. It is the minister's responsibility to offer new perspectives from which to consider masturbation within a wholistic context. When masturbation becomes constant, compulsive activity, blaming the church can replace taking responsibility to mature and grow in understanding healthy sexuality. Obviously, some of this work must be done on a one-to-one basis, where confidentiality is respected and trust between the minister and seeker is strong. The minister must discern whether or not outside counseling resources should be recommended in those cases where the residual effects of shame and guilt have paralyzed the seeker into a position of sexual inertia or dysfunction.

In most cases, however, this issue quickly becomes a nonissue as we accept our humanity and understand that the church, as well as the rest of society, is in the process of learning more and more about healthy sexuality. Evaluating individual acts of masturbation within the full spectrum of healthy Christian sexuality gives the seeker a new basis from which to determine his or her direction.

Birth Control

Seekers' Perspective

- "What do celibates really know about loving, spontaneous sexual intimacy, how essential it is to a vital marriage? What about the effects of too many children on the primary relationship of the husband and wife—or for that matter, on the kids themselves?"

- "Anyway, most Catholics are practicing birth control. It's a moot point."

- "It is irresponsible for the pope to be telling Third World nations that they need more babies. What about overpopulation, poverty, food shortages? It's hard to accept what the church teaches about justice and human rights when it is leading these developing nations into deeper poverty and turmoil by this outrageous, outdated interpretation of teachings on procreation."

- "For 25 years I thought I would go to hell because we could not risk having more children. We could hardly handle the eight we have. We had almost no adult, husband-wife relationship. Parenting all those kids was more than we could handle. I didn't receive the sacraments at any of my own kids' weddings because I thought I was such a sinner. Now I can't believe I let a priest who didn't even know what a good person I am judge me like that. How do I undo all those years of feeling unacceptable in God's eyes, of thinking I would burn in hell? Now I know that God knew we were doing the best we could."

- "My mother died while giving birth to her twelfth child, after the doctors had told her another pregnancy would kill her. At age fifteen, I felt rage toward my father because it seemed like he had killed her. At the same time, I became the mother of all *their* children. Don't tell me about birth control."

Church's Perspective

The prohibition of birth control for Catholics was reaffirmed by *Humanae Vitae,* which included the following: "...each and every act of marriage must always be open to the creation of new life. Any means to interrupt or prevent life is unacceptable." In more recent years, Pope John Paul II has reinforced this teaching.

The church does support methods of Natural Family Planning (NFP), relying on a process that determines those few days each month during a woman's menstrual cycle when she is able to conceive a child. Some see an inconsistency in a teaching that gives primacy to the procreational aspects of intercourse while encouraging couples to carefully schedule their lovemaking during those times when conception is impossible. Proponents of NFP methods insist it saves marriages, heightens sexual enjoyment, and is 90 percent effective in preventing unwanted pregnancies. NFP assumes a total commitment from both wife and husband, a predictable menstrual cycle, and an intense level of intimacy between partners that allows them to mutually control when their lovemaking will take place.

The church's teaching on birth control is entwined in an evolving history of development in understanding women, sexuality, and scripture. Once considered permissible only if procreation could result, sexual intimacy is now revered as a sacred gift. Woman's role has shifted from submission to participation in committed, sexual love. And the purpose of intercourse being open to new life places a strong emphasis on the developmental life and growth of both partners. "Planning and preparing for children is not something that can be done in a haphazard way today, given the social and economic conditions we face. That some couples will choose not to have children to further their own lives is a given, with or without the teaching on birth control. But that the church needs to respect and promote a type of responsible parenting to build up the Kingdom also seems to be a given."[14]

Pastoral Perspective

There are some Catholics who agree fully with *Humanae Vitae's* interpretation of authentic sexual expression. Others have found total peace, even enrichment, in their lives and their marriages through the use of Natural Family Planning. Most dioceses have active NFP organizations that promote ongoing educational programs for couples who seek to resolve this issue in full compliance with church teaching. These groups emphasize the sacredness of marriage and the involvement of both partners in the planning of their families. It is deeply rooted in mutual respect and prayer.

There are more Catholics, however, who cannot find the resolution in NFP. Consider those marriages where only one partner is open to this solution, or where NFP is not successful in limiting the number of children, resulting in too many children at the wrong time. There are those who take seriously *Humanae Vitae's* call to "responsible parenthood" and the individual's primary role in determining the full extent of what that responsibility entails. In two-career families, now the prevailing norm, husbands and wives find very little time for their own life of intimacy. Without intimacy, marriage drifts into a parenting cooperative, hardly a gift to either partner or to their children.

A May 1993 *National Catholic Reporter*/Gallop Poll showed that approximately 73 percent of all Catholic women use some method of artificial contraception. One has only to glance at the average parish roster to know that something has resulted in smaller Catholic families. The stereotypical large Catholic family of the past is no longer a reality in or out of the church. When the seekers raise this issue, our response is to help them understand the teaching and to revisit their own concepts of the sacredness of life, the purpose of marriage, and their call to discipleship. We encourage couples faced with this issue to frame their discussions within this context, to pray and reflect, to remain cognizant of the Holy Spirit's guidance, even if they must ultimately choose less than the ideal offered by the church. We also encourage them to become familiar with *Humanae Vitae* in its entirety, rather than grasping only the specific references to birth control. The document is a milestone in fostering an understanding of the sacred mutuality of marriage.

Abortion

Seekers' Perspective

- "I was young and I cannot undo what I did. How do I live without the promise of forgiveness for murdering my child? I cannot let go of the horror of that act, but where do I go to find peace?"

- "Why wasn't the church there for me when I was pregnant, filled with fear, shame, and guilt? I was afraid to tell anyone, even my parents."

- "What right does the church have to tell me what I can and cannot do with my body? Besides, the church can't say exactly when an embryo becomes a human being."

- "The church says you can kill in what they call a just war. What if this pregnancy is life-threatening to the mother?"

- "Why doesn't the church zero in more on the men who walk out on the lives of these mothers and their babies? Isn't that abandoning life too? Have you ever heard a homily about that? Why is all the shame heaped on the woman who feels trapped into this decision?"

- "This is an emotional issue. Some people rant and rave about abortion, yet see nothing wrong with capital punishment. Where's the consistency in that?"

- "A political football, that's all. It's made a mockery of the real issues involved. The church should be preaching more about our role in providing support for women faced with this decision. How many parishes invite them into their community activities? It's easier to set up shelters for them somewhere else. Then we don't have to deal with it...until it happens to be one of our own."

- "I'm a nurse and have seen the devastation in couples whose unborn child is diagnosed to be severely disabled, incapable of life out of the uterus. Twenty years ago those babies would have miscarried; now we hook the mother up to all kinds of devices that simply delay the inevitable: delivery of a premature child who dies before, during, or immediately after birth."

Church's Perspective

The church's prohibition of abortion for any reason is deeply rooted in its early formation. The one value that underlies all Catholic teaching is the sacredness of life. In 1974 the church reaffirmed its position on abortion:

The first right of the human person is the right to life....Hence it must be protected above all the others....The right to life remains complete in an old person, even one greatly weakened; it is not lost by one who is incurably sick. The right to life is no less to be respected in the small infant just born than in the mature person. In reality, respect for human life is called for from the time that the process of generation begins. From the time that the ovum is fertilized, a life is begun which is neither that of the father nor of the mother; it is rather the life of a new human being with his or her own growth.[15]

It is alarming to many Catholics that the church prohibits abortion even in those cases when the mother's life is in danger. The emphasis on the sacredness of human life is extended to all humans at all times. In principle, this means that neither the life of the mother or the child can be subjected to an act of direct suppression in order to save the other. In all situations, Catholics are obliged to make every effort to save both lives.

Pastoral Perspective

I have strong feelings on this subject, feelings that grow stronger as my ministry continually presents this issue to me. I am the mother of four adopted children and cannot imagine the world without their existence. As our grandchildren arrive, I am even more in awe of the sacredness of their lives. I think I know what it means to love someone so much you could die for them. And I have sent thousands of prayers heavenward in thanksgiving for the men and women who conceived my children. I have met two of them and thanked them directly.

As a Clinical Pastoral Education student in a large metropolitan hospital, I walked with couples who had to face impossibly difficult decisions regarding their pregnancies because of medical situations I had neither heard of nor contemplated before. Whether they were Catholic or not, the word *abortion* carried so many negative connotations that the couples could hardly bring themselves to say it. Weighing weeks or months of futile, high-technology efforts in a hospital against removing a nonviable fetus from the life-support of the womb looked to me more like parental anguish than abortion. Often they asked me to be there when it happened, to baptize their few-ounces baby and to be a consoling presence, to let them know they were good. Family coffers drained, children at home begging for their mother, and a hopeless survival prognosis would bring them to this point. The agonizing experience of birthing a dead or near-dead baby is hardly something anyone can pass judgment on under these circumstances. I could see no difference in the amount of grief, loss, or sense of failure that I experienced when I gave birth to a dead baby at home, in my bedroom nearly three decades ago. A child is dead and a parent's heart is forever changed. It is soul-stirring, grief-wracking stuff to deal with, whether or not it involves a decision.

I am only too aware that there are others who conceive and terminate pregnancies on whim. But I don't believe there are many, regardless of circumstances, who are unaffected by abortion. My pastoral concern is pulled toward that focus.

Once again, individually or as a church, we can use the Declaration on Abortion as a teaching tool, gaining insights about our response to the dilemma. This teaching is both challenge and admonishment to the entire Christian community, not only those faced with the immediate resolution of a pregnancy: "Every man and woman with feeling, and certainly every Christian, must be ready to do what they can to remedy the [sorrows and miseries which cause people to choose abortion]....One can never approve of abortion; but it is above all necessary to combat its causes...to do everything possible to help families, mothers, and children."[16]

These are powerful words that leave me wondering why their major application has been toward legal fights and protests, name calling and accusations. I am filled with gratitude for the wonderful Catholic ministries for women faced with unwanted pregnancies and for the excellent postabortion counseling provided by the church in many dioceses across our land. However, I have grown weary of listening to rhetoric that sounds more like hate than love, more like self-interest than self-investment. I often wonder how the abortion picture would change if every parish provided assistance and support in the care of children who are born with special needs, physical and mental disabilities. This would involve personal, relational assistance to provide not only respite for the child's care, but a shoulder to cry on when a weary mother or father can hardly take another day of heartache. To me, that is antiabortion ministry at its best. That is what Pope John Paul II seems to be asking of us in this declaration.

Within the context of community responsibility it becomes more difficult to wield judgment solely on those who are secondary victims of abortion, the women who have had them. We are all too aware of the singularly heavy load of guilt that has been placed on them. We invite the seekers to discuss the kinds of desperation that lead one to make that decision and the lack of cultural and church support available to most women during those times. We keep the ideal, the sacredness of all human life, in the fore of these discussions in order to promote comparisons of that ideal with prevailing societal and cultural attitudes. This very sacredness is also each individual's assurance of forgiveness by a compassionate God and a loving church community.

It is important during these group discussions that the invitation is extended to schedule a one-to-one appointment if anyone wants to discuss this matter personally. It is unfair to encourage a woman who is grappling with the enormity of this issue to discuss it in our group setting. Private sessions are very different from the group discussions on abortion. The pain is personal. The issue is not simply a church teaching; it is monumental to the individual seeker's life and her relationship with God. To put it simply and tragically, these are often women whose guilt has never allowed them to grieve the loss of their babies or to forgive themselves.

Private sessions result in long talks about the events of their lives that led up to the abortion, giving them an opportunity to reflect on their decision through the perspective of time and increased understanding. We invite them to embrace the same kind of grieving process that we would encourage for any woman who loses a baby through miscarriage. We point out the goodness that we see evidenced in their lives, the cherishment that God feels for them. It can be especially helpful, if and when the seeker is ready, to refer her to an understanding priest who will guide her through the deeply spiritual experience of sacramental reconciliation. And it may be necessary to help them find sensitive counseling by therapists who understand the devastation experienced by so many women who have had abortions, Catholic or not.

Abortion may be a symptom of a much larger picture of unresolved issues, including childhood abuse, dysfunctional families, lack of self-esteem, behavior compulsions, and other symptoms of unsuccessful lives.

(Our reflections result from our work with women who have come to us. I cannot speak to the lived experience of women who have neither access nor need to seek help regarding their abortions.) As with any other issue the seekers bring to us, even abortion becomes a catalyst to growth, self-understanding, and ongoing conversion in the seeker's relationship with God. Given permission to bring God into the process of their healing, these women evidence powerful sensitivity and compassion toward others as their own wounds heal. Some are called through their brokenness and healing to minister to others.

Homosexuality

Seekers' Perspective

- "When I began to realize I was gay I prayed all the time that God would let me be normal. I hated myself and even tried to commit suicide once. I didn't know where to go for help, for information, and ended up going to gay bars and hangouts just to find people like me. But that lifestyle scared me even more. Where do I belong?"

- "There are so many serious problems in our world. Why does the church continue to focus on these sexual issues?"

- "I used to make sick jokes about gays and lesbians; then I found out my brother is gay. His life has been horrible because of something he can't help. Those men in Rome don't know my brother and they don't know all the other people they are hurting either. How can they judge people like that?"

- "We are not promiscuous; our commitment to one another is permanent and we are faithful to each other. We celebrate our Christianity very consciously, yet the church says we are disordered. Like lepers, we are set apart from the rest of the sinners whose actions call forth no such label from the hierarchy."

- "Who's kidding who? Look at all the priests and seminarians and bishops who are gay. How can we defend anything that forces people to hide who they are?"

- "If sexuality is only acceptable when it is open to procreation, what about old married couples having sex? What about people having sex at certain times of the month when they know they can't conceive? Are they disordered?"

- "What about Catholics who only care about power and money, who are racially prejudiced? Those who support capital punishment? We never hear them condemned for their inclinations."

- "I am so sad, so humiliated by the church's continuing efforts to categorize gay and lesbian people. Who are they doing this for? Are they protecting God or us? I think God can handle all of us just fine, straight or gay. It's the church that has the problem."

- "Thank God for courageous bishops and priests who are able to listen to their consciences and the gospel. We need people to lead us all out of this mess. The church's credibility suffers every time another edict on sexuality comes out."

- "Don't they read the same psychological and medical information we do? And Jesus didn't have anything to say about homosexuality!"

- "What greater discrimination is there than to label people 'objectively disordered'? It makes me ashamed to be a Catholic. I feel like I should be out there apologizing to gay people for what the church says. It's easier to just leave altogether."

Church's Perspective

Church teaching has not changed; in fact, it has been reinforced and succinctly defined in official documents: Sexual intercourse that is not open to procreation is objectively evil. Any sexually relational activity between gay and lesbian Catholics is sin because it cannot lead to biological reproduction. Resting its theology on what the church has always determined to be *natural law,* official church teaching reflects the insistence of this procreational end to all sexual activity. In its implication, this precludes from the reach of homosexual men and women any possibility of lives lived in complete commitment and fidelity with an intimate other.

In a landmark document issued by Joseph Cardinal Ratzinger in 1986, the following was included, "Although the particular inclination of the homosexual person is not a sin, it is a more or less strong tendency ordered toward an intrinsic moral evil; and thus the inclination itself must be seen as an objective disorder."[17] The same document also states:

> It is only in the marital relationship that the use of the sexual faculty can be morally good. A person engaging in homosexual behavior therefore acts immorally....Homosexual activity is not a complementary union, able to transmit life; and so it thwarts the call to a life of that form of self-giving which the Gospel says is the essence of Christian living. This does not mean that homosexual persons are not often generous and giving of themselves; but when they engage in homosexual activity they confirm within themselves a disordered sexual inclination which is essentially self indulgent."[18]

The *Catechism of the Catholic Church,* first released in 1994, reinforces this teaching, while acknowledging that men and women with deep-seated homosexual tendencies do not choose their condition. It encourages respect, compassion, and sensitivity in our relationships with them while calling them to live in chastity.[19]

In a caring document called *Always Our Children,* the American bishops provide information and reassurance to families whose children struggle with their sexual identity, acknowledging the necessity for close parental involvement in the journey of discovery. Regarding the homosexual inclination, the bishops state: "Generally, homosexual orientation is experienced as a given, not as something freely chosen. By itself, therefore, a homosexual orientation cannot be considered sinful....God does not love someone any less simply because he or she is homosexual. God's love is always and everywhere offered to those who are open to receiving it." [20]

In a statement issued in 1991, now retired Archbishop John R. Roach supported official church teaching, adding an admonition that we must be careful to "avoid passing judgment on the inner moral state of any individual."[21]

The conciliatory tone of the bishops' message was interrupted in 1999 by the Vatican's censoring of Father Robert Nugent and Sister Jeanine Gramick, prohibiting them from continuing in their ministry to gay and lesbian Catholics. They have, for the past 20 years, devoted their lives to reconciling the chasm between the official church and its gay and lesbian children.

Pastoral Perspective

A major change evolving during the years of our ministry is the increased concern of homosexual and straight Catholics regarding these teachings. Most often, the outrage is voiced by seekers who are not gay, but who see these official teachings as unjust and discriminatory. Knowledge from other disciplines has brought all of us to new understanding of homosexuality. Accompanying our deeper understanding of human sexuality is the realization that we are all called toward a mature integration of our sexuality into our personhood. With this new discovery, more and more homosexual men and women are "coming out," embracing their sexuality as a gift from God. Shame is the greatest inhibitor to healthy sexuality. Labels and condemnation serve no purpose in the process of conversion into deeper relationship with a loving God.

During my Clinical Pastoral Educational training, I was assigned to the hospital's HIV/AIDS unit. My welcome from the doctor in charge began with, "I have no respect for your church because of what it does to these people," along with a warning that I needed to avoid anything that would heap shame on their heads. In the staffings and encounters that were to follow, I came to see Jesus in this man, not even a Christian, as he considered not only the physical, but the emotional condition of each patient. While not every HIV/AIDS patient is homosexual, most of those with whom I worked during that assignment were. They fended me off at first too; word of my "Roman Catholic" identity preceded me. Some were hostile. Then I became a curiosity. Their concept of the church didn't include a woman in ministry, and when I told them I had been divorced and remarried, their attitude changed. In some small way, I became one of them because I, too, was "tainted."

Their stories were sometimes more than I could hear, resulting in sleepless nights spent reliving their words, their pain, their gaunt, tear-stained faces. I learned about faith from those people, a faith that has to be discovered and learn to survive with no help from religion. Almost all of them revealed deep compassion rooted in the humiliation and cruelty projected upon them by unknowing, sometimes knowing, people and structures in their lives. I met God's grace in those gay people. How else can one explain their goodness in spite of the frustration of not being allowed what we all crave in our lives: committed, sustained intimacy in relationship with another? They ministered to me by their honesty, their eventual trust, and their good-natured encouragement to "keep doing whatever it is you do in the church." It pleased them that a woman with a broken past could represent the Catholic Church. Many revealed their status as "former Catholics," acknowledging that while the church was not a part of their lives, God was even more evident than before. They told stories of their families, of lost dreams, of exploitation, of lost love, of shame, of redemption, of caring and ministering to one another. One told me he had been a priest, from a faraway diocese, determined not to share his stigma with his fellow priests or his bishop. He would die alone during my time there, with no consolation from the church he had served all his life.

The distance between official church teaching and pastoral response on this issue seems insurmountable at times. If only we could move back from the rhetoric to the human being, beyond the category of sinfulness to the larger reality of human life lived in relationship with God, always called to new discovery, new birth, new direction. If we are not able to bridge this chasm, I fear we will lose the very people who will lead us out of this dilemma, those whose lives teach us all. Incarnational theology demands that we learn from them, an impossibility if they are not welcomed, indeed solicited to join us, talk with us, pray with us, weep with us. The American bishops remind us, "The Christian life is a journey marked by perseverance and prayer. It is a path leading from where we are to where we know God is calling us."[22] It is also a path that sometimes includes crucifixion for anyone who takes seriously the primacy of conscience "where we are alone with God whose voice echoes in our depths."[23] It is toward the authentic understanding of that voice that our pastoral focus must point. Only in mutual awareness that we are all the beloved of God does the invitation to journey with us become credible to gay and lesbian Catholics. That awareness must include validation and sensitivity to the frustration and hardship along the way. In the closing statement of *Always Our Children,* the bishops implore, "Though at times you may feel discouraged, hurt, or angry, do not walk away from your families, from the Christian community, from all those who love you. In you God's love is revealed."[24]

It is a lot to ask people who have been deeply wounded and judged to walk with us once again, but we cannot stop extending the invitation. We need their presence; we need them to share their stories with us, their heartache and their joy; we need their goodness, their creativity, their spirituality. We need to console them and to be consoled by them and we need to reconcile with them, perhaps over and over again, until we recognize God's presence in their unique human experience. Perhaps then we can stop labeling people by their sexual orientation and get on with building the kingdom together.

After all is said and done, it comes down to welcoming, the basic ingredient in any evangelization effort. We must get the word out through our parish communities that our homosexual sisters and brothers will be safe with us, will be respected by us, and will be equal to us. The invitation to Christian hospitality is expressed poignantly in these words by Bill Huebsch in his moving, crystalline style called prose sense:

> *In light of all of this,*
> > *what kind of pastoral response do we make*
> > *at the Basilica of St. Mary?*
> *I can summarize our response*
> > *in three clear principles.*
> *First, all persons who come to the Basilica*
> > *are treated with equal respect.*
> *This is true not just on the basis of sexual orientation,*
> > *but on socio-economic status,*
> > *Race, gender, religious affiliation,*
> > > *And a long list of other factors.*
> *Simply put, we do not discriminate at the Basilica.*
> *Second, we do not judge.*
> > *We do all we can to assist everyone*
> > *Who comes to us*
> > *To clarify their consciences,*
> > > *To know their vocations,*
> > > *And to discern the power of light*
> > > > *from the power of darkness.*

We offer support groups,
  prayer groups,
  ministry groups,
  a strong commitment to clear preaching,
    and other means—
      all to assist people in living their beliefs.
But in the end
  we trust our people.
We have learned over the years
  that the people, whether gay or straight,
    are generous,
    faithful,
    and searching.
We know the journey to God is not traveled alone
  and we do all we can to help people
    identify the experience of God in their lives
      and then to worship and live accordingly.
But we do not judge the decisions they reach
  in good conscience.
And third, we do now and we have always
  at the Basilica,
  called all who hear us
  to fidelity in relationships,
  to holiness,
  to integrity as persons,
  to charity as the highest virtue,
  and to a common life.
Our proclamation of the Gospel is clear as a bell:
  Who are you?
      Are you searching for God? We welcome you.
      Are you divorced? We welcome you.
      Are you an immigrant? We welcome you.
    You belong to us because you belong to Christ.
    Christ is the host at the Basilica and Christ welcomes all.
      Are you a family raising children?

> *Are you homeless?*
> *Are you handicapped in some way?*
> *Are you sick or on your deathbed?*
> *Are you a woman seeking her place in the church?*
> > *We welcome you.*
> *Are you gay or lesbian?*
> *Are you a widow?*
> > *Have you lost an important relationship?*
> > *Are you lonely and alone?*
> > *We welcome you.*
> *You belong to us because you belong to Christ.*
> *Christ is the host at the Basilica and Christ welcomes all.*
At the Basilica of St. Mary,
> *our pastoral response to homosexual persons*
> *is no different from our response to all others.*
At the Basilica, if you're a gay man or lesbian woman,
> *you are "mainstreamed."*
> *We treat you on a par with all others.*
We do not discriminate.
> *We do not judge.*
And we welcome all in the name of Christ.[25]

Women's Issues

Seekers' Perspective

- "It is a contradiction for the male church authority to preach human justice and dignity while denying the call of women to priestly ordination."

- "How can a church maintain relevancy to a modern world with its archaic concept of a woman's role?"

- "Every time the Vatican speaks out on this issue, it gets worse. Frankly I'm embarrassed to belong to a church that hasn't left the Dark Ages."

- "God is conceptualized as a father; women are denied ordination; canon law says women can't give homilies. Men make the rules; men carry out the rules; men enforce the rules. Men perpetuate the myth of "Holy Mother, the church." In reality it is "Holy Father, the church!"

- "It is painful to think of how different the church would be if women had been included as equals. Discrimination against women may have been a cultural norm at one time; it is inexcusable that we are carrying it into the new millennium."

- "If sexism is a sin, why do we keep enforcing it? What are they afraid of?"

- "Those of us who have daughters can't tolerate their being rated second class in their own church."

- "I come from a rural parish where the pastoral minister does all of the ministry during the week. On weekends she has no authority because of the young priest who is our pastor. He doesn't even know us."

Church's Perspective

In the 1994 apostolic letter entitled *Ordinatio Sacerdotalis,* Pope John Paul II reinforced the teaching of Pope Paul VI. The traditional position of a male-only ordained priesthood was upheld. There would be no more discussion on the subject. In a statement on February 13, 1998, the late Bishop P. Francis Murphy stated, "Despite the strength and clarity of Pope John Paul II's pronouncements, there remains much unrest and unease with the arguments given to support the traditional teaching, more questioning among Catholic theologians...and a large percentage of our Catholic people who are not in harmony with the teaching...."[26] In another address, Bishop Murphy refers to John's assurance that darkness will never overcome Light, indicating, "I draw strength from this and reflect on ways that may assist the official church in the new millennium...where bishops and others could discuss this issue without fear of being considered disloyal."[27]

As we enter the twenty-first century, the debate on women's ordination is officially closed. Yet women are playing more and more high-profile roles within the church. Some women are completing the same theology program required of seminarians; others are specializing in various theological and scriptural studies. Parish staffs are usually heavily dominated by women in numerous areas of ministry. Some are being assigned as parish administrators.

Many women accept their role in the church *as is*. They are content to minister and serve the people of God, confident that the Spirit is at work in the priest shortage, that change is in the making, that the church will one day acknowledge that there is no discrimination between male or female when it comes to priesthood.

Pastoral Perspective

Before we can minister to others who are smarting from this issue, we must painfully scrutinize the implications of these teachings on our individual lives. Few of my counterparts in ministry are free from the effects of the subordinate role the church affords them.

We cannot whitewash these teachings by stressing *the contribution of women in the life of the church*. What the seekers want to talk about is *the contribution of the church in the life of its women!* While many women continue to work toward change within the institutional church, and others simply cease trying to change the system, growing numbers are wearing out and leaving. Protestant seminaries are ordaining Catholic women whose call transcends their church membership. Women are gathering to celebrate Eucharist with a small "e," using prayers, scriptures, and casual circles of community as a substitute for the institutional church.

There may be some merit in pointing out that women play a lesser role in nearly all walks of secular life. However, the response is usually "But the church should lead society in fighting injustice." For every woman who struggles with her own faith commitment, her lived experience of church, there is ongoing confrontation with the restrictions placed on her gifts, talents, her ability to make decisions. This reality has to be validated for the seeker. Whether or not she can sustain that emotional and spiritual bombardment depends largely on the amount of support available from others within the church. This support comes from men and women, priests and lay ministers, even bishops.

It is asking a lot of a woman to suggest that she stay in and work toward change. Only those who have suffered the injustice of second-class citizenship in any society understand the daily pressure such a decision entails. Her focus must rest clearly on goals that are real and valuable to her, but probably not attainable in her lifetime. It is nearly impossible to maintain a healthy emotional and spiritual equilibrium without such a vision. Carolyn Osiek describes such an awareness: "Life is not as it was before, and can never be so again. It cannot return to the comfort of denial. One's self-image of loyalty and one's experience of oppression come to a screeching collision with one another and seem henceforth incompatible. How can I remain loyal to a person, institution, or tradition that has done this to me? But without that commitment, what do I have left? Who am I?"[28]

While we have to accept reality, there are discussions that prove helpful in stirring the embers of hope. Single-focused discussions on ordaining women at this particular time in the history of the church bear little fruit. We encourage the seekers to consider the role of priesthood itself. Can it possibly continue in its present form in light of the continuing decline of its members? Would the Holy Spirit allow the church to disappear because the ordained priesthood as we know it is diminishing? In what ways are women already called to priesthood, making significant strides and contributions in their ministries toward the realization of the kingdom? What would a priesthood open to all look like? How would it change the church?

Exploration of the history of ministry in the church helps the seekers find hope in the possibility that a change in the structure of priesthood may be the necessary prerequisite to a priesthood of service, whether the priest is a woman or man, married or single. Father Franklin O'Meara states, "The context of a theology of ministry for today is not decline, but expansion."[29] What a hope-filled message for all of us, men and women, called by baptism to service within the church! In O'Meara's clear overview of the development of ministry over the first two centuries of the church's experience, we find seeds of hope for the new millennium. Historical perspective often reveals to us an awareness of the Spirit of God at work in the present, instilling hope for the future. For many of us who stay and commit ourselves toward ridding the church of injustice in any form, there is the hope that our children will know a different kind of church, one more closely resembling the kingdom. There is great dignity in aligning ourselves with women and men of the ages who have dared to dream, to hope, and to work for change, albeit at great cost and personal sacrifice.

I have been blessed in ministry to have had numerous "ordinations" (validations of God's love working through me as a minister, and an acceptance of me as a sister in Christ in instances where only priests have trod before). The shortage of ordained men has called me to sacred ground: death journeys, grief ministry, emergency baptisms, pastoral counseling, nonsacramental anointing and confessions, faith exploration, and marriage preparation. The Catholic laity is open, responsive, and welcoming to women in these and all ministry activities. A number of years ago I was called to the deathbed of a lifelong parishioner, a very old woman named Vera. Still conscious, she acknowledged my presence with a smile. I prayed with her, rubbed her body with oil, and sat next to her in silence while she slept. Once, when she opened her eyes and looked at me, I asked her, "Did you ever dream that when this time came for you, the church would send a woman to be with you?" Her parting consecration to me was her response, "It's about time." The church was there for Vera in the presence of this humble spirit, sans ordination!

Change

Seekers' Perspectives

- "It just isn't the same church I belonged to when I was growing up."

- "Why are they so secretive about all the changes? How are we supposed to know what they are or why they changed everything? This is the first place I have found where someone explained what went on at Vatican II."

- "Why didn't they go further? They just scratched the surface."

- "What happened to all the people who went to hell for eating meat on Fridays?"

- "It was easier before, when we didn't have to think!"

- "They don't even call it Mass anymore. They call it Eucharist. The priest used to take charge up there. Now there are people going up there on Sunday mornings, doing everything. I've seen flutes, drums—even dancers—on the altar. Where will it stop?"

- "Why are they preaching about social justice? Isn't that messing up religion and politics?"

- "Is there anything the Catholic Church stands for anymore?"

- "With all these changes, are we any different from Protestants?"

Church's Perspective

Many of us were taught that an absolute and eternal truth existed in the church's laws and practices. The primary virtue was obedience; we were taught not to challenge or question what we were told. Many of these practices and teachings were actually the result of cultural, political, and historical situations having little connection with fundamental Catholic teaching. There was little opportunity to develop a historical perspective, a larger context in which to consider the rules and explanations. And the church was seen as the ultimate source of all truth, drawing little from the wisdom of other disciplines. In fact, the church became increasingly out of touch with cultural discoveries concerning human development, relationships, even our global environment. Vatican II changed many of those concepts, restoring our focus to one of discipleship and building the kingdom of God, as it had been in the early church.

The initial response to Vatican Council II was manifested by abrupt changes in the external identity of the church. Latin gave way to the language of the people, altars were turned around and stripped of statuary, and people were asked to participate in liturgies rather than just watch them. The Baltimore Catechism was replaced by colorfully illustrated books depicting a God who loved everyone. Catholics were used to operating on externally motivated control, to being told what to do and what was right. Vatican II brought into question issues and beliefs that Catholics never thought about, much less discussed. Confusion became a widespread Catholic experience.

The depth of meaning that underlies all the external changes brought about by Vatican II is only now being grasped by Catholic laity. Its thrust was not one of uncontrolled change, but of restoration. It called the church and its members to inner conversion, to renewed understanding of the sacredness of human conscience, to personal spirituality characteristic of the early church. Sadly, most of these changes were imposed without adequate education or explanation. The result is an entire generation of Catholics who are left bewildered and insecure by the church's new mode of spiritual direction. Once told their very salvation rested on obedience to this rule or that, they are now being told that God's love is unconditional. At a recent discussion of church professionals, the question was posited, "How many people would go to mass at all if they weren't worried about hell?" It is hard for people whose salvation has been held in abeyance for so long to believe that love can be a more powerful motivator than fear.

Pastoral Perspective

Discussions about change are intense because the seekers are like all Catholics: their lived experiences present differing points of view. It is a wonderful opportunity to point out the difficulty faced by a church characterized by "Here comes everybody!" Among Catholics there are different stages of faith development, different cultural backgrounds, a spectrum of ages, genders, and lived experiences. What is a burning issue to one may not seem relevant to another.

It is helpful for them to learn that the church has always changed, that any living organism has to change or it will die. The seekers are often surprised to learn the church has changed its teaching on a number of issues over the years. Interest charged for borrowed money was declared sinful in the twelfth century, but became acceptable seven hundred years later. The church executed heretics at one time; only recently has the pope denounced the death penalty. Defined by Pope John Paul II as "intrinsically evil," slavery was acceptable until the latter part of the nineteenth century. All of these changes resulted from new awareness developing within the faith community, ignited by knowledge gleaned from life events, education, and greater understanding of the gospel message. It is reassuring for Catholics to see that their experience of an unchanging church is not the reality of church throughout the ages. They begin to see the inevitably of debate between laity, clergy, even hierarchy, as changes take root, develop, and find implementation.

More numerous than the sceptics who condemned its changes are those who feel that Vatican II was a "breath of fresh air." They welcome the new vitality and vigor it brought to the church, but complain that renewal seems to have come to a standstill, in fact, seems to be sliding backward. They express their frustration with resignation: "You can't stuff toothpaste back into the tube. And you can't hide knowledge and discovery with outdated explanations and logic. We can't go back to the old way of doing things." They worry that all the positive effects of Vatican II will be lost, expressing concern about the future of the church if it loses relevance to lived experience and ongoing discovery of truth. These seekers speculate about who the next pope will be and how he will lead the church in the new century.

It will be helpful for facilitator and team to understand these strong, polarized reactions to change that will surface when seekers gather. It is essential that you reflect on your own experience of change and how it has affected your life as a Catholic. It can be difficult to minister to seekers who are distressed by an issue that actually pleases the minister. We need to identify our own biases in order to treat each seeker with acceptance. If we cut off their discussions by rationalization or our opinions, the seekers may never have another opportunity to bring these confusing issues into the open where they can be resolved.

Ironically, because of these in-depth discussions, both groups of seekers—those who value change and those who resent it—frequently tell us that for the first time they are able to hear opinions of Catholics on another side of an issue without feeling threatened or angry. Gentle humor often permeates these encounters as seekers experience support and acceptance from one another. Sides are less likely to be drawn if we are not ridiculed for saying what we feel and believe, if we don't have to defend our position. Gradually, it becomes evident that we all have a place in the church, and that the church will never stop redefining who it is. "I'm changing and I'm the church," a seeker observed, "so it figures that the church will change too."

We encourage the seekers to see the church from a global perspective, rather than assuming their parish experience typifies the church universal. It becomes obvious that a burning need for change in the church in the United States may not be a concern for the church on another continent. It helps them to see the need for the universal church to remain keenly aware of the impact of its teachings on cultures ranging from the very primitive to the technologically advanced. We become more tolerant of the slow pace with which church responds to human problems and conditions, and we see even more clearly the need for the sound development of conscience to help us through those rough spots where teaching may not meet lived reality.

It helps to make the seekers aware of the traditional, biblical, and historical legacy that has always allowed the church to adapt to diverse cultures in different ways, at different times. This is what being Catholic is all about. Addressing the tension between polarizing perspectives, Father Richard Fragomeni suggests we move toward a realization of *retrieving* significant aspects of our faith, rather than restoring old practices with little or no concern for their relevance in a post-Vatican II church. He cited parishes that have *retrieved* the practice of perpetual adoration in a way that incorporates the evolving awareness of eucharistic piety, the direct connection between Eucharist and justice. For every hour devoted to eucharistic adoration, parishioners commit to an hour of service to the poor, sick, or marginalized. In this way, pre-Vatican II Catholics have retrieved a meaningful faith experience, amplifying it with a broader understanding of Eucharist. Younger Catholics are drawn to the adoration experience by their interest in justice and older Catholics are becoming involved in justice ministry by their love of the Eucharist. The ritual, begun in the eighteenth century, is made relevant to the church's understanding of its mission today.[30]

Change is difficult for most people. It would be unfair to encourage anyone to reconcile with a church imagined to be rigid and unchanging in light of the vast potential for change looming on our immediate horizon. When I look at the changes that have taken place in the 15 years I have been in ministry, I am convinced that we can adjust to change and transformation within our church. It is hard to see the overall impact on the future church, yet we feel the resulting tension daily. Jesus taught us that there can be no transformation without some sort of dying. Most seekers realize the vast amount of change that has taken place in all other areas of their lives: transportation, education, technology, and gender roles. We have to help them integrate their perceptions of church into their entire lived experience. Thus, change becomes a natural part of their faith experience. It is a sign of life, of the Spirit at work in our midst. Our role is to challenge the seekers to accept the struggle as reality and to see in it a hopeful sign of a church that is truly alive. As it has for 2000 years, the Holy Spirit will guide us into the ebb and flow of life in the new millennium.

Confession (Sacrament of Reconciliation)

Seekers' Perspective

- "I still have nightmares about that black box; it is one of my most terrifying childhood memories."

- "It didn't make sense then and it makes less now, rattling off all those Our Fathers and Hail Marys even though I knew I'd be back in another week or two to list the same sins and receive the same penance."

- "Confession conjures up images of angry priests, fires of hell, God's wrath. I just can't do it anymore."

- "It's the first Catholic thing I quit doing and I quit as soon as I moved away from home."

- "Why not go directly to God?"

Church's Perspective

Of all the changes implemented by Vatican II, perhaps none were more welcome than those surrounding the sacrament of confession. Even the new name of this sacrament, reconciliation, signifies the depth of these changes. Millions of active Catholics have abandoned completely the practice of going to weekly confession. Along with the seekers, they may not even recognize the sacrament of reconciliation as it is practiced today. It has truly become a celebration of God's forgiveness and personal faith conversion. To describe confession in terms of celebration may be a contradiction to most Catholics who define the experience by unpleasant childhood experience. But it is an indication of the evolution of this sacrament. Gone is the black box; in its place there is free-flowing prayer and dialogue between the priest and penitent in an inviting atmosphere.

To heighten awareness of the communal aspect of sin and forgiveness, Vatican II offered two additional forms of this sacrament. The original form is still familiar; it consists of individual confession and absolution (words of God's forgiveness) between the priest and penitent. A new form that has become popular in some dioceses and churches during special times of the year, such as Advent and Lent, is a communal gathering for prayer, music, and scripture. This is followed by individual confession of sins and absolution.

The third form, used in special circumstances that preclude the availability of a sufficient number of confessors (priests) is very much like the second with one exception: General absolution is given for sins contemplated internally by each penitent. There is no individual encounter with a priest.

Clearly, the church stresses that it is God who forgives sins, but the church also teaches that sin affects our relationships with one another. As did the early Christians, we need to acknowledge our sinfulness and request forgiveness within the context of community. In the reconciliation, the priest represents the community while promising God's forgiveness to the penitent, calling her to conversion and recommitment to discipleship.

Pastoral Perspective

I was amused recently when a young priest who had been ordained only two years came to see me after visiting the church to which he had just been assigned pastor. He was very excited about almost everything until he came to the confessional. He had never been in the infamous "black box"! He had grown up in a parish that discontinued its use in favor of face-to-face visits with the confessor. That was also the norm in the seminary. His first inclination was to put the confessional on a "Things to Do" list, waiting until a later date to make the change. However, it became an immediate need when he realized that he could not sit in that black box. He assured me that it was impossible for him to celebrate a sacrament in such a mysterious, nonrelational manner.

I have come to consider the return to the sacrament of reconciliation a key to the return of most seekers. Those who come to us with pain, anger, and hurt feelings need to experience God's healing. When properly prepared, most seekers find this sacrament a turning point in their reconciliation journey. It is our responsibility to help them develop a new understanding of this sacrament. This may include inviting them into the reconciliation room where they can sit and discuss questions and observations, or an invitation to a communal service of reconciliation where they can make the choice to participate or merely observe. The significance of a ritual that marks this pivotal moment in a faith journey is very powerful to many seekers. In Chapter 4, we describe the way we present this sacrament to the seekers during our Catholics Coming Home series.

For many, their negative memories are a strong impediment to returning to this sacrament. We state the following very clearly to anyone considering taking the *risk*: (1) Catholics should know something about their confessor. It is important that he be understanding, fair, and sensitive to the apprehensions or fears of the penitent. We recommend priests who are supportive of this ministry and who will celebrate this sacrament in a way that emphasizes God's forgiveness and healing. It is important that the seekers learn to assume responsibility in choosing confessors with whom they feel safe, at ease. We do not recommend that seekers approach an unknown priest for this sacrament. (2) We encourage seekers to call a priest for an appointment, especially for their first celebration of this sacrament after a long period of time. This allows for a more relaxed atmosphere and eliminates the pressure of standing in line or catching the priest when he is already committed elsewhere and cannot devote appropriate time or attention to the seeker.

For those whose childhood experiences have been particularly traumatic, it may be impossible to return to confession. They need to be assured that they are welcome to journey with the faith community, trusting their newfound relationship with a loving God and a loving faith community to rebuild their experience of this sacrament.

Baptism

Seekers' Perspective

* "What kind of church sends a child to hell because the parents don't go to church."

* "I miscarried and my baby was never baptized. Where is my baby now?"

* "I was pregnant and the priest wouldn't marry us before our baby was born. Then he wouldn't baptize our baby because we weren't married. Now he won't marry us because we are living together. We don't want our baby going to limbo, but the church isn't making this very easy!"

- "I called to schedule our baby's baptism and the first question I got in response was, "Are you a registered, contributing member of the parish?""

- "Immersion? What is the Catholic Church coming to, dunking all those people at the Easter Vigil!"

Church's Perspective

Although we may trivialize the prevailing misunderstanding about this sacrament in view of the larger scope of conflicting issues in the church, my hospital ministry reveals the depth of anguish caused by lack of knowledge about baptism. Nearly thirty years ago, I suffered a violent miscarriage just past the first trimester of my pregnancy. The fetus was disposed of without consulting me, a common practice in those days. Days later, a friend came to console me. She expressed no concern for the loss of my child, only horror and concern because my baby had not been baptized, raising an entirely new dimension of grief I hadn't yet contemplated! I have devoted specific attention to helping women and couples grieve the loss of their unborn children because of this experience. Always, the question of baptism is raised. Fundamental beliefs that connect baptism with salvation raise chilling concerns among parents and families. Our theology of a loving God has yet to permeate the hearts of these good people.

The church teaches that baptism, together with confirmation and Eucharist, are the sacraments of initiation into the Catholic faith community. Like all sacraments, it signifies a milestone in our faith journey, with God and the community. It ritualizes belonging while celebrating the power of our inner sacredness to overcome the human inclination to choosing selfishly (short definition of original sin!). That power is called grace. Each baptism is a sign to the faith community, reconnecting its members to that same power within each of them. More than any other sacrament, baptism is considered within the context of belonging, being nourished spiritually by the body of believers. The relationship is mutual throughout the lifetime of the baptized person, a relationship based on regard for the sacredness of one another, our interdependency with one another. The core of our belonging is Jesus Christ. In a way, through baptism we become his hands and feet and heart, called to live out his life in our own. Baptism calls us to eat, breathe, think, pray, and worship in a community-oriented mindset. From that day forward, we are part of a whole, and it is the grace within the whole that forms and guides us.

The concept of original sin rests in the propensity of all human beings to place self first, to pull away from others and *help myself.* When carried to extremes, this self-centered attitude isolates us from others. It prevents us from discovering our inner dependence on God and our interdependence with one another; it prevents us from caring about the welfare of others. In short, this tendency prevents us from putting our sacredness into practice.

In baptism, the community celebrates the reality of another person being embraced by God's love and the life of Jesus Christ within them, the arrival of another person who will help to bring about God's kingdom. Vatican II stressed that not only does baptism free us from our original inclinations toward sinfulness or selfishness, but that it begins a new relationship with the Church. Bonding the recipient to the church forever, baptism calls forth blessings and responsibilities on community and recipient.

In the past, church teaching indicated that children who died before reception of this sacrament would spend eternity in a place called limbo, an ambiguous destination where they would never experience the face of God. The church encouraged parents to have their children baptized as soon as possible in order to assure them of salvation. This teaching is the root of fear among many Catholic and Protestant Christians to this day, a gnawing uncertainty about what happens to their deceased children or to unbaptized adults.

There are many legends about how limbo entered our theology, but the church recognizes today that there is no theological certainty about such an eternal destination. Baptism has moved beyond the narrow definition of the sacrament as saving one from limbo or hell to one of expansiveness, inclusion in a way of life that offers belonging, peace, and redemption.

Because of this emphasis on community, many parishes are now asking that parents of children being presented for baptism be active participants in the parish community, and that they attend preparation classes that will help them grow into their primary role as community representatives for the child. This preparation can be an evangelizing experience for a couple whose church affiliation has been limited or nonexistent. If they are arbitrarily turned away, it becomes a moment of departure from the church for them, their child, and future generations of the family.

Catholics who attend the Easter Vigil Service are becoming familiar with full immersion baptisms. Because the church offered only the pouring of water for centuries, some may find this new way of celebrating baptism uncomfortable. However, adult candidates are drawn to immersion and new Catholic sanctuaries across the country are being equipped with baptismal areas that accommodate this new rite. The fonts become a significant architectural focus, their flowing water conveying to all who enter a sense of Christ's presence in the community. Parents of infants are usually invited to choose which method they prefer for their child's baptism. I was delighted when our grandson was baptized by immersion last year, casting a very different emphasis on the words and prayers of the liturgy. Logan seemed to enjoy it very much!

Pastoral Perspective

Seekers are primarily relieved to learn that they don't have to believe in limbo anymore! Discussion about a loving, compassionate God reveals the inconsistency presented in a God who sentences anyone to eternal punishment because they weren't baptized. I have come to think of God's love in terms of grandparenting; ask any grandparent whether it would be possible to separate them from their love for their grandchildren and you will know why. Yet grandparents come to these sessions worried that their grandchildren are going to suffer, wondering how they can force their children to have them baptized. I draw on their limited, human love, to help ease their concern.

Baptism needs to be discussed in the context of relationship with community. Taken out of the community context, it becomes something done to us by a God who has no other way to express redemptive love for us, or a secular tradition that will have little or no effect on the newly baptized. Those who are caught up in serious worry about this issue should not be treated lightly. While the subject of baptism conjures up images of happiness, celebration, and joy to most of us, the fear and dread it raises in some cannot be ignored or minimized.

Conscience

Seekers' Perspective

- "How do we know what's right if the church doesn't tell us what to do?"

- "Deep inside, I know what is right for me, but the church tells me I have to do something else."

- "Why should I do good if others can get away with anything?"

- "I thought all the church teachings came from God. How can the church change them?"

Church's Perspective

In addition to the Vatican II documents noted in Chapter 4, a wonderful insight into the church's teaching on conscience is contained in a pastoral letter from Bishop Michael Pfeifer, O.M.I. A gentle, but firm affirmation of the sacredness placed by the church on one's conscience, it says in part:

> At the very heart of God's scriptural revelation and his dealings with humanity is the clear and ringing message that God has made us free. There is a hope in the Creator's gift that we should come in freedom to love God and to seek union with Him above all else....The only love that God wants is a love that is freely given from the heart. No sacrifice, no rule-keeping, no...attitude can substitute, and no one else may force our decision.
>
> If we are created so radically free by God, how can anyone tell us what to believe? How can anyone finally command how we are to behave? No one can. God will not, even though He awaits our free, loving response....
>
> The name we have given to that faculty, that place, that secret tribunal which God will not violate, and no other power can coerce, is conscience. Here is the place whereby we discern right from wrong in a spirit of striving to be faithful to God's natural law and the gospel teaching of Christ in the concrete circumstances of everyday life....
>
> Since that is so, it is clear that our conscience must be well-formed, that is, knowledgeable and practiced, in seeking God's

will. The formation of conscience involves us in a constant dialogue with God's scriptural revelation, with the ongoing tradition
and official teaching of the church. It also implies a dialogue with
our experience and understanding of the daily demands which
face us as individuals and as a community. Prayer for the guidance
of the Holy Spirit is of vital importance in the process of conscience formation....

The church offers its guidance to the whole community according to the best available resources at its disposal. One can always
rely on this official teaching at least not to lead us astray even if a
final word cannot be given. It is this assurance which obliges
Catholics to open themselves up to what is taught, ready to give
assent and obedience. But, just as the teaching is not final, both
church authorities and Catholics in general must be open to ongoing exploration and even revision when greater clarity emerges....

Where does this leave the ordinary person? In all cases of non-
infallible official teaching we retain the responsibility to seek truth
and goodness in our lives. Official teaching must be addressed to
the whole Catholic world. For that reason it cannot take into
account the specific circumstances of each person who seeks sincerely to hear the church's guiding word and to live accordingly.
The well-formed conscience will always strive to be based on the
gospel principles of Christ, and on the best teachings of the
church. Prayer, study, reflection and consultation are of vital
importance in conscience formation."[31]

Pastoral Perspective

Our ministry places serious emphasis on this right of conscience
clearly described by Bishop Pfeifer. It is a turning point for many seekers. Because they know they can think and respond as adults, they
begin to sense freedom from past hurt and anger. There is a glimmer
of hope that issues and concerns can be explored not through anger
and resistance, but through a mature and realistic response. There are
others who are uncomfortable with this newfound freedom. They have
relied for so long on church authority to think and choose for them
that they feel insecure about thinking and choosing for themselves.
They may confuse decisions of conscience with what is commonly

called *situation ethics,* choices determined solely by what seems right at the time.

At first glance, this new freedom seems to some to be the easy way. Further discussion, however, reveals the responsibility that goes with the freedom. It can be much easier to follow rules blindly than to discern what God is asking of someone when there aren't prevailing rules. Integrity is increased when we develop a pattern of assuming responsibility for our lives, the good and the bad, instead of relying on external governances to control our behavior. We remind the seekers that prayer, reflection, scripture, and consultation are the primary foundation to any Christian process of conscience formation and decision. And we encourage them to become comfortable with these new concepts before they make new decisions that will affect their lives, even those involving reconciling with the church.

Hidden Issues

The stated issues of alienation expressed by some seekers may not be the only ones, or even the most significant issues that separate them from the church. Some have issues that are not directly connected with the church. They are more difficult to identify and even more difficult to address. John S. Savage suggests that some individuals leave the church because of anxiety and anger that is not directly related to the church.[32] These emotions can be triggered by any event that causes estrangement, within the family, between friends, at work—anywhere and with anyone. When a church-related event occurs, the pain surfaces and is focused toward the church or clergy. The individual then faults the church for not responding during the time of crisis. There is resulting movement away from the church as the cause of pain is transferred from its original source to the church.

We find this to be true in our own experience with the seekers. It is easier to say that one has stopped coming to church because of confession or the hierarchy than to face other more personal and painful nonchurch related issues. Our pastoral response is to create an atmosphere that allows personal exploration and reflection on those deeper issues of alienation. With free-flowing discussion in a trusting atmosphere, the expressed causes of alienation often give way to the deeper issues, which may involve family problems, lack of self-esteem, childhood shame, abuse, personal or family chemical dependency. These issues are not always appropriate topics for the group process. For those whose issues lie deeply buried even from themselves, or who dare not risk exposing their vulnerability within the group setting, it is our job to offer gentle invitations to explore more personally the roots of their church alienation. It may be necessary to encourage professional counseling where they can receive the appropriate attention to their specific situations.

Chapter 6

Called to Reconcile, to Forgive, to Heal

Reconciliation is not a new concept in the church; it has always been at the core of our existence as a people committed to the fulfillment of Jesus' mission. Real reconciliation is not confined solely to the "little black box." Rather, as described by Monika Hellwig, "...continuing reconciliation, sacramental in a broad and true sense, is happening in people's kitchens and family rooms, and bedrooms, on streets, in buses and where they shop, in offices, factories, and farms, in playgrounds, theaters and hospitals, on Monday, Tuesday, and the rest of the week. That is where the church lives and breathes and plays its role in the redemption."[1]

While our focus has been on the seekers and their process of reconciliation, the underlying experience of alienation and the need for forgiveness is familiar to all of us. The gospel calls us to much more than coexistence; we are called to live in intimacy with our God and with one another. Intimacy always includes the risk of pain, misunderstanding, and isolation. Reconciliation is the key to knowing the goodness in others in spite of these risks, and becomes the way in which we begin to experience the reality of a relationship with a loving God. Through the experience of genuine reconciliation we become free of the burdensome concepts of God that stifle growth and our ability to live at peace with ourselves and in unity with one another. We learn about reconciliation during times when it is most needed. When we bar people from our churches we deny them and ourselves the powerful lessons that can be learned from the process of reconciliation. Dennis Woods warns us, "Those who undertake a ministry of reconciliation have to stay alert for those special opportunities that must be seized as teaching moments or moments of consciousness raising or recognition."[2]

Reconciliation does not happen automatically; it is not accomplished through one experience or liturgy, and it is not possible without honest dialogue between all concerned. It is a process that continues as long as there is discord in our lives. Sacramentally, reconciliation becomes a powerful conversion experience for seekers who have reflected and prayed about their lived journeys. Far removed from the old "grocery list" confessions, they are sacred experiences for penitent and confessor. We need to expand the reality of this sacramental process to include living lives of reconciliation in our parish communities. Caught up in the activity and program focus so prevalent in today's parishes, we sometimes lose sight of who we are and what we are about. Active Catholics worship together, attend meetings and social events together, but rarely are models of resolving differences, living in intimate relationship with one another. People come and go, carrying their stories with them, their gifts lost to the community.

Eucharist is a primary experience of reconciliation in those parishes where liturgies are truly a celebration of God's love and forgiveness. When we can accept our own brokenness and vulnerability, our dependence on God's love and forgiveness, we have no need to place barriers between ourselves and others. As the beloved of God, we neither perceive nor reflect judgment on who is "in" and who is "out." Rather than a reward for lives lived according to rules and regulations, Eucharist becomes a triumphant explosion of joy reflecting God's presence and power in a broken body made whole once again. As with the sacrament of reconciliation, we must give flesh to the sacrament of Eucharist through true communion as described by Jean Vanier:

> Communion is the to and fro of love. It is the trust that bonds us together, children with their parents, a sick person with a nurse, a child with a teacher, a husband with a wife, friends together, people with a common task....Communion is not static; it is an evolving reality. Trust is continually called to grow and to deepen, or it is wounded and diminishes. It is a trust that the other will not

possess or crush you but rejoices in your gifts and calls you to growth and to freedom....One who is weak, who lives in true communion with another, will not see his own weakness as something to be judged, as something negative, he will sense that he is appreciated, that he has a place.[3]

That place for baptized Catholics is at the table, where the Body of Christ finds completion. And so we must reconcile with one another. We cannot afford to sit smugly in our pews, measuring holiness by outward appearances and theological yardsticks. We are all seekers, carrying doubt and a sense of failure deep within our hearts. Our holiness is defined by embracing lived reality, not by church attendance. For some, that holiness comes at a very dear price. We need to support one another, provide ongoing opportunities for discussion, healing, and forgiveness. We need to welcome the broken and those who can't afford to fill their envelopes. We need to provide a spiritual resting place for those who are tired from their journey. And we need to learn from them, for they have much to teach us. In one of my favorite evangelization messages, Bishop Michael Sheehan calls us to a new way of *being* church to one another:

No more unfriendly, hurried coldness at the doors and in the pews of our churches, let there be life.

No more insensitivity to the prophetic teachings of the church on justice and peace, let there be love.

No more refusal to share with others the good news of Jesus Christ and the importance of his body, the church, let there be joy.[4]

We must live in the hope that Bishop Sheehan's words will take on the flesh and blood of lived Catholic experience. Only then will our parishes be transformed into reconciling communities, opening the doors to those who have left and enriching the lives of those who remain.

Efforts to make our parishes places of life, love, and joy begin with a focus on relationships rather than on activity and programs. We need to be flexible and risk trying something new, to listen with Christ-filled hearts and serve with the hands and feet and mind of Jesus. Our focus must remain on the recipient and the gospel message, not on the program itself, certainly not on those who administer it. The word *program* can be indicative of too much expectation, too much direction, too much control. Programs often have to meet timetables, budgets, and human agendas, the very things that stifle the work of the Holy Spirit! According to Monika Hellwig, our task as reconciling communities "...requires growth to maturity in faith in which judgments can really be made from inner conviction according to the mind and heart of Jesus and under the impulse of the Spirit."[5]

For 15 years, we have seen seekers' lives changed by this faith maturation process as they come to grips with their own sacred authority and God's relentless love for them. It is an awesome gift to be a part of their conversion experience, a gift that enriches our lives, informs our ministry, and reveals the ongoing presence of God's Spirit. The seekers are our teachers, our divining rods in determining our course. They have forced us to rely more on God's Spirit and less on ourselves. And they have taught us about forgiveness. True reconciliation cannot happen without forgiveness. Unfortunately, it is often the seeker who has to do the most forgiving. It is a painful reality that requires opening old wounds, acknowledging the grievousness of wrongs done to shattered souls. Only then can forgiveness take place. Only then can wounds and breaches be healed. Anything less leads to ongoing alienation and victimization. Forgiveness is a painful journey toward freedom and resurrection; it is a path on which we must walk tenderly with one another, in and out of church.

In a recent address to the National Federation of Priests Councils, Auxiliary Bishop Robert Morneau of Green Bay, Wisconsin, offered the gathered priests "two suggestions, and only two": "Be a listener, be a lover...If we listen and love, if we follow the way of Jesus in doing the will of the Father—acting always with justice, loving as tenderly as possible, walking confidently in faith (Mic 6:8)—we will fulfill our pastoral responsibility well."[6] Through baptism, all Catholics are called to be a priestly people, called to be listeners and lovers! What impact the church could make in this century if we could each live out that holy order.

The dawning of a new millennium presents us with a milemarker. We are being called to see forgiveness and reconciliation in new and broader contexts than we have ever considered them before. As our universe gets smaller and our lives get busier, we cannot forget that first and foremost we are pilgrims on a journey. Catholics are committed, Christ-centered, loving people whose increasing participation in the living church is at the root of its sacramentality. Efforts to bridge the gaps and heal the wounds among ourselves will enhance our ability to influence unity in the secular community. We do not reconcile only to tolerate, but rather to learn from one another, to see the face of God in new people, experiences, and challenges.

It is in the universal sense of the word *Catholic* that we live as reconcilers within our church communities. The unleashed power of ongoing reconciliation forges together not only a people, but all that is good within them. Through reconciliation, fear of differences is replaced with new awareness of individual sacredness; fear of weakness is replaced with dramatic proof of the power and strength of love; fear of error is replaced with the assurance of God's forgiveness and guidance toward all that is truth, all that is good.

If you have a family member or friend who is an inactive Catholic...

- Listen to them and validate their experience.

- Be nonjudgmental, affirming, accepting, and patient.

- Let them see your own faith working in your life.

- Share some of your own doubts and struggles with them.

- Love them unconditionally. (God does!)

- Don't push or force them into coming back.

- Don't argue about their reasons for not going to church.

- Do not place limits on Jesus' gift of salvation for all of us. Do not question their salvation.

- Encourage programs and liturgies in your parish that will welcome everyone.

- Always provide *invitation,* never *confrontation!*

If you want to minister to inactive Catholics...

- Do all the above, plus:

- Be willing to accept their anger or blame without taking it personally or becoming defensive.

- Address inactive Catholics in the secular community.

- Reach out in a way that respects the seekers' privacy and dignity.

- Become familiar with the issues that alienate people from the church. Check your own feelings about these issues.

- Take a good look at your own parish community. Perhaps you have people who feel alienated among your regular members. Start with them!

- Promote liturgies and programs that are sensitive to inactive Catholics and their issues.

- Be pastorally sensitive, compassionate, concerned, tender, caring, and reconciling. Be lovers!

- Develop a catalog of resources: diocesan/community programs, counseling, support groups, and so on.

- *Listen, listen, listen!*

- Use prayer, team support, and processing.

- Consider joining or forming a reconciling team in your own parish or in collaboration with neighboring parishes.

If you are an angry or inactive Catholic, or someone who has been hurt by the church...

- We are sorry.

- Remember that as a baptized Catholic, you are a member of the church. God does not abandon you as you struggle with faith issues, life issues, not even when you fail. God's love, forgiveness, and peace are always available to you, in or out of the church.

- Seek out a place and means to express your anger and confusion; find church representatives who will listen to you and who are role models you can respect, not just authority figures.

- It's all right to "shop around" on Sunday mornings. Find a parish where the worship and community feel comfortable for you, where you feel welcome, and where you can share *your* gifts.

- We ask your patience and forgiveness. As church, we are human; we make mistakes.

- Find a good *adult* education program to update your faith and theology. Explore the church's history, it's constant change and evolution over centuries, and its reaction to and interaction with cultural influence.

- Start with one step. Don't give up. Reach out and continue your search, no matter how small each effort may seem. Nourish your spirit through prayer and scripture.

- Be patient with yourself. Rest in God's love. Trust the Holy Spirit to work in your life, to get you through the hard spots.

- Accept Jesus' gift of salvation; no strings attached.

- Pray, for yourself, the church, for all of us.

- Know that you are a part of our daily prayers.

- Always remember: **You are the beloved of God!**

I am grateful to all who open their hearts to the seekers and to the seekers who are ready to risk coming home again. It is my prayer that our combined journeys will bring us closer to a day when the church will be fully immersed in the sacredness of human life, reveling in and extolling the beauty of the human condition, thus revealing all that we can be while revealing Jesus to one another. On that day, the kingdom of God will be at hand!

Notes

1. Sharing the Gift

1. All scripture references are from the *New American Bible.*

2. Penelope J. Ryan, *Practicing Catholic* (New York: Henry Holt, 1998), 201.

3. Norbert F. Gaughan, *Troubled Catholics* (Chicago: Thomas More Publishing, 1988), 133.

2. Tell Me the Story

1. Carrie Kemp, "Tell Me The Story of Jesus," in *Another Look* (Washington, D.C.: Paulist National Catholic Evangelization Association, 1992).

3. What Are You Bringing Them Home To?

1. *Go and Make Disciples, A National Plan and Strategy for Catholic Evangelization in the United States* (Washington, D.C.: National Council of Catholic Bishops, 1993).

2. M. Scott Peck, *A World Waiting to Be Born* (New York: Bantam Books, 1993), 352.

3. Judith Ann Koller. *A User Friendly Parish* (Mystic, Conn.: Twenty-Third Publications, 1998), 10.

4. The Reflection Journey

1. Dennis Linn, Sheila Fabrican Linn, Matthew Linn, *Good Goats, Healing Our Image of God* (Mahwah, N.J.: Paulist Press, 1994), 3, 18–19.

2. Dick Westley, *Redemptive Intimacy* (Mystic, Conn.: Twenty-Third Publications, 1989), 49.

3. Westley, 52.

4. *Exploring the Sunday Readings* (Mystic, Conn.: Twenty-Third Publications), published monthly.

5. Charles E. Bouchard, O.P., *Whatever Happened to Sin, The Truth About Catholic Morality* (Liguori, Mo.: Liguori Publications, 1996), v.

6. Thomas Bokenkotter, *A Concise History of the Catholic Church* (Garden City, N.Y.: Doubleday/Image Books, 1979), 433.

7. James Dunning, *New Wine, New Wineskins* (New York: Sadlier, 1981), 23. (adapted)

8. Robert Bellah, et al., *Habits of the Heart* (New York: Harper & Row, 1985). (adapted)

9. Mitch Finley, *Time Capsules of the Church* (Huntington, Ind.: Our Sunday Visitor Press, 1990), 84.

10. Finley, 79.

11. *Open Wide the Doors, How to Prepare for Jubilee Year 2000,* film by Resources for Christian Living (Allen, Tex.: Thomas More Publishing, 1998) and the U. S. Bishops' Secretariat for the Third Millennium.

12. Jim Castelli, "Vatican II, 30 Years on the Road from Rome," in *U.S. Catholic* (Chicago: Claretian Press, September 1995), 6–13.

13. Castelli, 11. Reprinted with permission from *U.S. Catholic.* For more information, call 1-800-328-6515.

14. Leonard Foley, O.F.M., "Vatican II: The Vision Lives On!" in *Catholic Update* Issue CO393, (Cincinnati: St. Anthony Messenger Press, March 1993).

15. *Catholic Bulletin* (now *Catholic Spirit*), Official Publication of the Archdiocese of Saint Paul and Minneapolis, July 19, 1990. Quote from Catholic News Service.

16. Austin Flannery, O.P., *Vatican Council II, Constitutions, Decrees, Declarations* (Northport, N.Y.: Costello Publishing, 1996), 178–79.

17. Bill Huebsch, *A Spirituality of Wholeness* (Mystic, Conn.: Twenty-Third Publications, 1992), 101, 103.

18. Henri J. M. Nouwen, *The Return of the Prodigal Son, A Story of Homecoming* (New York: Doubleday, 1992), 71.

19. Carrie Kemp, "Divorce and Remarriage in the Catholic Chruch" in *Another Look* (Washington, D.C.: Paulist National Catholic Evangelization Association, 1992).

20. Jean Vanier, *Becoming Human* (Mahwah, N.J.: Paulist Press, 1998), 43.

21. Flannery, 554.

22. Susan Blum, *Text, Study Guide, Implementation Process for "Go and Make Disciples": A National Plan and Strategy for Catholic Evangelization in the United States* (Manassas, Va.: National Council for Catholic Evangelization, 1993), 23.

5. The Issues That Separate

1. Raymond F. Collins, *Christian Morality* (Notre Dame, Ind.: University of Notre Dame Press, 1986), 3.

2. Michael Bayly, *Rainbow Spirit* (Minneapolis: CPCSM), April 1998.

3. Quoted in *Catholic Bulletin* (now *Catholic Spirit*), Official Publication of the Archdiocese of Saint Paul and Minneapolis, March 19, 1992.

4. Flannery, 102.

5. Quoted in *National Catholic Reporter,* Kansas City, Mo. February 19, 1999.

6. F. Barry Brunsman, *New Hope for Divorced Catholics* (San Francisco: Harper & Row, 1985), 3.

7. James J. Young, C.S.P., *Divorcing, Believing, Belonging* (New York: Paulist Press, 1984), 167.

8. Pope John Paul II, *Christian Family in the Modern World* (Washington, D.C.: National Conference of Catholic Bishops, December 15, 1981), para. 84.

9. Young, 167.

10. Francisco Javier Urrutia, S.J., The "Internal Forum Solution," in *The Jurist* (Washington, D.C.: The Catholic University of America, 1980), Vol. XL.

11. Brunsman, 3.

12. Fran Ferder and John Heagle, *Your Sexual Self, Pathway to Authentic Intimacy* (Notre Dame, Ind.: Ave Maria Press, 1992), 11.

13. Bishop William Borders, *Pastoral Letter on Human Sexuality* (Baltimore: Archdiocese of Baltimore, March 25, 1987).

14. Ryan, 113.

15. Sacred Congregation for the Doctrine of the Faith, *Declaration on Procured Abortion: Questio de abortu,* November 18, 1975, para. 11, 12.

16. John Paul, para. 26.

17. Joseph Cardinal Ratzinger, *Letter to the Bishops of the Catholic Church on the Pastoral Care of Homosexual Persons* (Vatican: Congregation for the Doctrine of the Faith, October 1, 1986), para. 3.

18. Ratzinger, para. 7.

19. *Catechism of the Catholic Church* (Vatican: Libreria Editrice Vaticana, 1994). para. 2357–59.

20. *Always Our Children* (Washington, D.C.: United States Catholic Conference, 1997), Publication No. 5-131, p. 6–7.

21. Archbishop John R. Roach, quoted in *Catholic Bulletin* (now *Catholic Spirit*)(Archdiocese of Saint Paul and Minneapolis, September 16, 1991).

22. *Always Our Children,* 5.

23. Austin Flannery, O.P., Pastoral Constitution on the Church in the Modern World *(Gaudium et Spes),* in *Vatican Council II, Constitutions, Decrees, Declarations* (Northport, N.Y.: Costello Publishing Company, 1996), 178.

24. *Always Our Children*, 13.

25. Bill Huebsch, *Homosexuality: A Catholic Appraisal, 1999,* pp. 12–14. I am grateful to Bill for allowing me to quote from his as yet unpublished work.

26. Bishop P. Francis Murphy, address to the 26th Annual East Coast Conference for Religious Education in Washington, D.C., February 13, 1998.

27. Bishop P. Francis Murphy, address at Fall Ministry Day, Diocese of Rochester, New York, October 19, 1998.

28. Carolyn Osiek, R.S.C.J., *Beyond Anger* (New York: Paulist Press, 1986), 12.

29. Thomas Franklin O'Meara, O.P., *Theology of Ministry* (New York: Paulist Press, 1983), 208.

30. Father Richard Fragomeni in an Advent retreat for lay ministers and priests in the Archdiocese of Saint Paul and Minneapolis, November 30, 1999. Father Fragomeni is a priest of the Diocese of Albany and Chair of the Department of Word and Worship at Catholic Theological Union.

31. Bishop Michael Pfeifer, O.M.I., in a pastoral letter, *The Freedom of Catholics: An Official Church Teaching,* published by the Diocese of San Angelo, Texas in 1986.

32. John S. Savage, *The Apathetic and Bored Church Member* (Pittsford, N.Y.: LEAD Consultants, 1976), 55–70.

6. Called to Reconcile, to Forgive, to Heal

1. Monika K. Hellwig, *Sign of Reconciliation and Conversion* (Wilmington, Del.: Michael Glazier, 1986), 28.

2. Dennis J. Woods, "Reconciliation of Groups," in Peter E. Fink, S.J., *Alternative Futures for Worship,* Vol. 4, Reconciliation (Collegeville, Minn.: Liturgical Press, 1987), 37.

3. Vanier, 43.

4. Bishop Michael Sheehan, in a pastoral letter, *Making Evangelization a Priority,* published by the Diocese of Lubbock, Texas in 1985.

5. Hellwig, 23.

6. Auxiliary Bishop Robert Morneau, address to National Federation of Priests Councils, Tempe, Arizona, April 21–24, 1999, quoted in *Origins,* CNS Documentary Service.

Index